LITERATURE FROM CRESCENT MOON I

Sexing Hardy: Thomas Hardy and Feminism
by Margaret Elvy

Thomas Hardy's Jude the Obscure: A Critical Study
by Margaret Elvy

Thomas Hardy's Tess of the d'Urbervilles: A Critical Study
by Margaret Elvy

Stepping Forward: Essays, Lectures and Interviews
by Wolfgang Iser

Lawrence Durrell: Between Love and Death, Between East and West
by Jeremy Mark Robinson

Andrea Dworkin
by Jeremy Mark Robinson

German Romantic Poetry: Goethe, Novalis,
Heine, Hölderlin, Schlegel, Schiller
by Carol Appleby

Cavafy: Anatomy of a Soul
by Matt Crispin

Rilke: Space, Essence and Angels in the Poetry of Rainer Maria Rilke
by B.D. Barnacle

Rimbaud: Arthur Rimbaud and the Magic of Poetry
by Jeremy Mark Robinson

Shakespeare: Love, Poetry and Magic in Shakespeare's Sonnets and Plays
by B.D. Barnacle

Feminism and Shakespeare
by B.D. Barnacle

The Poetry of Landscape in Thomas Hardy
by Jeremy Mark Robinson

D.H. Lawrence: Infinite Sensual Violence
by M.K. Pace

D.H. Lawrence: Symbolic Landscapes
by Jane Foster

The Passion of D.H. Lawrence
by Jeremy Mark Robinson

Samuel Beckett Goes Into the Silence
by Jeremy Mark Robinson

In the Dim Void: Samuel Beckett's Late Trilogy:
Company, Ill Seen, Ill Said and Worstward Ho

by Gregory Johns

Andre Gide: Fiction and Fervour in the Novels
by Jeremy Mark Robinson

The Ecstasies of John Cowper Powys
by A.P. Seabright

Amorous Life: John Cowper Powys and the Manifestation of Affectivity
by H.W. Fawkner

Postmodern Powys: New Essays on John Cowper Powys
by Joe Boulter

Rethinking Powys: Critical Essays on John Cowper Powys
edited by Jeremy Mark Robinson

Thomas Hardy and John Cowper Powys: Wessex Revisited
by Jeremy Mark Robinson

Thomas Hardy: The Tragic Novels
by Tom Spenser

Julia Kristeva: Art, Love, Melancholy, Philosophy, Semiotics
by Kelly Ives

Luce Irigaray: Lips, Kissing, and the Politics of Sexual Difference
by Kelly Ives

Hélène Cixous I Love You: The Jouissance of Writing
by Kelly Ives

Emily Dickinson: *Selected Poems*
selected and introduced by Miriam Chalk

Petrarch, Dante and the Troubadours: The Religion of Love and Poetry
by Cassidy Hughes

Dante: *Selections From the Vita Nuova*
translated by Thomas Okey

Friedrich Hölderlin: *Selected Poems*
translated by Michael Hamburger

Rainer Maria Rilke: *Selected Poems*
translated by Michael Hamburger

Andrea Dworkin

ANDREA DWORKIN

Jeremy Mark Robinson

CRESCENT MOON

Crescent Moon Publishing
P.O. Box 393
Maidstone
Kent
ME14 5XU, U.K.

First published 1994. Second edition 2008.

Printed and bound in Great Britain.
Set in Palatino 10 on 13 pt.
Designed by Radiance Graphics.

British Library Cataloguing in Publication data

Robinson, Jeremy Mark
Andrea Dworkin
I. Title
305.42092

ISBN 1-86171-126-3
ISBN-13 9781861711267

Contents

Acknowledgements

Thanks to Andrea Dworkin,
and to authors quoted and their publishers

Abbreviations

Andrea Dworkin:

M	*Mercy,* Arrow 1990
IF	*Ice and Fire,* Flamingo 1987
I	*Intercourse,* Arrow 1988
P	*Pornography,* Women's Press 1984
OB	*Our Blood,* Harper & Row, New York 1976
RWW	*Right-Wing Women,* Women's Press 1983
War	*Letters From a War Zone,* Secker & Warburg 1988

Preface

For this second edition of *Andrea Dworkin*, I have opted not to rewrite the book. The text is a response to the astonishing power of Dworkin's writing and work. She's a one-woman revolution. Reworking the book would probably turn it into something different, so I've kept the freshness of the initial response. The format – a single, continuous paragraph – which was meant to emulate the style of Dworkin's own novels (not her non-fiction), I have also left alone.

She's passionate, she's very passionate, she's coming on strong, that's what she does, she comes on strong and she's very passionate; nothing will stop her, it seems, from writing; she's a whirlwind of writing, a witch who whirls up worlds of words; she creates worlds using words, all writers do that, but she writes more passionately than most; it's a cry, her work is a cry, a shout, a scream, it's passionate, she knows how to do it, she knows how to write, she writes and she writes, she writes and then she starts to really *write*, her writing is pure writing, it's *written*, she gives it all, she gives it her all, she gives her writing her all because that's how she writes that's how she's always written, she's always written like that and never in any other way; she's always written at full speed, at full anger, with a violence that grabs your head, it slices you up, you can't be the same afterwards, she writes immensely passionately, enormously passionately, she's one long passionate cry, a scream, a wail heard in the rain-sodden snowbound wind-howling bleak streets of New York City, heard echoing down the dreary midnight tunnels in the subway, heard over the bridges somewhere near Queens or the Bronx or Brooklyn, screaming sounds that are words pushed into poetry, she writes like that, she writes like screams, like people screaming in pain, she writes so passionately it takes your head off, it lifts you up, it's idealistic, it's strong, it's very powerful, she's powerful, Dworkin's powerful, some people are scared, fear her vehemence, as she says in this self-interview: 'Q: People are surprised when they meet you. That you're nice. A: I think that's strange. Why couldn't I be nice?'[1] and Michael Moorcock says of her when he met her: '[f]rom her books I had thought of her as good-hearted, benign. She's little but very plump and she always wears overalls, as indeed I do. There she was in overalls and I thought she looked sweet. Cute. I know that sounds terrible and funny because here was Attila the Hun in most people's imaginations. I think she has a lovely face, there's beauty there'[2] and Dworkin responds to Moorcock: 'it's true I'm pretty nice in my own life. It tickles me that he says I'm sweet

1 Dworkin: "Nervous Interview", 1978, 57
2 Michael Moorcock & Andrea Dworkin: "How We Met", *The Independent on Sunday*, 19 July 1992, 61

and cute. He's right – I am!' (in ib.) but she never stops hacking away at it, at *it*, her problem, everyone's problem, what she sees as everyone's problem, what she sees as the central problem of life, which is violence, or men, or men and their violence, the violence of men, she sees that as central, as pivotal, as mechanical, as metaphysical, as mystical even, as physical, It is violence she hates, that's her problem, it's everyone's problem, my problem is everyone's problem, she says, she screams, that's her message, it's the same message throughout her works, throughout her books and lectures, her screams in the snowbound city of wind by night, that's her scream, you can hear her scream, echoing along the dark alleys in the in-between zones in the nowhere-city, that's her passion, her passionate plea, her scream, her cry of warfare, the war against men, or their violence, or the male system, or how men use the system, they abuse it, that's what she attacks, relentlessly, again and again, she never stops, that's her passion, that's her vocation, to talk like that, to never stop talking, to keep talking so that she is not talked out, talked over, talked away, she won't be talked away, she won't be stopped, that's what men do, she says, or if not men then the male system, call it patriarchy, call it masculinism, call it male power relations, give it any name, ('[w]e do not have a cultural dialogue on social values: we have a perpetual male monologue' (War, 244), that's her target, it's always the same target, true, it has different names, and each name connotes something different, subtly or massively different, but still, basically, it's the same target, the same prick to kick against, the same people, or the same system, it has many guises, down the ages, from the witchcraft hunters of Old Europe to the Nazis in 1930s Germany, they have many names, they are mainly men, but not always, not always men, not simply just men, but others too, others collude, others are complicit, they are 'involved', they get involved, they involve themselves, through no fault of other own, sometimes, perhaps they don't know what they do, perhaps they do it for all sorts of reasons, perhaps they are not aware of their male/ masculine/ patriarchal bias, perhaps they don't realize they are spouting patriarchal views or masculinist dogma, perhaps they don't know why they do it, but they do it, it's not just men, then, not just men, but also others, women yes, and children, but men mostly, it's mostly men, there's a question about that, you only have to look at culture to see that, or at art, or at the judicial system, or look at politics and politicians, and in rape, it's mostly men that rape, and 'all men benefit from rape, because all men benefit from the fact that women are not free in this society' (War, 142); that's Dworkin's point, that's her target, the violence of men, their sexual exploitation of women, the way they continually exert their power over women, where, '[i]n theological terms, God raised man above all other creatures; in biological terms, man raised himself. In both systems of thought, man is at the top, where he belongs; woman is under him, literally and figuratively, where she belongs', as Dworkin writes in "Pornography and Male Supremacy" (War, 228), for feminists, somehow men or the masculinist society, 'forget' what life is, or as Luce Irigaray puts it: '[t]he entire male economy demonstrates a forgetting of life, a lack of recognition of debt to the mother, of maternal ancestry, of the women who do the work of producing and maintaining life',[3] life for many women, some feminists claim, is continuous violation of one sort or another, or as Suzanne Gibson puts it in a review of a book on women's rights: '[i]n the name of human culture, tradition and religion, women are genitally mutilated, bought and sold as commodities, forced into marriage, tortured and imprisoned in the home, executed without trial by menfolk who think them unchaste, compelled to reproduce, denied rights to their children, debarred from economic independence, excluded from political participation';[4] for Dworkin, the lie of pornography is men believing that women desire sexual violence – a view held by men 'to the utter bewilderment of women throughout the ages' (P, 166) and Luce Irigaray concurs: in an interview, Irigaray comments that when one surveys 'what is presented as 'female fantasies' by magazines, sexology books, pornography, etc, one only finds, in fact, induced images, and not an 'imaginary' which would correspond to the specificity of female sexuality. There are

3 Irigaray, 1994, 7
4 Suzanne Gibson: "The right to a language", review of Joanna Kerr, ed: *Ours By Right: Women's Rights as Human Rights*, Zed Books 1993

nothing but rapes, violence, penetrations described as breaking and entering, female orgasms functioning as the proof of male power, an over-evaluation of the size of the male sex, etc'[5] for Dworkin, men have superiority and women don't, women don't have what men have, or women have (had) it taken away from them, things have been stolen from women since time immemorial, claims Dworkin, writing: '[t]he principle that whatever can be stolen can be sold applies not only to women as such, but also the sexuality of women. The sexuality of women has been stolen outright, appropriated by men – conquered, possessed, taken, violated; women have been systematically and absolutely denied the right to sexual self-determination and to sexual integrity' (War, 229), women don't have it because they are not allowed to have it, it being power, or subjectivity, or identity, or separateness, or difference, or their own culture, art, science, politics, religion, their own institutions, their own not-male things, things that are not dipped into, controlled, manipulated and exploited by men; men hate difference, no one can be different from them, and if they are different then they don't exist, blacks don't exist, Jews don't exist, or women, or homosexuals, or the physically or socially disabled, or abused, or exploited; so when she begins her most famous book, *Pornography: Men Possessing Women*, Dworkin starts with the denial of subjectivity: men, she says, have the power of self, of being a self, of being able to say 'I am', she writes: '[t]he first tenet of male-supremacist ideology is that men have this self and that women must, by definition, lack it'; it is a self that can have anything it needs, Dworkin says, writing: 'it is entitled to take what it wants to sustain or improve itself, to have anything, to requite any need at any cost' (13); we see this everywhere in history, this imperial imperative, where men explore and exploit the world, travelling wherever they like, converting the peoples there to their own religion and politics and economics, for no one must be different, men hate different beings, things not-themselves, Dworkin calls this *cunt*,

5 Luce Irigaray, "Women's Exile", in Cameron, 1990, 92

she quotes Kate Millet,[6] who says that women's sexuality becomes 'cunt... our essence, our offense';[7] Dworkin says women become 'sluts, cows (as in: sexual cunts' *Pornography, 200);* Dworkin calls the phenomena of hatred *cunt,* meaning that which is different from men, difference in itself, something to be hated: what? you're *different*? how can this be? this is what men hate; for difference, cited so often by feminist such as Luce Irigaray, Helene Cixous, Julia Kristeva and Monique Wittig, infuriates men; why? it's because they can't control what is different from them, there is no way of controlling it, except by violence, which is why violence is employed so often, for, when in doubt, men resort to violence, but not just men, others too, but men, as we say, men mostly; men use violence where words will not do the trick; the trick is do the violence without anyone knowing, but we know about violence, we find out about violence, violence is difficult to hide, it comes out, it rears its 'ugly head', as people say, using yet again a phallic metaphor for the inrush of violence into life, people say 'sex rears its ugly head again', the head being the penis, sex being the penis, this is what Dworkin says often, she says it a lot, because she's passionate, she's angry, she's vehement, she can take on anyone and decimate them, it seems: don't take on Andrea Dworkin, she'll decimate you; Dworkin says that the 'penis in pornography is the penis in rape is the penis in sex is the penis in history' (War, 241), which is clearly wrong, for here she equates pornography, rape, sex and history, and sexual acts are not always pornography, and sexual acts between people are not always rape either; Dworkin says the penis is the basis thing in sex, it's what does the fucking, the penis *is* fucking, and what the penis does in fucking is fucking, she writes, in *Pornography*: '[c]ommonly referred to as "it," sex is defined in action only by what the male does with his penis. Fucking – the penis thrusting is the magical, hidden meaning of "it," the reason for sex... In practice, fucking is an act of possession – simultaneously an act of ownership, taking, force; it is

6 Dworkin's method of analyzing literary texts is similar to Kate Millett's second wave feminism in *Sexual Politics,* both identify the author with his/ her characters; both 'ventriloquise' and parody the texts by quoting and rewriting the texts. (Still, 1993, 23)
7 Kate Millet, 1973, 95

conquering... In the male system, sex is the penis, the penis is sexual power, its use in fucking is manhood' (23), and, again, Dworkin writes that '[i]n pornography, the penis is characterized as a weapon: sword, knife, scissor, gun, pistol, rifle, tank, various instruments of torture, steel, rod, cattle prod; and all these weapons are used in place of the penis or in conjunction with the penis' (War, 240-1), but Dworkin is not being totally accurate here, for although those connotations are present, and although pornography can be read in this way, and in so many others ways, there is not one *single* reading of pornography as penis-thrusting, rather, pornography has multiple readings/ meanings, like any other human construction; for other women writers, the penis is loved, beloved, exalted, as with Tuppy Owens, who has worked in conventional soft-core pornography and the new 'women's pornography', and she loves the penis: '[l]et's hope that my sex mag which *can't* show dicks (Smiths and Menzies won't allow them to be shown in their exciting, excited state), won't also be a waste of time. It's a travesty! Dicks are delectable, incredible biological structures. The whole apparatus, the size, the way it fits inside, and the precariousness of it all, makes me wonder why people bother to take an interest in anything else in life at all. That so many cocks go unloved and uncherished by women these days is an unbelievable waste of resources, and also senseless human cruelty';[8] Owens' exaltation of the penis is about as far away from Dworkin's polemical anti-pornography feminism as is possible; Dworkin finds this sort of wistful, slavish adoration of the penis repugnant, for it is just the sort of response of male sexuality and male art and male pornography and male culture that must be squashed, that is so dangerous; for Dworkin, simply, 'sex is defined in action only by what the male does with his penis', and so is to be condemned (*Pornography*, 23), sex and the penis and fucking and so on are all part of the same male mystery, in Dworkin's view, and it's a holy mystery, like the mystery of violence, a holy mystery, like Jesus' Incarnation, something always to be guarded, to be religiously defended, as Dworkin writes in *Intercourse*: '[t]he penis needs the protection of the law, of awe, of power' (176), it's some great secret, like some great

8 Owens: "Sex On My Mind", in Assister, 125

secret in the temple, male power,[9] embodied in the phallus, it's the holy mystery that has to be hidden away in the temple, locked away, eternally hidden from view, yet continually alluded to, by metaphor, by allusion, by allegory, by myth, this is one of the secrets of male power, the 'empire of the phallus', as Luce Irigaray calls it,[10] hidden away, yet constantly mythicized, each society, each age, mythicizing it anew, this is Dworkin's view, the Romans and Greeks mythologizing phallic power in deities such as Jupiter and Zeus, those wild, rampant gods who spent much of their time pursuing and raping women, or the Aztec and Inca worlds, or the Celtic warrior gods, each deity being some incarnation of male/ phallic power, a power that must always remain secret, taboo: '[t]he fathers know that taboo is the essence of power: keep the source of power hidden, mysterious, sacred, so that those without power can never find it, understand it, or take it away... the fathers maintained, as they always have, that the power of manhood is in the phallus: keep it covered, hidden; shroud it in religious taboos; use it in secret; on it build an empire, but never expose it to the powerless, those who do not have it, those who would, if they could but see its true, naked, unarmed dimensions, have contempt for it, grind it to nothing under their thumbs' Dworkin says (War, 216-7), yet, at the same time, the penis as phallus is very visible in culture, in a million 'phallic substitutes (from deodorant and lipstick to car and nuclear warheads); it is the vagina, according to French feminists (in particular Luce Irigaray) which has been silenced, negated, decentred, written out; the penis is exalted as the emblem of presence, while the vagina is all absence, the vagina is a cultural hole or vacuum which cannot speak, while the phallus, the 'transcendent signifier', is all mouth and speech;[11] as Margaret Whitford says of Luce Irigaray's philosophy: 'Western systems of representation privilege *seeing*: what can be seen (presence) is privileged over what cannot be seen (absence) and guarantees

9 Michel Foucault wrote: 'For power, secrecy is not in the nature of an abuse, it is indispensable to its operation.' 1981, 86

10 Luce Irigaray: "The poverty of psychoanalysis", in Irigaray, 1991, 96

11 Some feminists have criticized French feminists' insistence on the womb and labia, ignoring the clitoris, the organ of 'pure pleasure'. Sayers, 131; Naomi Schor: *Breaking the Chain: Women, Theory and French Realist Fiction*, New York 1985; Still, 1993, 32

Being, hence the privilege of the penis which is elevated to the status of the Phallus';[12] the phallus is not everything in male power: the testicles also signify holy manhood – strong, 'true' men have 'got balls', (the Pope, before he's proclaimed Pope, has to be medically examined to prove he is 'properly hung'); yet the veil of the temple has been rent in twain, and it reveals... male violence, this is what Dworkin says, and this is one of the reasons, perhaps, why feminism upsets so many men, because they feel suddenly exposed, they feel the cold wind of exposure around their balls, their temple veil has been kicked in, they have been found out, undone, their powerbase uncovered, ransacked, fragmented, shattered, because when you bring the phallus out of its bejewelled shrine and black marble sarcophagus everyone cackles, because it looks ridiculous, the thin ice breaks, the rug is whipped out, the house of cards collapses, and the power of the phallus is even more ruthlessly upheld and defended; rape is a violation of the body, or as Umberto Eco says, '[r]ape does not respect the body of someone else';[13] Robin Morgan writes: 'rape is the perfected act of male-sexuality in a patriarchal culture – it is the ultimate metaphor for domination, violence, subjugation, and possession' (82); Dworkin says that male violence, male rape, male dogma and male ideas lie behind *everything*, so that nobody can escape, not on the streets, on the cold New York streets, where screams are not heeded, echoing down endless concrete tunnels, and nobody can escape in the houses either, in the primacy and secrecy of their own emotions, there, too, male hate and male violence seeps into everything, infecting it, this is what the French feminists say too, they say that culture is everything, that education and socialization counts for everything, that the body is something but not everything, that one is not 'born a woman', one 'becomes a woman', meaning, we come back to this eternally, that culture and education influences people more than their biological make-up, that the body is crucial but not everything, so that, even alone, even living alone, one is filled up with the culture of male violence, that you can't escape, that it is a part of our Western system, perhaps a part of

12 Whitford, 1991, 88
13 Umberto Eco in *Le Monde*, 5 October 1993, and in Owen, 1994, 54

all systems, all systems everywhere, the system which is life which is infected from bottom to top with male ideas, male hate, male values and male violence; there is a logic in patriarchy, Dworkin claims, and it is a logic that favours men, or as she puts it in *Right-Wing Women*: '[w]omen's social condition is built on a simple premise: women can be fucked and bear babies, therefore women must be fucked and bear babies. Sometimes, especially among the sophisticated, "penetrated" is substituted for "fucked": women can be penetrated, therefore women must be penetrated. This logic does not apply to men, whichever word is used: men can be fucked, therefore men must be fucked; men can be penetrated, therefore men must be penetrated. This logic applies only to women and sex. One does not say, for instance, women have delicate hands, therefore women must be surgeons. Or women have legs, therefore women must run, jump, climb. Or women have minds, therefore women must use them. One does learn, however, that women have sex organs that must be used by men, or the women are not women: they are somehow less or more, either of which is bad and thoroughly discouraged. Women are defined, valued, judged, in one way only: as women – that is, with sex organs that must be used' (63-64); and again, Dworkin writes: '[w]omen are for fucking and having children. Fucking gets you dead, unless you have children too' (ib, 144); the act of penetration, as other feminists have noted, defines hetero-sexuality, where 'penile-vaginal penetration' equals possession, 'being 'had', 'possessed', 'taken', 'fucked' as two feminists call it,[14] and penetration is thoroughly socialized ('sexuality 'is a social construct, gendered to the ground' says Dworkin's companion in feminism, Catherine MacKinnon),[15] or as the Leeds Revolutionary Feminist Group put it: '[n]o act of penetration takes place in isolation. Each takes place in a system of relationships that is male supremacy',[16] for some feminists, penetration can be

14 Sue Wilkinson & Celia Kitzinger: "Contemporary Rehabilitations of Heterosexuality", in Griffin, *et al*, 1994, 78
15 MacKinnon, 1987, 149
16 Leeds Revolutionary Feminist Group: "Political Lesbianism: The Case Against Heterosexuality", in Onlywomen Press, 1981, 7

termed 'compulsory' or 'abusive' or 'consensual',[17] while for others, and Dworkin would agree with them, penile penetration can 'feel like one more invasion,'[18] and it can be difficult to rebel against 'the coital imperative' of intercourse;[19] Dworkin's friend John Stoltenberg argues for heterosexual lovemaking which does not include intercourse; it's not just heterosexuality that is 'compulsory', as Adrienne Rich noted,[20] it is sexuality itself that is compulsory, because '[w]omen are expected to be in, or to want to be in, a sexual relationship',[21] and not just women: everyone is expected to be sexual, and for Dworkin being sexual is equated with being fucked, no one can escape from it, it seems, so that everyone is branded socially by what they do sexually: thus, old people are defined by their non-sexual activity and jokes are made about the non-performance of their genitals; children are defined as non-sexual, and all manner of controversies are ignited when the words 'sexuality' and 'children' appear in the same sentence; in the media, in magazines and TV programmes, in films and radio shows, people are depicted either in or not in a sexual relationship, and the sexual relationship takes precedence over all others, over friendship, over being a child or a parent, over business and social relationships; everyone is expected to be in, or to want to be in, a sexual relationship, and when someone isn't interested, the media hounds them, by making fun of them, by lampooning the individual's non-sexual status; sex (fucking, in Dworkin's terminology) is the norm – anything outside of that is regarded suspiciously; when celebrities such as pop singer Cliff Richard doesn't seem particularly interested in rutting away, suspicions are aroused: is he gay? perverted? impotent? and so on; and as for the idea of friendship, holding hands, dancing, sleeping together, being together, all this means a sexual relationship is going on: in the media and society, holding hands

17 R. Rowland: "Radical Feminist Heterosexuality: The Personal and the Political", in Wilkinson, 1993, 77; W. Holloway: "Theorizing Heterosexuality: A Feminism", *Feminism & Psychology*, vol. 3, no. 3, 1993, 412-7
18 Gill & Walker, 1993, 70
19 A. Sebestyen, "Sexual Assumptions in the Women's Movement", in Friedman, 1982, 235
20 Rich: "Compulsory Heterosexuality and Lesbian Existence", in Rich, 1980
21 Becky Rosa: Anti-monogamy: A Radical Challenge to Compulsory Heterosexuality?", in Griffin *et al*, 1993, 110

or doing the things romantic, sexual couples do is not allowed unless one *is* a romantic, sexual couple;[22] towards the end of *Pornography* she puts her basic credo another way: '[i]n the male system, women are sex' sex is the whore. The whore is *porne*, the lowest whore, the whore who belongs to *all* male citizens: the slut, the cunt' (202); Dworkin reckons that women are being fucked over, fucked up, fucked dead, and it is happening in pornography, which is the cultural expression of something (women's subordination) that's happening in real life, in homes over the real world, where 'according to the FBI a woman is battered every eighteen seconds' (War, 286), '[a] woman is raped every three minutes, nearly half the rapes are committed by someone the woman knows. Forty-four percent of the adult women in the United States have been raped at least once' (War, 308), there are the battered and the batterers, for, and Dworkin, and pornography is the tip of the iceberg called violence, and if the horrors that occur in pornography are bad, then the horrors women undergo are vile beyond words, because pornography, in Dworkin's view, is an abomination: 'our genitals are tied up, they are pasted, makeup is put on them to make them pop out of a page at a male viewer. Millions and millions of pictures are made of us in postures of submission and sexual access so that our vaginas are exposed for penetration, our anuses are exposed for penetration, our throats are used as if they are genitals for penetration. In this country where I live as a citizen real rapes are on film and are being sold in the marketplace... women are penetrated by animals and objects for public entertainment, women are urinated on and defecated on, women and girls are used interchangeably so that grown women are made up to look like a five-or-six-year-old child surrounded by toys, presented in mainstream pornographic publications for anal penetration' (War, 277) and again, in this extract from 1978's "Pornography and Grief": '[o]ne can know everything and still be stunned and paralyzed when one meets a child who is being continuously raped by her father or some close male relative. One can know everything and still be reduced to sputtering like an idiot when a woman is prosecuted for

22 Becky Rosa: Anti-monogamy: A Radical Challenge to Compulsory Heterosexuality?", in Griffin *et al*, 1993, 107

attempting to abort herself with knitting needles, or when a woman is imprisoned for killing a man who has raped or tortured her' (War, 21); for Gayle Rubin, it is wrong, perhaps, to concentrate on violence in pornography, because the mass media are more violent: Rubin, finds films more violent than pornography, and so why focus on violence in pornography? 'If the problem is violence,' Rubin asks, 'why single out sexually explicit media?'[23] Dworkin is clearly someone who *cares* about her subject, violence against women in all its many forms, she clearly is extremely angry about the situation, and sees her books and speeches as a contribution to the revolution that will change the state of affairs, as she writes in the introduction to her collection of speeches and essays, *Letters From a War Zone*: 'I wrote them [the essays and speeches] to communicate and to survive: as a writer and as a woman; for me, the two are one. I wrote them because I care about fairness and justice for women. I wrote them because I believe in bearing witness, and I have seen a lot. I wrote them because people are being hurt and the injury has to stop' (War, 5), for Dworkin, writing is an act of revolution, and the life and the writing are one, so that it's a continuum: the novels, the short stories, the speeches, the essays and the interviews, it's all a part of the same revolutionary and radical feminist view of life; Hélène Cixous also speaks piquantly of writing, regarding writing, like Dworkin, as essential to living: 'I need writing... I need writing to celebrate living';[24] but, even as we follow Dworkin on the trail of the decimation of pornography, violence and various forms of abuse, we must be wary when she speaks of 'woman' in 'real life' ('on the streets', so to speak) and 'woman' in art and pornography, for, as French feminists keep telling us, 'woman' in 'real life', as in 'we women', is not identical to (indeed, has an ambiguous relationship with) 'woman' in art/ pornography/ representation; that is, we must keep reminding ourselves of other feminists' view on what (a) 'woman' is; 'woman' is, for instance, a 'writing-effect', for the feminist Alice Jardine, an element in cultural discourse or a text; it's important,

23 Gayle Rubin: "Misguided, Dangerous and Wrong: an Analysis of Anti-Pornography Politics", in Assister & Carol, eds, 24
24 Cixous: "The Art of Innocence", Cixous, 1994, 95

as Monique Wittig notes, to make a distinction between the various interpretations of 'woman' and 'women': '[o]ur first task... is thoroughly to dissociate "woman" (the class within which we fight) and "woman," the myth. For "woman" does not exist for us; it is only an imaginary formation, while "women" is the duct of a social relationship'.[25] It may be simplistic to speak terms of the ratio of male to female artists, this may be a too-simplified version of gender politics, but it is true, that when one trawls culture, one finds that most artists revered by culture, most writers, most philosophers, composers, architects, and so on, are male; when one looks at a few books, one sees just how much of culture, proportionally, is male or masculine – anthologies, for instance, reveal a severely masculinist bias: an anthology allows the editors to select from a welter of material, but anthologies of artists, whether composers' notes on music-making, or poets, or painters, are male, so, in *The Oxford Book of Seventeenth Century Verse*, we find a host of poets, some 'great', some indifferent, some poor, but all male: Robert Herrick, Richard Crashaw, John Donne, Michael Drayton, George Herbert, Ben Jonson, Henry Vaughan, Andrew Marvell, etc; the books on 'great' painters of the world also draw on masculinist, white, First World, Western artists: Picasso, Rembrandt, Michelangelo, Vermeer, Angelico, Constable, etc; if you look in the index of almost any book, you'll see mainly male names; Dworkin notes that, still, men hold positions of power: '[t]he government in all its aspects – legislative, executive, judicial, enforcement – has been composed almost exclusively of men. Even juries, until very recently, were composed almost entirely of men. Women have had virtually nothing to do with either formulating or applying laws on obscenity or anything else. In the arena of political power, women have been effectively silenced';[26] the male system is a cultural edifice which makes it easier for men to get ahead rather than women, women are second class citizens, if they have citizenship at all, because for years women were not citizens, they could not even vote, imagine it! life in a *democracy*, equal rights for all and all

25 Monique Witting: "One Is Not Born a Woman", speech at the Feminist as Scholar Conference, May 1979, Barnard College, New York
26 "For Men, Freedom of Speech; For Women, Silence Please", War, 223)

that, and yet women don't get to vote! and it's only recently, really, that women have got the vote; how ridiculous the whole thing is, and people talk, nowadays, of *post-feminism*, as if feminism were over, as if feminists have run their course, as if feminism has done all it could, when there is still so much to do, still so much to change; what things?, all manner of things, from violence to values, from culture to coercion, from penis to pornography, so much has to be change, and Andrea Dworkin wants to change, yet, she says, her books are not 'prescriptive', they do not say do this or do that, they are 'descriptive', that is, they describe the surrounding cultural environment; for Michael Moorcock, Andrea Dworkin is an inspiration; she does not dictate, Moorcock says, but simply reflects what is already there in contemporary culture: 'Dworkin says her books are not prescriptive but descriptive. While continuing to expand the boundaries of feminism, she argues from a humanistic and idealistic perspective both intellectually stunning and stylistically eloquent';[27] Moorcock writes on a more personal note: 'I think feminism is the most important political movement of our times. People think Andrea's a man-hater. She gets called a Fascist and a Nazi – particularly by the American left, but it's not detectable in her work. To me she seemed like a pussycat... She has an extraordinary eloquence, a kind of magic that moves people';[28] Dworkin is a very positive writer, always driving onwards for revolution, change and radical thinking, in the introduction to *Letters From a War Zone*, she writes: 'I am more reckless now than when I started out because I know what everything costs and it doesn't matter. I have paid a lot to write what I believe to be true. On one level, I suffer terribly from the disdain that much of my work has met. On another, deeper level, I don't give a fuck' (War, 4), and her life's work balances the individual suffering of the writer with the larger, worldwide suffering of women's subordination, so that, she says, one becomes, on a personal level, immune to pain, while on the larger, global level, the pain of women and children around the world continues to grow, and

27 Michael Moorcock: *Casablanca*, Gollancz 1989, 134-5
28 Michael Moorcock & Andrea Dworkin: "How We Met", *The Independent on Sunday*, 19 July 1992, 61

continues to make her madder and madder: 'I wrote them [the essays and speeches] because I believe in writing, in its power to right wrongs, to change how people see and think, to change how and what people know, to change how and why people act. I wrote them out of the conviction, Quaker in origin, that one must speak truth to power. This is the basic premise in my work as a feminist: activism or writing' (War, 5); here Dworkin posits her work as a crusade, that's the newspaper term for her kind of polemic, a 'crusade' against silence and violence, against cruelty and inequality, and certainly Dworkin is often portrayed in the media as a crusader, someone who really believes in herself, in her convictions, someone wholly committed, as few others are, to a radical change; Michael Moorcock, in his piece on Andrea Dworkin (*New Statesman*, 1988) writes: [w]hat she fights against, in everything she writes and does, is male refusal to acknowledge sexual inequality, male hatred of women, male contempt for women, male power';[29] for Dworkin, there is injustice where there doesn't need to be injustice: she is not talking about the unfairness of death, or the human condition as grounded in biology or Nature; she's talking about the injustices that people create, the endless tortures, either physical or psychological, tortures which simply do not have to be there: '[t]he women's movement is like other political movements in one important way. Every political movement is committed to the belief that there are certain kinds of pain that people should not endure. They are unnecessary. They are gratuitous. They are not part of the God-given order. They are not biologically inevitable. They are acts of human will. They are acts done by some human beings to other human beings' ("Feminism: An Agenda", War, 134); her idealism is balanced by a healthy cynicism regarding mainstream and mass politics; rightly, Dworkin regards the political left and right, and the people who call themselves liberal or radical, with suspicion: in *Pornography*, and elsewhere, she notes how, for the moral right-wing, pornography is secret, sinful, for 'secret buying and selling of women, secret profit, secret pleasure', while for the left, pornography is portrayed as free fun, about sexual liberation (P, 208), so that what's hidden at the heart of

29 Moorcock, 1989, 135

leftist or right-wing philosophies on pornography is commerce/ money/ capitalism, for '[c]apitalism is not wicked or cruel when the commodity is the whore' (P, 209), in Dworkin's view, when the corporations of crime syndicates are 'selling cunt', it's OK; Dworkin despises the leftist/ liberal stance which says that pornography is pleasure and freedom and pleasure and freedom are OK in a liberal society; if male sexuality wants pornography or pleasure, it must have it, so it produces it and consumes it; Dworkin articulates the thoughts of many feminists when she speaks of women in work: '[i]n the workplace, sexual harassment fixes the low status of women irreversibly. Women are sex; even filing or typing, women are sex' (RWW, 67); for Dworkin, the connections between sex and money are sinister and powerful, especially in the realm of work and economics, where the relations between sex and power and money say so much about the relations between the sexes, where men still earn more than women in similar jobs, where women do much of the real work of the world, where the corporate structure favours men, where the economy of a nation is geared towards men's benefit, as Dworkin writes: '[f]eminists know that if women are paid equal wages for equal work, women will gain sexual as well as economic independence; but feminists have refused to face the fact that in a woman-hating social system, women will never be paid equal wages; men in all their institutions of power are sustained by the sex labor and sexual subordination of women. The sex labor of women must be maintained; and systematic low wages for sex-neutral work effectively force women to sell sex to survive. The economic system that pays women lower wages than it pays men actually punishes women for working outside marriage or prostitution, since women work hard for low wages and still must sell sex. The economic system that punishes women for working outside the bedroom by paying low wages contributes significantly to women's perception that the sexual serving of men is a necessary part of any woman's life; or how else could she live? Feminists appear to think that equal pay for equal work is a simple reform, whereas it is no reform at all; it is revolution' (ib, 67); for Dworkin, we live in a societal system thoroughly dominated by men: she claims that men dominate in the realms of the economy, health, organized religion, art, etc (P, 203); for Dworkin, sex and power are interlinked in male culture, and pornography is the expression of that power relation between men and women, as Alison Assister writes: '[p]ornography, for her, becomes a Foucauldian discourse of power. Similarly, in the work of constructivists – and Andrea Dworkin falls into this camp on this issue – women working in the sex industry lose all agency. They become 'victims' of the power-knowledge complex: pornography. Their ability to choose what they do is lost. In fact, neither rapists, on the one hand, nor sex workers, on the other, are victims; rather, both are agents actively choosing what they do';[30] in Dworkin's reading of contemporary culture, the sexual subordination of women is central to the overall subordination of women – in the realms of economy, class, status, race, age, etc, but other feminists question the insistence on sexuality as the site of every conflict or suppression in culture, as Christobel Mackenzie says: '[i]f women like sex, we are not always the perfect victims of violent or coercive males. If women like sex, then sex isn't the 'price' of the things women 'get' from men (home, marriage, love, security, etc.). Most of all, if some women like sex, then the women who have only endured sex for the sake of their relationships have been lying to themselves, selling themselves for no good reason',[31] the assertion of many feminists that women like sex undermines some of Dworkin's arguments, which seems to be that just about all sex with men is horrible and subordinating, and if Dworkin doesn't say that outright – indeed, to say so outright would make her a laughing stock – it is the idea behind much of her writing; in *Letters From a War Zone*, in particular, Dworkin attacks male culture, and, in doing so, seems to be suggesting that all forms of sexual contact with men are problematic, if not subordinating. For some feminists, focusing on the pornography issue means vital energy is directed at only one issue, when there are many others that need attention; '[p]orn is just one product in the big social supermarket,' writes B. Ruby Rich,[32] adding, '[w]hy is pornography so important, finally? Is it

30 Assister: "Essentially Sex: A New Look", in Assister, ed, 103
31 Mackenzie: "The Anti-sexism Campaign", in Assister, 142
32 B. Ruby Rich: "Anti-Porn: Soft Issue, Hard World", Village Voice, 20 July 1982, in *Feminist Review*, eds, *Sexuality: A Reader*, 347-8, 350

important enough to be consuming all our political energy as feminists?... whether symptom or cause, pornography presents an incomplete target for feminist attack. The campaign against pornography is a massive displacement of outrage that ought to be directed at a far wider sphere of oppression'; and Julienne Dickey says that there 'are also other dangers in making a centrality of the pornography position. Focussing so strongly on sexual imagery can lead to feminist struggle being co-opted by the right, thus defusing the very real threat that feminist ideas and practice pose to the patriarchal structures of society. It can divert feminist attention, resources and energy away from other sites of struggle, such as socio-economic problems, women's inequality in every sphere – and the appalling but non-pornographic content of the rest of the media' (in Chester, 165); and another feminist, Claudia, says that the concentration on pornography as production displays awareness of other important modes of labour by women: '[i]t is remarkable how sudden feelings of empathy and identification with 'exploited' women surge up in the breasts of feminists when they think of workers in the sex-industry... It is even more remarkable how feminists never identify in this way with cleaners, child-minders and factory works; that is, those 'hidden' women who create the conditions that keep the feminist in the 'alternative' lifestyle to which she has become accustomed';[33] when the establishment – politicians, the media, etc – speak of feminism they usually mean, without saying so, the white middle class feminism of France or Anglo-America; it is important to remember that however important issues such as pornography and men-women conflict are, the issue of racism is regarded by many feminists as much more important to address;[34] Dworkin, though, looks around, sees what is going on, and tries to capture some of it, some of the meanings and events that are going on, all the time, everywhere, and here, especially here, wherever here is, here is where you are, that's right, right here, and now, at this time, before any other time, Andrea Dworkin's books aim to describe what is going on now and here, in this time

33 Claudia: "Fear of Pornography", in Assister, 133

34 C. Moraga & G. Anzaldúa, eds: *This Bridge Called My Back: Writings by Radical Women of Color*, Kitchen Table, New York 1983; B. Christian: *Black Feminist Criticism*, Pergamon, Oxford 1985; P.H. Collins: *Black Feminist Thought*, Unwin 1990

and in this place, and what she sees is not good, she sees things going on that are not good at all, though there are good things too, there must be good things, or, rather, Dworkin thinks that there *could* be good things, there should and must be good things, and she wants those good things to happen, she is supremely idealistic, her idealism comes out all the time, squashed out from under the edges of her rage, her idealism makes itself known, more especially in her fiction, where she doesn't have to be sober, whereas in the non-fiction and the critical studies she is more sober, more controlled, more restrained, but in the fiction she lets her idealism range free, and a very powerful idealism it is too, listen to her here, she's writing in *Mercy* about Rebecca, a 'ruthless crusher of a dyke' out on the streets: 'I see her on the street, gold lamé against a window, I see her shimmering, and I go with her for thanks and because she is grand, and I find out you can be free in a gold lamé dress, in jail, whoring, in black skin, in hunger, in pain, in strife, the strife of the streets, perpetual war, gritty, gray, she's the wild one with freedom in her soul, it translates into how you touch, what's in your fingers, the silk in your hands, the freedom you take with who you got under you... and what you give is ambition, the ambition to do it big, do it great, big gestures, free – girls do it big, girls soar, girls burn, girls take big not puny' (108), this is Dworkin at her most idealistic, writing of 'girls' burning through the streets of New York City, which is what she does, which is what Andrea Dworkin herself does, in her works, and especially in her fiction, where her idealism burns very brightly, indeed, so brightly you can't look, it's like an angel's landed right in front of you, on the sidewalk, an amazing angel burning so brightly, a rage of fire, the fire of rage, red stuff, anger, anger and blood, red stuff, on the sidewalk, in New York or Bombay or Seoul or Sao Paulo, all across the world, the red stuff, which is blood, which in Dworkin becomes the blood of rage, the red rag waved at a bull, coming again and again, this blood, holy blood, it's part of Dworkin's rage, her rage against the world, against life when it gets incredibly difficult, but against people mostly, not the 'human condition', her rage is not really against being human, a flesh and blood body, but against the constraints put on it by systems, values, attitudes, ideas, dogmas, structures, strictures, institutions, religions, cultures, arts, laws, constraints which Dworkin reacts against violently, for she is really a liberal, in some sense, a liberal, fighting for 'freedom', though she might dislike the term 'liberal', perhaps, preferring, perhaps, 'radical', coming out of the 60s, the late 60s, the decade when masses of people became seriously politicized, her novels, *Ice and Fire* and *Mercy* each deal with women working at the heart of 60s radicalism, the 60s liberalism which wanted to overturn the status quo; of this era, Dworkin writes in *Right-Wing Women*: 'at the very end of the sixties, women who had been radical counterculture terms – women who had been both politically and sexually active – became radical in new terms: they became feminists' (95), and she quotes Robin Morgan: '[w]e have met the enemy and he's our friend. And dangerous';[35] this is where 60s Dworkin's radical thinking comes from, the late 60s, and her idealism is really fierce; radical not liberal is the right term for Dworkin's philosophy, perhaps, or perhaps just plain passionate, but not liberal, no, for the 'liberal' she despises, as epitomized in writers such as Norman Mailer, one of the big brash macho Amerikan writers she hates, as she writes in *Right-Wing Women*: 'Norman Mailer remarked during the sixties that the problem with the sexual revolution was that it was put into the hands of the wrong people. He was right. It was in the hands of men. The pop idea was that fucking was good, so good that the more there was of it, the better. The pop idea was that people should fuck whom they wanted: translated for the girls, they wanted that girls should want to be fucked – as close to all the time as was humanly possible. For women, alas, all the time is humanly possible with enough changes of partners. Men envision frequency with reference to their own patterns of erection and ejaculation. Women got fucked a lot more than men fucked' (88-89), for Dworkin, here, men's ideas of multiple fucking depends on how many times they can orgasm and get erections, while for women it means promiscuity, many partners, i.e., in Dworkin's parlance, being branded a whore, but the idealism of the 60s affected men and

35 Robin Morgan: "Goodbye to All That", in *Going Too Far*, Random House, New York 122

women differently, Dworkin contests: it meant something different for women than for men, but this was the era which formed much of Dworkin's thinking, it was the era in which she spread her wings and began to rage hard; the *zeitgeist* of the late 60s was summarized by Dworkin in *Right-Wing Women* thus: '[o]ne did not have to read Wilhelm Reich, though some did. A bunch of nasty bastards who hated making love were making war. A bunch of boys who liked flowers were making love and refusing to march. These boys were wonderful and beautiful. They wanted peace. They talked love, love, love, not romantic love but love of mankind translated by women: humankind)', Dworkin goes on to explain the position of the 'girls' in this late 60s idealism, which can be read as an account Dworkin's own formative years: '[t]he girls were real idealist. They hated the Viet Nam War and their own lives, unlike the boys', were not at stake. They hated the racial and sexual bigotry visited on blacks, in particular on black men who were the figures in visible jeopardy... but still the black man was the figure of empathy, the figure whom they wanted to protect from racist pogroms. Rape was seen as a racist ploy: not something real in itself used in a racist connect to isolate and destroy black men in specific and strategic ways, but a fabrication, a figment of the racist imagination. The girls were idealistic because, unlike the boys, many of them had been raped: their lives were at stake. The girls were idealists especially because they believed in peace and freedom *so much* that they even thought it was intended for them too' (89-90); you see here something of Dworkin's idealism, which is a life-or-death idealism, an ideology of going to extremes, of laying one's life, not just one's beliefs, on the line, a philosophy in which the stakes are the highest – life itself; but Dworkin's idealism is founded firmly on people, on humanism and humanity, Dworkin gets excited most often not by ideas, but by experiences, and by people in particular, people excite her, she can't deny it, she loves them, certain people, people she cares for, people she loves, passionately, really passionately, so she cares for them and they excite her, they thrill, certain people, the blond boy in *Ice and Fire*, or the boy in *Mercy*, of whom the narrator writes '[h]e was the pure present, a whirling dervish of innocence, a minute-to-minute boy incarnating innocence, no burden of memory or law, untouched by convention' (137); in *Ice and Fire* there is a tremendously passionate description of the narrator's lover, N, a description which is so enthusiastic, so heartfelt, it recalls the heights of the Elizabethan era, the paeans to beloveds of William Shakespeare, Edmund Spenser, Sir Philip Sidney, Christopher Marlowe and Michael Drayton, or perhaps, going further back, to the courtly love poets (Giraut de Borneil, Arnaut Daniel, Bernard de Ventadour), or to the Italian *stilnovisti* (Dante, Cavalcanti, Guinicelli) or back before them, to the Goddess and Muse of love poets, Sappho – indeed, Dworkin's description of N recalls Sappho, the Sappho who wrote of love so strong it was like the wind shaking oak trees on a mountainside: '[s]he is very beautiful, not like a girl. She is lean and tough like a gang of boys... Women pursue her. She is aloof, amused. She fucks everyone eventually, with perfect simplicity and grace. She is a rough fuck. She grinds her hips in. She pushes her fingers in. She tears around inside. She is all muscle and jagged bones. She thrusts her hips so hard you can't remember who she is or how many of her there are. The first time she tore me apart. I bled and bled... Women want her. So do men. She fucks everyone... She dresses like a glittering boy, a tough, gorgeous boy. She is Garbo in *Queen Christina* but run-down and dirty and druggy, leaner and tougher' (*Ice*, 46-47); such energetic and direct exaltations of a lover recalls Edmund Spenser's breathless adulation of Elizabeth I in *The Faerie Queene*, or John Donne apostrophizing his beloved in his *Songs and Sonnets*, or Dante's hymn to Beatrice in the *Vita Nuova* or Petrarch's polished *canzone* to the deeply-desired Laura in his *Rime Sparse*, or, more recently, Hélène Cixous' evocation of a female beloved in her fictional text *Souffles* (*Breaths*, 1975): '[h]er beauty strikes me. Produces streaming. Makes me flow. She seduces my forces. Gentleness. Gives me the desire to complete her. Emptying me. Destroys and recommences me';[36] Dworkin is distinctly of this school of lovers, this cult of love poets, but it is always an erotic, sensual love closely aligned with a passionate, radical political feeling, so that love is not love on its own in Dworkin's work, but love coupled with politics,

36 Cixous, 1994, 50

sex mixed with radicalism; so in *Ice and Fire*, the narrator, another 'Andrea', as in *Mercy*, speaks of life as an adventure, as a painful but also exhilarating experience, and, indeed, like Arthur Rimbaud, Dworkin's protagonists are trying to 'deschool the senses', trying to dive as deep as possible into life, into experience, and pure experience becomes the key note in Dworkin's fiction, this total immersion (immolation) in life, this diving into the flux or river of life, as Heraclitus put it, a grappling with Love and Strife, the twin poles of Empodecles' cosmological view, or, in the modern, post-Baudelairean/ post-de Sadean view, the poles of sex and death, the aim being so piquantly outlined by Rimbaud in his famous 'lettre du voyant' of 15 May 1871: 'I say one must be a *seer*, make oneself a *seer*. The Poet makes himself a *seer* by a long, gigantic and rational *derangement of all the senses.* All forms of love, suffering, and madness'[37] – this is, to the letter, the goal of Dworkin's protagonists, this totality of experience: the adolescent poet from Charleville in provincial France continues: '[h]e searches himself. He exhausts all poisons in himself and keeps only their quintessences. Unspeakable torture where he needs all his faith, all his superhuman strength, the one accursed – and the supreme Scholar! – Because he reaches the *unknown*!'[38] how accurately this describes Dworkin's characters, this intense sense of being alive, summed up by the quote from one of Pier Paolo Pasolini's poems: 'I love life so fiercely, so desperately' (*Ice*, 85), a doctrine that is expressed in the rage of *Letters From a War Zone*, and in Dworkin's novels thus: '[w]e fuck for drugs. Speed is cheaper than food. We fuck for pills. We fuck for prescriptions. We fuck for meals when we have to. We fuck for drinks in bars. We fuck for tabs of acid. We fuck for capsules of mescaline. We fuck for loose change. We fuck for fun. We fuck for adventure. We fuck when we are hot from the weather. We fuck for big bucks to produce our movie. In between, we discuss art and politics' (*Ice*, 41); and there's the political activists the narrator works with in *Mercy*; she works with them, and the work is passionate work, work she passionately believes in, work she

37 Rimbaud, 307. See Harold Bloom, ed: *Arthur Rimbaud*, Chelsea House Publishers, New York 1988; Enid Starkie: *Arthur Rimbaud*, Faber 1973; Charles Chadwick: *Rimbaud*, Athlone Press, 1979
38 Rimbaud, ib., 307

finds fascinating and holy, work which is important too, very important, important because it usurps the status quo, it subverts the establishment, it pulls the carpet from under the feet of the politicians, it upsets them, it makes them itch and howl, this is what Dworkin's protagonists want, this subversion and protest, eternal protest, because nothing is good enough, not yet, not everywhere anyway, not everywhere in the world; Dworkin's idealism is connected with sex, because her protagonists fall in love with the political activists, and the sex and the love become part of the subversion and the protest, such as in this extract from *Mercy*, where love and politics are bound up together, so that brilliant sex is melted in with brilliant political activism, the two are eternally entwined in Dworkin's work: 'you take the body, the divine body, that their hate disfigures and destroys, and you let it triumph over murder and rage and hate through physical love and it is in the purest democracy, there is no exclusion in it. Anything, everything, is or can be communion. I-Thou. Anything, everything, can be transformed, transcended, opened up, turned from opaque to translucent' (M, 168); this is Dworkin at her most idealistic, for she counters her ruthless polemical criticism of patriarchy with fervent idealism, which appears in her lectures and talks and speeches as well as her fiction, and her speeches are powerful (Dworkin is 'a remarkably effective public speaker' says Lisa Duggan),[39] where she says, in "I Want a Twenty-Four Hour Truce During Which There is No Rape": '[i]ntimacy is worth having. Tenderness is worth having. Cooperation is worth having. A real emotional life is worth having', but she adds: '[b]ut you can't have them in a world with rape... You can't have equality or tenderness or intimacy as long as there is rape, because rape means terror" (War, 169); there is the dream behind all her work, a utopian dream of absolute beauty and absolute love and absolute togetherness and absolute passion: 'I wanted a grand sensuality that encompassed everyone, didn't leave anyone out. I wanted it dense and real and full-blooded and part of the fabric of every day, every single ordinary day, all the time; I wanted it in all things great and small. I wanted the world to tremble with sexual feeling, all stirred up,

39 Duggan: "Censorship in the Name of Feminism", in Chester, 79

on the edge of a thrill, riding a tremor, and I wanted a tender embrace to dissolve alienation and end war. I wanted the world's colors to deepen and shine and shimmer and leap out, I didn't want limits or boundaries, not on me, not on anyone else either; I didn't want life flat and dull, a line drawing done by some sophomore student at the Art League. I thought we'd fuck power to death, because sexual passion was the enemy of power, and I thought that every fuck was an act of passion and compassion, beauty and faith, empathy and an impersonal ecstasy' (169); in Dworkin, everything is mixed up together – sex, death, politics, passion, pain and utopia – it has to be this way, it has to be 'all or nothing' for her, absolutism or extremism is her credo, and in each of her books she goes to extremes, '[e]verything I feel I feel absolutely' says the narrator of *Mercy* (81), and the pair in *Ice and Fire* (N and the narrator) says: '[w]e are dazzled with the universe and its sense of humour' (*Ice*, 45); she pushes, she pushes things as far as they will go, and then she nudges them even further; this extremism annoys a lot of people: *don't go too far!* they cry, for they have never gone to extremes, they have never known absolute beauty or extreme passion; they say, in their voices which severely suppress emotion, *don't go too far*, or platitudes such as *everything in equal measure*, they yearn for 'harmony', 'balance', 'fairness', and Andrea Dworkin, they moan, goes 'too far', she writes too madly and powerfully and hysterically, they say, she is too mad with fury for men, they say, she goes too far; of course she does, but, clearly, she ain't gone far enough, not enough yet, not enough for all those radical changes she'd like to see happen, not far enough yet, there's still a long way to go, but she keeps her idealism, erotic and furious it is, together, both erotic and crazy, always the two, always mad with passion and passionately mad, but the madness is not all fierce, it's often tender, tender love, she evokes tender fucking, as D.H. Lawrence called it in *Lady Chatterley's Lover*, or 'mercy-fucking', in Lawrence Durrell's phrase,[40] a form of fucking that ain't about power-power-power, it's a kind of fucking portrayed in *Ice and Fire*: 'I met my beautiful boy, my lost brother, around, somewhere, and invited him in... We were like women together

40 in Lawrence Durrell: *Quinx*, Faber 1985

on that narrow piece of foam rubber, and he, astonished by the sensuality of it, ongoing, the thick sweetness of it, came so many times, like a woman: and me too: over and over: like one massive, perpetually knotted and moving creature, the same intense orgasms, no drifting separateness of the mind or fragmented fetishizing of the boy: instead a magnificent cresting, the way a wave rises to a height pushing forward and pulls back underneath itself toward drowning at the same time: one wave lasting forever, rising, pulling, drowning, dying' (*Ice*, 123), Dworkin, like D.H. Lawrence, can't resist resorting to the old oceanic metaphor for the orgasm, orgasm as molten water, juice, surging waves, orgasms like the cut to the shot of the ocean in old Hollywood movies; and again, in this passage from *Mercy*, there's more idealism and lovemaking, where the narrator writes superbly and poetically of the idealism and passion of being in love shot through with extraordinary lovemaking: '[a]nd fuck meant all kinds of making love – it was a new word. It was fucking if you got inside each other, or so near you couldn't be pulled apart. It was joy and risk and fun and orgasm; not faking it; I never have. It didn't have to do with who put what where. It was all kinds of wet and all kinds of urgent and all kinds of here and now, with him or her. It was you tangled up with someone, raw. It wasn't this one genital act, in out in out, that someone could package and sell or that there was an etiquette for. It wasn't some imitation of something you saw somewhere, in porn or your favourite movie star saying how he did it. It was something vast, filled with risk and feeling; feeling; personal love ain't the only feeling there's feelings of adventure and newness and excitement and Goddam pure happiness – here's need and sorrow and loneliness and certain kinds of grief that turn easy into touching someone, wild, agitated, everywhere – there's just liking whoever it is and wanting to pull them down right on you, they make you giddy, their mere existence tickles you to death, you giggle and cheer them on and you touch them – and there's sensation, just that, no morality, no higher good, no justification, just how it feels. There's uncharted waters, you ain't acting out a script and there's no way past the present, you are right there in the middle of your own real life riding a wave a mile high with speed and grace and then you are pulled under to the bottom of the world. The whole world's alive, everything moves and wants and loves, the whole world's alive with promise, with possibility; and I wanted to live, I said yes I want to live' (172); here, Dworkin's narrator is like Ursula in D.H. Lawrence's fabulous *The Rainbow*, where she prowls in the surf like a wolf and cries 'I want to go!': '[s]he stood on the edge of the water, at the edge of the solid, flashing body of the sea, and the wave rushed over her feet. 'I want to go,' she cried, in a strong, dominant voice. 'I want to go.' She prowled, ranging on the edge of the water like a possessed creature, and he followed her... she turned, she walked to him. 'I want to go,' she cried, in the high, hard voice, like the scream of gulls. 'Where?' he asked. 'I don't know'';[41] where? where does Ursula Brangwen want to go? she doesn't know, she just knows she 'wants to go', it's the same with Rimbaud, with all (usually young) outsiders, outcasts, rebels without a cause, the ones that won't 'fit in', the disenfranchized, the alienated, the dispossessed, the figures out of Dostoievsky, Rimbaud, Gide, Miller, Huysmans, Baudelaire, Camus, and now Dworkin; the outsiders/ dispossessed who 'want to go', they don't know where, where doesn't count, it doesn't matter 'where', just anywhere, anywhere'll do, and nowhere, nowhere'll do – Tangiers, Mexico, Lima, Paris, St Petersburg, Bombay – anywhere, all-place, no-place, because once you get into this state, there's no escape, it's a hell, an in-between zone, neither here nor there, and there's no way out, there's no exit, 'no one here gets out alive' as the Lizard Idiot put it, there's nothing to do and nowhere to go, 'nothing happens' as Jude knows in Thomas Hardy's *Jude the Obscure*, 'it's awful!' as Estragon cries in *Waiting For Godot*, and the way out (or in) for Dworkin's characters is to write, write, write, to write and keep on writing, this is her way: *to write her way out of Hell*; and so, in Hell, she, I mean her characters, her texts, go mad, you have to go mad – creativity and madness become synonymous, they're part of the same thing (from shamanism onwards madness, psychosis, creativity, genius, magic, poetry and prophecy are part of the same thing); so how mad she is, really, Andrea Dworkin, how mad she is in her fiction, how simple, how

41 *The Rainbow*, 531

she simplifies things, how idealistic, too, madly idealistic she is, yet she has to be, she has to be idealistic, artists have to be, at times, from time to time, to counter the shit, to counter the constant flow of junk that threatens to smother the world, artists have to be idealistic, and we love them when they are (Rimbaud, for instance, the ruffian poet who burned brighter than most), or Sappho, wild woman poet of love, whose way of loving shakes the trees on a mountainside, in her vivid metaphor, or Jean Genet or Franz Kafka, writers who expose the brutalities of the system). These are the writers that Dworkin admired in her youth, they are her 'influences', if she has any 'influences' – she speaks of these writers in "Loving Books: Male/ Female/ Feminist" (1985): 'I live a strange life, but often the strangest thing about it is that I still love books, and have faith in them and get courage from them as I did when I was young, hopeful and innocent... The books I loved when I was younger were by wild men: Dostoevsky, Rimbaud, Allen Ginsberg among the living, Baudelaire, Whitman, the indecorous. I read Freud and Darwin as great visionaries, their work culled from the fantastic, complex imagination' (some of the 'great writers' are put in the novel *Ice and Fire* as epigraphs: quotes from Spinoza – 'Neither weep nor laugh but understand', Dostoievsky, Baudelaire, Kafka – 'Coitus as punishment for the happiness of being together', Pasolini – 'I love life so fiercely, so desperately'); like other writers, Dworkin was ambitious, and burned to be a writer; writers such as Julie Burchill have written of their youthful desires to be a writer, but when one compares Julie Burchill and Andrea Dworkin, one sees that Burchill is a waspish, relatively unimportant journalist, while Dworkin is one of the few writers who comes close to the fervour and idealism of the young Arthur Rimbaud; Dworkin writes: '[w]hen young, I never thought about being homosexual or bisexual or heterosexual: only about being like Rimbaud. *Artiste* in the soon-to-be-dead mode was my sexual orientation, my gender identity, the most intense way of living: dying early the inevitable end of doing everything with absolute passion' (War, 63); Dworkin has a profound view of writing and art: she believes writing is important, that it is not something you do as a sideline, that writing is central to her life, and to a society's well-being, that the writer is someone who *acts*, that writing is an *act*, not an idea, not something invisible and flimsy, but an act, much as André Gide said that 'in the beginning was the deed', not the Word, but the Act: in her essays on censorship, free speech, civil rights and obscenity, Dworkin writes: '[p]olice in police states and most great writers throughout time see writing as act, not air – as act, not idea; concrete, specific, real, not insubstantial blather on a dead page' ("Against the Male Flood: Censorship, Pornography, and Equality", War, 255), and Dworkin knows, as too few others do, of the number of writers and journalists who are arrested, imprisoned and shot: International PEN, for instance, monitors over seven hundred writers who are imprisoned or attacked in 95 countries worldwide; the conditions of the cells in which these writers and journalists are forced to live are horrific;[42] the price of writing, of wanting to become a writer, Dworkin knows, can be very high: indeed, as the narrator of *Ice and fire* finds out, one pays with one's life to be a writer, writing is a life's work, a life's *act*, an act which puts all of one's life on the line, an act in which one dares everything, risks everything; Dworkin is this kind of writer (there are too few of them) and this is perhaps another reason why Dworkin is so reviled in some quarters – simply because she is so passionate, because she risks everything, because she throws her whole self, leaving nothing back, into her work, so her work contains so much of *her*, and critics and newspaper commentators and pundits simply cannot deal with that, or do not wish to, or don't know how to; Dworkin is the sort of writer who cannot go along with tabloid pundits and broadsheet journalists who get upset by the word *fuck*, who get uptight when a novel uses 'dirty words' too often, yes, this is all very well, oh yes, the word *fuck is* 'shocking', isn't it? no it isn't, *fuck* isn't 'shocking', at all, for

42 A piece by International PEN describes what happened to a journalist jailed in the Western Sahara: 'For nine years the man in the Western Sahara lived in a two square metre cell with seven other men. The only light came in through two tiny holes. Prisoners were fed lentils and beans during the day and gruel at night. They were routinely tortured. Many went mad; many died. They were not allowed to write, and yet they did write. They used their half bar of soap to write plays on their trousers and memorized the plays before they washed the trousers. They found scraps of paper and wrote poetry, using thick coffee for ink.' Joanne Leedom-Ackerman *et al*, International PEN: "Writers in Prison", in Ursula Owen, ed: *Index on Censorship*, May/June 1994, 106

there are far more important issues to discuss, and the brutal treatment of reporters and writers worldwide is far more pressing a matter for discussion, another inspirational artist for Dworkin was the painter Frida Kahlo; for Dworkin, Kahlo is 'the great painter of primal female pain' whose 'paintings are the most vivid renderings by any woman of the female screwed, gashed, wounded', who, married to Diego Rivera, the Mexican artist, 'painted what it was like being fucked by him';[43] Dworkin quotes Diego Rivera's testament of his relationship with Kahlo: '[i]f I loved a woman, the more I loved her, the more I wanted to hurt her. Frida was only the most obvious victim of this disgusting trait';[44] for Dworkin, as for many feminists, Kahlo's paintings are the astonishing record of a woman's incredibly painful relationship with a man: '[s]he painted the suffering, enraged; she created an iconography of the *chingada* [literally the "screwed one"] that was resistance, not pornography; knowing herself to be the screwed one, she made an art of passionate rebellion that shows the pain of inferiority delivered into your body – the violence of the contempt... Kahlo paints the woman vividly wounded, dripping blood; in one, *A Few Small Nips*, painted in 1935, a naked woman (except for one sock and one shoe) is on a bed, gashed all over; she is alive, wide-eyed, her boy animated in curves and subtle, living contortion; a man stands upright next to the bed, he is fully dressed, even wearing a hat, and he holds a knife in his hand; he is aloof, indifferent, blank; and the blood in blotches and smears is all over her body and spreads out over the walls and over the floor in spots and smears even past the boundaries of the canvas to the frame. Kahlo shows the unspeakable pain of being *alive* and female, penetrated like this';[45] Kahlo's art is that of an outsider, someone who inhabits the edges of society, a place that is perhaps the feminist 'wild zone'; as Whitney Chadwick wrote: '[w]hen it came to sharing in the collective mythology of Surrealism, women experienced themselves as outsiders';[46] Léonor Fini saw herself as that archetypal female outsider, Lilith, the mythic witch of Western

43 Andrea Dworkin: *Intercourse*, 211-2
44 Rivera, quoted in Hayden Herrera: *Frida*, op.cit., 183
45 Dworkin: *Intercourse*, 212, 223
46 Whitney Chadwick, *Women Artists and the Surrealist Movement*, 129

religion: 'I know that I belong with the idea of Lilith, the anti-Eve, and that my universe is that of the spirit';[47] looking at Surrealist concepts of eroticism from the alienated viewpoint of the female Surrealist artist, Ithel Colquhoun painted some ironic parodies of Surrealist sexuality, such as her *The Pine Family*, which depicts three male torsos made of pine logs, each with the penis lopped off; Colquhoun's painting sends up Freudian psychoanalysis and the grotesque notion of castration; some critics say that Dworkin emphasizes sexuality too much, or rather, pornography, but this perspective, Dworkin would maintain, is the masculinist one, the prudish one, where even to mention sexuality is to be regarded suspiciously: this extract from an interview she conducted with herself is instructive: 'Q: I mean, any Freudian would have a field day with your work. Penis envy, penis hatred, penis obsession, some might say. A: Men are the source of that, in their literature, culture, behaviour. I could never have invented it. Who was more penis obsessed than Freud? Except maybe Reich. But then, what a competition that would be. Choose the most penis obsessed man in history. What is so remarkable is that men in general, really with so few exceptions, are so penis obsessed. I mean, if anyone should be sure of self-worth in a penis-orientated society, it should be the one who has the penis';[48] and, again, in *Pornography*, Dworkin claims, extraordinarily, that there is a continuity between men and their penis, that the man is the penis, or vice versa, as she writes: '[m]en renounce whatever they have in common with women so as to experience no commonality with women; and what is left, according to men, is one piece of flesh a few inches long, the penis. The penis is sensate; the penis is the man; the man is human; the penis signifies humanity' (*Pornography*, 54); Dworkin seems to regard the penis as some powerful 'weapon', where she really means the phallus, the phallus being the penis as cultural artifact, the cultural significance of the penis, not the biological slip of flesh, yet Dworkin harps on about the penis, as if it has a mind of its own (a comic rendition of the penis is that it does have a mind of its own, and men are often described as thinking with

47 Léonor Fini, quoted in Xavière Gauthier: *Léonor Fini*, op.cit., 74
48 Dworkin: "Nervous Interview", 1978, War, 58-59

their dicks rather than their brains), so in *Pornography* she writes: '[v]iolence is male; the male is the penis; violence is the penis or the sperm ejaculated from it' (55), but, again, Dworkin is wrong, for violence is patently not 'male', there are many forms of violence, and violence *per se* is not 'male', male-gendered, or rather, it is gendered, culturally, as male, for it is true, as Dworkin elsewhere attests, that men are more violent than women, or, rather, to further qualify the statement, societies worldwide are perhaps generally orientated towards masculinism, towards systems of action and thought that favour masculinism, but that doesn't mean, as Dworkin says, that 'violence is male', no, not at all, and then, in the next sentence, she claims that 'the male is the penis', well, sure, men have dicks, but is that all men are, dicks? just dicks? maybe, maybe men are just dicks in the same way that Dworkin sees women in pornography as just cunts, but this is plainly ridiculous, and when Dworkin's polemic boils down to bold but idiotic assertions that 'the male is the penis' or that 'violence is male' she renders her arguments void, because although we love bold assertions when Dworkin asserts one step too far and falls flat on her face, how disappointing it is; a big problem which Dworkin does not really tackle is the question of texts or artworks in themselves; like other modernists, Dworkin believes in the 'transparency' of a text, that is, the text is merely a vehicle for the author's intentions/ emotions/ ideologies, that is, the text is a mirror of the soul, a mode of communication in which what is written is what the author really thinks and feels; Dworkin does not employ the methodology of postmodernism or cultural studies, which sees texts as having multiple meanings, meanings which shift continually, meanings which are affected by all manner of considerations – of context, ideology, economics, race, class, status, identity, gender, and so on; Dworkin deals with such themes and economies, but does not investigate how they impress upon a text, so when she reads certain pornographic texts, she does consider the many factors that affect the text, she simply reads the text directly, reacting to it, as if the text is exactly as it is meant to be, as if it is devoid of a socio-ideological context; Dworkin's battleground of life, certainly, is very much centred in sexuality, in sexual politics, in the rewriting of sexual *mœurs*, sexuality is where she investigates culture, her surroundings, yet, and this is crucial, Dworkin does not hate sex, no, she loves sexuality, loves lovemaking, loves the wildness and power and passion of lovemaking, meaning 'the wild us outside and free or stretched out together body to body and carnal, mutual; not this fucking tame stupid boring tie me up then fuck me' (M, 151), she's bored with men and their depictions of sexuality, at times Dworkin would agree with Luce Irigaray that 'woman can come without any help from you', the 'you' here being Freud and/ or all men,[49] Dworkin doesn't mean that type of fucking, but something like this, from *Mercy*, where she writes passionately of lovemaking, lovemaking so deep and wonderful it produces burning: '[a]nd the light burns me clean too, the light and the heat, from the sun and from the sex. Could you fuck the sun? That's how I feel, like I'm fucking the sun. I'm right up on it, smashed down it, a great, brilliant body that is part of its landscape, the heat melts us together but it doesn't burn me away, I'm flat on it and it burns, my arms are flat up against it and it burns, I'm flung flat on it like it's the ground but it's the sun and it burns with me up against it, arms up and out to hold it but there is nothing to hold, the flames are never solid, never still, I'm solid, I'm still, and I'm on it, smashed up against it. I think it's the sun but it's M and he's on top of me and I'm burning but not to death, past death, immortal, an eternal burning up against him and there are waves of heat that are suffocating but I breathe and I drown but I don't die no matter how far I go under. You've seen a fire but have you ever been one – the red and blue and black and orange and yellow in waves, great tidal waves of heat, and if it comes toward you, you run because the heat is in waves that can stop you from breathing, you'll suffocate, and you can see the waves because they come after you and they eat up the air behind you and it gets heavy and hard and tight and mean... But I don't get burned up no matter how I burn. I'm indestructible, a new kind of flesh. Every night, hours before dawn, we make love until dawn or sunrise or late in the morning when there's a bright yellow glaze over everything, and I drift off into a coma of sleep, a perfect blackness, no fear, no

49 Luce Irigaray: "The poverty of psychoanalysis", in Irigaray, 1991, 93

memory, no dream, and when I open my eyes again he is in me and it is brute daylight, the naked sun, and I am on fire and there is nothing else, just this, burning, smashed up against him, outside time or anything anyone knows or thinks or wants and it's never enough' (M, 90-91); Andrea Dworkin is very angry, always angry, it seems, though this is not true, this is to stereotype her, to see her as simply the ubiquitous 'right on' feminist, dressed in boots and dungarees, this is how newspapers and journalists present feminists, because they have no space, they say, to write in a more detailed manner, so they use stereotypes, it's a way of getting something across, and it's what makes Andrea Dworkin and feminists angry, because they are continually being denigrated, it's one backlash after another, all reactionary thinking, from one extreme to the other, with all the liberals in the middle screaming BE FAIR!, they want everyone to be 'fair', no one must get upset, it must all be calm and polite, so when Andrea Dworkin gets angry, they can't deal with it, it upsets the equilibrium of their lives, it subverts their lives, it overturns their complacency, as Michael Moorcock writes: '[w]hat seems to annoy people is the power with which she presents her arguments, the relentless refusal to compromise, to ignore the injustices and cruelties of male power';[50] critics often lay into Dworkin personally – they mention her the size or shape of her body, her stereotypical feminist appearance (dungarees), and, often, they question her sexuality – she's a lesbian, they say, or she's bisexual, or she hates men but lives with a man (John Stoltenberg), or has men as companions, which some radical lesbians think is wrong, to collude with men, which is ridiculous, and critics wonder about her sexuality, because, as in so much of humanist criticism, they think the personality of the author is important, whereas, for cultural theorists, the text is primary, so discussion of the sexual 'preferences' or character of the author is not the issue, but, on the few occasions when she has discussed her own sexuality, Dworkin produces dollops of irony, as in the self-interview "Nervous Interview": ''Q: If you could sleep with anyone in history, who would it be? A: That's easy. George Sand. Q: She was pretty involved with men. A: I would have saved her

50 Michael Moorcock,1989, 167

from all that. Q: Is there any man, I mean, there must be at least one. A: Well, ok, yes. Ugh. Rimbaud. Disaster. In the old tradition, Glorious Disaster' (War, 61); picking Sand and Rimbaud to fuck is of course a stylish choice – they are powerful European writers – and Dworkin is sure to make all the right sort of references (Dostoievsky, Rimbaud, Bronte, Genet); the first chapter of Dworkin's *Pornography* is a feminist manifesto, a manifesto of radical feminism, fraught with problems for many feminists, because Dworkin bases so much of her feminism on biology, and feminists such as Elaine Showalter, Julia Kristeva and Bonnie Zimmerman are very critical of those feminists who found their view of things on biology and essentialism (where 'anatomy is textuality'),[51] some of the feminists who do include Shere Hite and Nancy Friday, with their surveys of the sexual antics of women and men, and also Luce Irigaray, the marvellous French feminist who writes so powerfully, like Dworkin, about the injustice and pain that women experience at the hands of men, and who founds some of her feminism on biology, on the body, and this is always a problem, because it leads too much towards the right, politically, some feminists think, it becomes too right wing, too materialistic, it takes materialism in the wrong direction, although, as Dworkin and Irigaray would say (as would Cixous), the body is very important, and it's men who control the body, and the weapons they use varies from coercion to persuasion to cultural influence to violence, we are back with violence again; this aspect of feminism – the crusade against rape and violence, an important part of many feminist and women's groups, is relatively easy to identify, violence is hard to hide, as we have said, except in the home, except in domestic violence, which is horrifyingly widespread, it's everywhere, much more than anyone thinks, really, and Dworkin assures us in her books that this violence is everywhere, and in *Pornography* she notes how men use physical strength to exert their power over and above everyone else, and that this violence is protected, nay,

51 Elaine Showalter: "Organic or biological criticism is the most extreme statement of gender difference, of a text indelibly marked by the boy: anatomy if textuality... Simply to invoke anatomy risks a return to the crude essentialism, the phallic and ovarian theories of art, that oppressed women in the past.' "Feminist Criticism in the Wilderness", in Showalter, 1986, 250

exalted, by men, as she writes: 'Laws and customs protect it; art and literature adore it; history depends on it'; the distribution of wealth maintains it' (15); and we see this male violence everywhere, it is what happens in the 'wild zone', as Elaine Showalter calls it,[52] where it is celebrated in countless works of art and culture; the masculinist cults of violence are explored in Dworkin's works, from *Woman Hating* through *Our Blood* to the novels *Ice and Fire* and *Mercy,* the cult of violence is everywhere, and it is carried out, as Dworkin notes in the first chapter of *Pornography,* by all manner of weapons, implements that are now familiar to us from psycho slasher gore movies and other forms of pornography: '[t]he symbols of terror are commonplace and utterly familiar: the gun, the knife, the bomb, the fist, and so on' (15); Annie Blue of Women Against Violence Against Women says: '[w]e see all pornography as violence against women';[53] throughout *Pornography,* Dworkin isolates the ways in which men terrorize women, with all manner of implements, called 'tools', all euphemisms for the penis (swords, weapons, guns, bombs, missiles, rockets), and she tells how men terrorize women with their aggression and brute strength, and the apotheosis of male aggression for Dworkin is rape, and rape forms the basis of *Ice and Fire* and *Mercy,* these fictions are all about rape, about how women struggle through rape, through successive rapes, continual rapes, how women are continually raped by men, and, again, we have to continually remind ourselves of the reductionism and simplicity of Dworkin's argument, this extremism which places men against women, with nothing in between, this ruthless gender dichotomy which forms the basis of Dworkin's polemic, which she returns to, throughout her work, and rape is at the centre of it, as rape is at the centre of so much feminism; rape and pornography, these two issues are part of the same masculinist dogma of power, for feminists, so that they see marriage as 'sanctified rape', or as Dworkin puts it, 'Marriage as an institution developed from rape as a practice' (19), while Luce

52 Elaine Showalter: "Feminist Criticism in the Wilderness", in Showalter, 1986, 262-3; Jeanne Addison Roberts: *The Shakespearean Wild: Geography, Genus and Gender*, University of Nebraska Press, Lincoln, Nebraska 1991, 1-5
53 quoted in Sarah Baxter: "Women Against Porn", *Time Out*, London, 23 March 1988

Irigaray says that rape is everyone's problem, it not just concerns the raper and the raped and those close to them, Irigaray writes that '[i]f there were civil rights for women, the whole of society would be the injured party in the case of rape or all the other forms of violence inflicted on women; society, then, would be the plaintiff or co-plaintiff against the harm caused to one of its members',[54] in Irigaray's view, which is basically right, rape is society's problem, not something that happens to one or two people, because, as feminists have stated in the 1970s, the personal is political, and rape is therefore political as well as personal attack, political oppression as well as personal oppression, a wound in society's body, not just the raped's body; the man rapes the woman, says Dworkin, and this occurs all the time, and indeed, rape is not a new phenomenon, for women, it seems, have always been raped, since time immemorial, since the very beginning, for one can quite believe that men who didn't get their way sexually probably raped women; we don't know what people got up to tens of thousands of years ago, but in the mediæval era, where we have written records, we know that rape was common, as Marion Wynne-Davies writes: '[i]n mediæval Europe a woman was often abducted and sexually penetrated in order to force an unwanted or unsuitable marriage, thereby enabling her abductor to take possession of her lands and inheritance. Legally this was seen as the theft of property by one man from another, and once wedlock occurred very little redress was obtainable; indeed, the marriage redeemed the offender from any punishment',[55] rape, like its legal counterpart, heterosexual marriage, has been linked to property, economy and materialism since earliest times, and woman-hating was commonplace in the mediæval epoch, as Howard Bloch notes: 'the topic of misogyny... participates in a vestigial horror practically synonymous with the term *mediæval*, and because one of the assumptions governing our perception of the Middle Ages is the viral presence of antifeminism', and Bloch concludes: '[t]he discourse of misogyny runs like a rich vein throughout the

54 Irigaray: *Je, tu, nous*, 88
55 Wynne-Davies: ""The Swallowing Womb': Consumed and Consuming Women in *Titus Andronicus*", in Valerie Wayne, 131

breadth of mediæval literature',[56] woman-hating may have been so commonplace, so deeply ingrained in the Bible, in courtly love poetry, in hymns, liturgy and ritual, in proverbs and legends and romances, that it would have been obvious, and to draw attention to it at the time may have seemed ridiculous, as indeed, some people groan and tut when attention is drawn today to feminist issues, to inequality and so on; maybe sexism is still so prevalent today, so deeply embedded in various cultures around the globe, that when one goes against it, one is laughed at, or people groan, or yawn, or get angry, because you've disturbed the status quo, you've upset the norms and well-worn assumptions which are a part of contemporary life, and have been for millennia; for feminists, rape is the expression of this woman-hating, a violent eruption of a feeling that is damn near universal, as Susan Brownmiller writes: '[r]ape became not only a male prerogative, but man's basic weapon of force against woman, the principal agent of his will and her fear';[57] Dworkin returns to the subject of rape all the time, for pornography is based on rape, this is her central thesis in her non-fiction books, that pornography, which is the 'graphic depiction of whores', as she terms it, is the expression of male hatred of women, it is the manifestation of the power relations between men and women, pornography is the artistic expression of rape, Dworkin claims, it is the æstheticization of rape, the poeticizing of violence, it is pure desire, pornography, desire let loose, gone mad, really wild, so that rape is normal, so that women always want sex, from the male viewpoint, or as Dworkin writes: '[h]e says that the female wants to be raped; he rapes. She resists rape; he must beat her, threaten her with death, forcibly carry her off, attack her in the night, use knife or fist; and still he says she wants it, they all do' (18); and again: '[m]en have created the group, the type, the concept, the epithet, the insult, the industry, the trade, the

56 Howard Bloch: "Medieval misogyny", *Representations*, 20, Autumn 1987, 1; on misogyny in literature, see: Katharine M. Rogers: *The Troublesome ,Helpmate: A history of misogyny in literature*, University of Washington Press, Seattle 1966; Eleanor C. McLaughlin: "Equality of souls, inequality of sexes: woman in medieval theology", in Rosemary R. Ruether, ed: *Religion and Sexism: Images of woman in the Jewish and Christian traditions*, Simon & Schuster, New York 1964, 312-66

57 Brownmiller: *Against Our Will*, 5

commodity, the reality of women as whore' (War, 237); Beverly Brown agrees with Dworkin that pornography as a concept is violence against women: the 'harms feminism wishes to mark' writes Brown, 'do not depend for their seriousness on being or resulting directly in acts. The harms indicated by pornography's relation to a 'sexist society' are serious in themselves;'[58] for Dworkin, as for Catherine MacKinnon, rape and male force is *made sexy*, this is how it works: violent male sex, like masculine power, is eroticized, thus enabling men to have more of it; Sheila Jeffreys concords with Dworkin's view of the damaging effects of patriarchy and pornography: '[a]nother reason for women's opposition is that we have all, as women, been trained to eroticise our own subordination and to call that pleasure and freedom. The sexual liberals argue that if we have a sexual response to anything then that must be good and positive. This is clearly not true, since women can orgasm during rape and sexual abuse, and men do so when torturing and killing women, as in Vietnam';[59] Rosalind Coward reckons that '[m]ost women still prefer the sublimated masochism of romance to explicit pornographic material and feel uneasy rather than envious about men's use of pornography';[60] for Dworkin, the notion of 'romance', as found in 'women's magazines', in Mills & Boon 'bodice rippers', in romantic sit coms, is a soft version of pornography; Dworkin lays into rape as the theology and practice of masculine power, and she is right, for it is still mainly men who rape, the incidents of women raping men are very few and far between, it is mostly men that rape, still, always, nearly always, nearly always men that rape, men that do the raping, it is men but still nobody seems to realize this, the courts don't, they say, well, 'she was asking for it', they still use those arguments, yes, it's shocking, but some still think that way about rape, just as some men still believe in violence, and some men still think we should have nuclear weapons, and men anyway still stockpile and test and develop nuclear weapons, at billions of dollars per year, per month, per week, per day, male violence costs a lot of money, and money too

58 Beverly Brown: "A Feminist Interest in Pornography – Some Modest Proposals", *m/f*, 5/6, 1981, 12-13
59 Jeffreys: "The censorship of revolutionary feminism", in Chester, 138
60 Rosalind Coward: "Porn: What's in it for women?", *New Statesmen*, 13 June 1986

is at the heart of the rape cult, the rape culture, for money is power, as Dworkin and (nearly) all feminists note, money, they say, is patriarchal power in action, power made manifest, for money and exchange and trade form the basis of Western (global) life, forms the basis of capitalism and commerce, and money is at the heart of the masculine power system, and women still earn a fraction of what men earn, and there are still far far more men in the top jobs or even medium to high jobs in institutions such as law, politics, the media, manufacturing, education, the arts, it's still the men, the 'suits' as they're called, the men in the dark conservative suits, and what keeps the economic structure of the rape culture buoyant is, Dworkin says, the consumer, the one who buys all the pornography: '[f]inally, the ultimate colluders in the legitimizing of pornography, of course, are the consumers. In 1979 we had a $4-billion-a-year industry in this country. By 1985 it was an $8-billion-a-year industry. These consumers include men in all walks of life: lawyers, politicians, writers, professors, owners of media, police, doctors, maybe even commissioners on presidential commissions' (War, 282); the consumers of pornography are also the legislators, Dworkin claims, or in Catherine MacKinnon words, 'it was the rich who used to own pornography exclusively, the men who created the structures of our life... they are looking at the pornography, they are defining the state; they are looking at the pornography, they are writing the laws... the rape laws!';[61] but this power inequality is by no means everything in the feminist debate, the notion of 'equal pay', indeed, Luce Irigaray thinks that the abstraction 'equality' can only mean *at best* the equality of salaries, so that women will be paid the same as men, nothing else, Irigaray says, can be 'equal', instead, there must eternal *difference*, in gender, from the sexual to the cultural; Irigaray says that difference must be emphasized, but her theory of difference is based, like the metaphysics of Dworkin, on sexuality, sexuality lies at the heart of the feminist discourse of feminists such as Dworkin, Irigaray, Cixous, Millet, Griffin, Hite, they emphasize sexuality more than other factors, and this is a problem, this reduction, ultimately, to sexual matters, it reminds one of Freud, who also

61 Lesley White: "A porn fighter", *The Sunday Times*, 12 June 1994, section 9, 6,

sexualized the world, so that a tower was no mere tower, but a phallic object, connoting a penis, and a cave was no mere cave, but a vagina; it's the same with the Marquis de Sade (Dworkin explores his horrific writing in *Pornography*), Georges Bataille, Henry Miller, D.H. Lawrence, Charles Baudelaire, Wilhelm Reich, Havelock Ellis, the Kronhausens, and so on; these people (again, mostly male) eroticize the world, and everything becomes, ultimately, reduced to sex, or the penis, sex is reduced to the penis, the penis is at the centre of fucking, as Dworkin says time and again, the penis which is also a mirror, a phallic reflector of male desire, the phallus as mirror, reflecting male subjectivity, a product of masculine narcissism, a 'transcendent signifier' feminists call the phallus,[62] it's the holy of holies, and it's a mirror, in the Lacanian psychological system, associated with language and desire,[63] and it silences women who do not have access to the 'transcendental signifier',[64] and for Madeleine Gagnon, the phallus is symbolic of male narcissism: '[t]he phallus... represents repressive capitalist ownership, the exploiting bourgeois... The phallus means everything sets itself up as a mirror. Everything that erects itself as perfection',[65] men need their mirrors, Dworkin says, and how accurate she is, writing of the male: '[i]n fucking, he is enlarged. As Woolf wrote, she is his mirror; by diminishing her in his use of her he becomes twice his size. In the culture, he is a giant, enlarged by his conquest of her, implied or explicit. She remains his mirror and, as Woolf postulated, "...mirrors are essential to all violent and heroic action." In culture, his sexual power is his theme. In culture, the male uses the female to explicate his theme',[66] or to sex and death, for there is always a counterpart or opposite or companion to masculine theories, so they speak of sex *and* death, sex and *death*, the two together, calling it different names down

62 Luce Irigaray: *Speculum of the Other Woman*, tr Gillian C. Gill, and *This Sex which Is Not One*, tr Catherine Porter, both Cornell University Press, New York 1985; see also: Dorothy Leland: "Lacanian psychoanalysis and French feminism: toward an adequate political psychology", *Hypatia*, 3 (3), Winter 1989, 81-103
63 Gagnon: "Corps I", *La venue à l'écriture*, UGE, 10/18, Paris 1977; in Marks, 180
64 Cora Kaplan, 1986
65 Gagnon: "Corps I", *La venue à l'écriture*, UGE< Paris 10/18, 1977, and in Marks, 1981, 180
66 Dworkin: *Pornography*, 23-4; Virginia Woolf: *A Room of One's Own*, Harcourt, Brace & World, New York, 1957, 36

the ages, from love and death or the love-in-death in the Arthurian myths of Tristan and Isolde, to the orgasm of Surrealism, the same melding of love and death, or, as Dworkin would say, sex and pain, and this sex and pain is called pornography, the two go together, sex and pain, it's the two things together, chained together, in 'binary logic', so that feminists such as Helene Cixous have argued, rightly, that masculine 'binary logic', which constantly opposes terms such as 'masculine' and 'feminine' is very limiting, it is two-term logocentrism, which reduces everything to 'yes' or 'no', or sex and death,[67] death's at the heart of masculinist culture for Dworkin, as she writes in "Why So-Called Radical Men Love and Need Pornography": '[m]en love death. In everything they make, they hollow out a central place for death, let its rancid smell contaminate every dimension of whatever still survives. Men especially love murder. In art they celebrate it, and in life they commit it' (War, 214), and here she's right, for in art death is celebrated: Shakespeare celebrates death, makes it the key mystery in *Hamlet, King Lear* and *Macbeth*, and any number of (male) writers and artists make death central: Goya, Picasso, Mailer, Miller, Petrarch, Homer, de Sade, Freud, Nietzsche, Luther, Bataille, de Musset, Hugo, Cervantes, etc, and for Dworkin male culture is built upon this centrality of death, where the slow death and the quick death are both erotic, where death is celebrated – in Hollywood movie stars, for instance, who 'live fast and die young', as the cliché has it, or war heroes, or martyrs, or serial killers, or the deaths celebrated each night in a million cop and detective TV shows, around the globe, the killing at the beginning of the show, to upset the status quo of suburbia, followed by the police marksmen shooting the murderer at the end of the 50 minutes, the more grisly the death the better the effect, the more 'explicit' the special effects, the greater the enjoyment, i.e., viscerality and violence make for good TV, good cinema, good copy, and, as Dworkin notes, all this glorification of death is OK *as long as it's happening to someone else*, i.e., *not in my street, no way, no thank you*, i.e., serial killers are fine and

67 Helene Cixous & Catherine Clément: *The Newly Born Woman*, University of Manchester Press 1985, 63f

good fun on the sofa of an evening, as long as they're maiming in other cities, other countries, but not on your own doorstep, not in your own bedroom, as Dworkin writes: '[i]n male culture, slow murder is the heart of eros, fast murder is the heart of action, and systematized murder is the heart of history. It is as if, long, long ago, men made a covenant with murder: I will worship and serve you if you will spare *me*; I will murder so as not to be murdered' (War, 215), and in "Pornography and Grief" (1978), she writes: '[t]he fact is that the process of killing – and both rape and battery are steps in that process – is the prime sexual act for men in reality and/or in imagination' (War, 22), ah, but here, yes, she goes too far, with this blanket generalization, for it is clearly untrue, for, although death and murder are celebrated in every form of culture, from highbrow Wagnerian opera to the lowest of the lowbrow US soap opera, killing or death is not 'the prime sexual act' for men, no, it isn't, Dworkin gets it wrong here, she goes for the jugular and it wasn't the jugular at all, it was a mistake; rape may be one of the messages that culture sends out, but it is not the only message, so Dworkin's insistence on the primacy of rape and subordination misses out other issues: when Dworkin says (in "Violence Against Women: It Breaks the Heart, Also the Bones"): '[r]ape, battery, incest, torture, murder, sexual harassment, prostitution, and pornography are acts of real violence against us enjoyed by our husbands, fathers, sons, brother, lovers, teachers, and friends' (War, 180), we can see how she melds modes of representation (pornography) and actual events (rape), and it's a powerful connection, seemingly so obvious, because in Dworkin's rhetoric it is a seamless link, yet it is this link, this conflation, that is so hotly disputed among feminists, and there is certainly no consensus on it at all, and, while most (if not all) feminists (or people) would concur with Dworkin that the other 'acts' Dworkin lists – rape, battery, incest, torture, murder – are 'acts of real violence', it is the inclusion of pornography (and, by extension, most if not all art) that causes most controversy among feminists; Roland Barthes is another apologist, like Georges Bataille or André Breton, for pornography, claiming that the pornographic image has no 'punctum', no magic spot where presence or dynamics are created, where the thing depicted comes alive, and is not a mere 'motionless object' or fetish;[68] and it is the male who orchestrates the whole affair, for pornography, like high art, is made by and for the male, from a male point of view with a male point of view in mind during production and consumption, and it is this masculinized world that Dworkin explores, and because pornography is founded on erotic desire, Dworkin ends her feminist manifesto (the first half of chapter one of *Pornography*) by talking about sex; men, she says, have 'the power of sex', and the woman becomes a 'sexual object', because the male is always the *subject* of art and pornography, because women are denied subjectivity, so they have no self, they are always objects, and the male gazes at her, it is always, as Laura Mulvey said in her famous article, the *male* gaze looking at the *female* object; in Dworkin's view, men take away from their sense of self an identity, so that if women do not act like men, men not only can't understand them but will not tolerate them: '[i]n his [the male's] view, she is not a woman unless she acts like a woman as he has defined woman' (P, 65), so that, when women step outside of men's definitions, they upset patriarchy, they enter a realm of disinformation and subversion, or the 'wild zone'; Dworkin is absolutely right when she says that men fetishize things, so that telephones, cars, guns, knives, beds and all objects can become sex objects, aids to sexual encounters, as Dworkin rites in *Intercourse*: '[p]enetration was never meant to be kind. In pornography, scissors, razors, knives, and daggers are poised at the entrance to the vagina' (223), and art is the ultimate fetish, as Julia Kristeva says,[69] art is the ultimate fetishized object, and so is pornography, because pornography is part of art, and art is part of pornography, the two, art and pornography, are part of a continuum, many feminists have seen this, that there is no dividing line, really, between art and pornography, but for the establishment, for the judges and government, there is a dividing line, it is called 'the line', and the boundaries between art and pornography are constantly

68 Barthes: *Camera Lucida*, Flamingo 1984, 57; Belinda Budge: "Joan Collins and the Wilder side of Women", in Gamman, 110
69 Julia Kristeva says, 'isn't art the fetish *par excellence*, one that badly camouflages its archeology?', Kristeva: *Revolution in Poetic Language*, tr Margaret Walker, in *The Kristeva Reader*, 115

policed, pornography is 'policed', the governments of the world 'police' pornography, they review it and talk about it and forge the boundaries between art and pornography, between what is acceptable and what is not acceptable, and it seems that quite a bit of pornography is 'acceptable', it must be 'acceptable' to the government, because they have not banned it from the shelves of bookshops and newsagents, only some kinds of pornography are banned, only those kinds that really 'shock', child pornography, certain S/M, or homosexual stuff, but the other kinds, the so-called 'soft porn', is allowed, is allowed to be bought with a copy of a daily newspaper, so that the daily newspapers and soft pornography are set side by side with each other, just as in video shops Walt Disney can be rented next to pornographic films, the two are part of a continuum, art merges into pornography, and though the boundaries shift, continually, they are part of the same thing, the same phenomenon, which is culture, which is artistic expression, call it what you will, to justify it, to justify the whole enterprise, it's art, it's pornography, it's part of the same thing, which is patriarchal art, that is, art by and for men, or, rather, whoever makes it, it is contextualized as masculine, it assumes a masculine reader, as art has done from Greek tragedy to the latest Hollywood movie, they assume masculine audiences, they create masculine viewpoints, so that the notion of a truly 'feminine', a gendered female viewpoint seems to be impossible, that is, to put it another way, can there be a truly 'feminine' art, or a truly 'feminine' sexuality, or a truly 'feminine' response, utterly outside of the masculine world or the masculine art or the masculine context, can there be something truly 'feminine', anything truly 'feminine', anything outside of patriarchal culture, can there be, in other words, a female 'wild zone', a cultural space utterly non-male? It's a big question and feminists hotly debate it, because it's pretty hopeless, really, if there is nothing outside of men and masculine culture or patriarchy, it's depressing, because it means that something is limited, something is suffocating us, we can't escape from patriarchal constraints, it's a question Julia Kristeva tackles, writing that the notion of 'woman' exists on the edge of patriarchy, so that 'woman' is a witch, a specialist in being an outsider: 'woman is a specialist in the unconscious, a witch, a baccanalian, taking her *jouissance* in an anti-Apollonian, Dionysian orgy. A *jouissance* which breaks the symbolic chain, the taboo, the mastery. A *marginal discourse*, with regard to the science, religion and philosophy of the *polis* (witch, child, underdeveloped, not even a poet, at best his accomplice)',[70] Ann Rosalind Jones describes Kristeva's notion of the 'outsider' culture of women, of women as 'witches' thus: '[w]omen, for Kristeva... speak and write as "hysterics," as outsiders to male-dominated discourse, for two reasons: 'the predominance in them of drives related to anality and childbirth, and their marginal position vis-à-vis masculine culture. Their semiotic style is likely to involve repetitive, spasmodic separations from the dominating discourse, which, more often, they are forced to imitate';[71] and, certainly, in pornography, in Dworkin's monomanic view, there is only one response, one reader, one context, one theme, one idea, one protagonist, one personality, and that is male; the woman is simply an object, to be used, like any other object (a telephone, a car, a gun, a camera), the woman is fetishized, as Dworkin writes, so that the man can do what he likes: '[t]he male, through each and every one of his institutions, forces the female to conform to his supremely ridiculous definition of her as sexual object. He fetishizes her body as a whole and in its parts. He exiles her from every realm of expression outside the strictly male-defined sexual or male-defined maternal. He forces her to become that thing that causes erection, then holds himself helpless and powerless when he is aroused by her. His fury when she is not that thing, when she is either more or less than that thing, is intense and punishing' (22), and pornography is all about male lust, or erection, says Dworkin: '[p]ornography does not exist to effect something as vague as so-called erotic interest or sexual arousal; it exists specifically to provoke penile tumescence or erection' (War, 241), but she is wrong here, for pornography has other functions or effects, not simply to do with erection; and when women are worshipped, even when they are set on pedestals, says

70 In Kristeva: *The Kristeva Reader*, 154

71 Ann Rosalind Jones: "Writing the Body: L'Écriture féminine", in Showalter, ed, 363

Dworkin, the result is stereotypical and limiting, for the woman is put in a position she, again, has not chosen, so that even Goddesses, such as Ishtar or the Virgin Mary, are stuck in pigeonholes, as Dworkin explains in her book *Right-Wing Women*: 'this premise about a biologically based morality is used, the woman-superior model of antifeminism is operating to keep women down, not up, in the crude world of actual human interchange. To stay worshipped, the woman must stay a symbol and she must stay good. She cannot become merely a human in the muck of life, morally flawed and morally struggling, committing acts that have complex, difficult, unpredictable consequences. She must not walk the same streets men do or do the same things or have the same responsibilities. Precisely because she is good, she is unfit to do the same things, unfit to make the same decisions, unfit to resolve the same dilemmas, unfit to undertake the same responsibilities, unfit to exercise the same rights. Her nature is different – this time better but still absolutely different – and therefore her role must be different. The worshipping attitude, the spiritual revelation of women that men invoke whenever they suggest that women are finer than they, proposes that women are what men can never be: chaste, good. In fact men are what women can never be: real moral agents, the bearers of real moral authority and responsibility. Women are not kept from this moral agency by biology, but by a male social system that puts women above or below simple human choice in morally demanding situations. The spiritual superiority of women in this model of ludicrous homage isolates women from the human acts that create meaning, the human choices that create both ethics and history. It separates women out from the chaos and triumph of human responsibility by giving women a two-dimensional morality, a stagnant morality, one in which what is right and good is predetermined, sex-determined, biologically determined' (206-7); many feminists have been critical of Andrea Dworkin, because, first of all, *Pornography* was a powerful book, that touched on something central in feminism, and, secondly, because there was much that feminists thought was wrong with Dworkin's polemic, and then, later on in the 1980s, Dworkin and Catherine MacKinnon pushed their bill in North America, a move that created a lot of comment among feminists, for versions were suggested for the cities of Minneapolis, Boston, LA and Indianapolis, where it became law for a while;[72] Maggie Humm summarized the Dworkin-MacKinnon objective thus: 'Andrea Dworkin and Catherine MacKinnon argue that if pornography is designated as a civil offence (which their MacKinnon-Dworkin Ordinance in Minneapolis aimed to do) then the chance for alterations in the legal reproductive/ sexual objectification of women could occur',[73] the idea being a 'civil remedy', not to do with censorship or obscenity laws, but everything to do with the empowerment of people;[74] for Liz Kotz, Dworkin and MacKinnon 'conflated the fantasmatic and the real', and over-simplified the pornography issue;[75] Lynne Segal and Clare Whatling say it's dangerous that Dworkin and MacKinnon collaborated with right-wing politics;[76] for others, MacKinnon worked to carry out the wrong kind of censorship, and in Canada the statute banned the wrong people, 'prominent homosexual and lesbian authors';[77] for Gayle Rubin, the insistence on pornography, and the use of sensational examples of pornography, is offensive: '[i]t is politically reprehensible and intellectually embarrassing to target pornography on the basis of inflammatory examples and manipulative rhetoric',[78] and certainly Dworkin's writing on pornography is inflammatory, literally burning with rage; for other feminists, the Dworkin-MacKinnon Ordinance is too literal, too simple, too ignorant of many other issues that affect pornography, or that pornography is a part of, or as Avis Lewallen writes: 'Dworkin's pornography-equals-rape argument ignores all the other discourses through which power is mediated

72 Gillan Rodgerson & Linda Semple: "Who Watches the Watchwomen?" Feminists Against Censorship", in Bonner *et al*, eds, 268
73 Maggie Humm, *Feminism: A Reader*, 82; see also R. Tong: *Feminist Though*, Unwin Hyman 1989
74 Lesley White: "A porn fighter", *The Sunday Times*, 12 June 1994, section 9, 6,
75 Liz Kotz: "Complicity: Women Artists Investigating Masculinity", in Gibson, eds, 107
76 Lynne Segal: "Does Pornography Cause Violence??: The Search For Evidence", in Gibson, 8; Clare Whatling: "Who's read *Macho Sluts*?", in Still & Worton, ed, 195
77 Ronald Dworkin: "A New Map of Censorship", in Owen, 11-15
78 Gayle Rubin: "Misguided, Dangerous and Wrong: an Analysis of Anti-Pornography Politics", in Assister & Carol, eds, 24

– of which pornography is just one, if important, constituent',[79] so that their bill of rights does not help, in fact it hinders feminism, in some ways, and then there is the question of censorship, which is a minefield of complex arguments, which the Dworkin-MacKinnon Ordinance tackles and does not solve, because on the one hand, Dworkin, Itzin, MacKinnon *et al* are against censorship of any kind, and yet, on the other hand, they are advocating a form of censorship with their Ordinance; Dworkin wrote: '[t]he law that Catherine A. MacKinnon and I wrote making pornography a violation of women's civil rights recognizes the injury that pornography does: how it hurts women's rights of citizenship through sexual exploitation and sexual torture both' (War, 272); are you going to ban all pornography, then? but what *is* pornography? and who decides what is and what is not pornography, or if women are being 'subordinated' by/ through the use of pornography, as Dworkin maintains? Julienne Dickey writes: '[t]here is no doubt that media sexism contributes to our feelings about ourselves and our expectations, inevitably placing limits on our achievements and our enjoyment of life. But if we were to ban things on the grounds that they contribute to women's lowered expectations and negative self-image, then surely we should ban anything which presents women in stereotyped roles. The portrayal of women as engaged solely in the service of men – at home, at work, at play – is all-pervasive, and arguably more damaging to women's self-estimation than the (statistically rarer) instances of explicit pornography' (ib., 164); the policing of the Dworkin-MacKinnon is problematic, as Annie Blue of Women Against Violence Against Women acknowledges: '[w]e'd like a law that uses this radical feminist definition of its function in society. It's a double-edged sword, because it would give more power to the police and state, but in this present climate, it's the best of two evils. What else have we got?'[80] Catherine Itzin is with Dworkin and MacKinnon in some ways: Itzin, for example, see no conflict between being against censorship and for the

79 Avis Lewallen: "*Lace*: pornography for women", in L. Gamman & M. Marshment, eds: *The Female Gaze: women as viewers of popular culture*, Women's Press 1988
80 quoted in Sarah Baxter: "Women Against Porn", *Time Out*, London, 23 March 1988

censoring of pornography – as Itzin puts it: 'I have now had an insight into the *meaning* of pornography... I can see now that the 'freedom' of pornography is posited on the 'censorship' of women: that the price of the 'freedom' given to those who publish and purchase pornography (men) is freedom denied to its objects',[81] for Itzen, pornography is violence because it silences women, it denies them a voice, it is a question of language, and the relation between language/ culture and life – as Itzin writes, summarizing the argument of Dworkin's *Pornography*: '[i]ts key message... is that pornography has nothing to do with sex, but rather with the silencing of women, the denial of the humanness of women, the 'death' of women. Pornography is violence',[82] this view of Itzin's sees pornography as cultural violence, as a cultural manifestation of the power relations between men and women; '[w]omen are the population that dissents most, through silence... Being beaver, pussy, cunt, bunnies, pets, whatever, that is silence' writes Dworkin (War, 249) and Luce Irigaray says that if the vagina is regarded as a 'hole', it is a 'negative' space that cannot be represented in the dominant discourse, thus to have a vagina is to be deprived of a voice, to be decentred or culturally subordinated, and so Irigaray replaces Lacan's mirror with a vaginal speculum),[83] seen this way, then, there is no hypocrisy in being against censorship but for the censoring of pornography, because pornography is the expression of the male-female power relation, so that, developing her argument from Dworkin's *Pornography*, Itzin writes: '[t]here still persists an 'illusion' that there is no provable connection between pornography and violence... The truth – the irony – is that pornography *is* violence' (ib., 43), and this is where the Dworkin-MacKinnon Bill comes in, by focussing not on the content of this or that piece of pornography so much as on the implications within pornography of male subordination of women: the issue that arises, then, is based on civil or human rights, not on æsthetic or censorship issues; in other words, the Dworkin-MacKinnon bill is centred on humanity, on basic human

81 Itzin: "Sex and Censorship: The Political Implications", in Chester, 42
82 Itzin, in Chester, 42
83 Luce Irigaray, "Women's Exile", in Cameron, 1990, 83; and Luce Irigaray: *Speculum of the Other Woman*, tr Gillian C. Gill, Cornell University Press, New York 1985

(civil) rights, not on questions of 'obscenity' or 'censorship; Luce Irigaray says that the 'right to human dignity' would require 'an end to the commercial use of their bodies or their images',[84] because for Dworkin, the very *existence* of pornography is offensive and subordinating, that is, where there is porn, there is oppression and subordination, and subordination cannot be wiped out until pornography is wiped out – as Dworkin says in many speeches and short texts: 'pornography annihilates our chance for freedom' ("Why Pornography Matters to Feminists", War, 205), it's an extraordinary statement, really, and reveals the full extent of Dworkin's radical feminism: that, so important and central does Dworkin regard pornography, she says women cannot be 'free' until pornography is eradicated, this is extreme, perhaps the most extreme view on pornography around, more extreme than, say, D.H. Lawrence, who spoke very radically about pornography, but Dworkin goes much further, she reckons that life itself is imperilled by pornography, as if pornography was a disease seeping into every aspect of life, which is indeed Dworkin's view, because she believes that '[w]omen are an occupied people' and that pornography is terrorism, a constant terror to women – 'all over this country a new campaign of terror and vilification is being waged against us' ("Pornography: The New Terrorism", War, 200), and if pornography still exists there will be no release from the oppression, as Dworkin asks at the end of her speech of 1977: 'how, surrounded by this flesh of our flesh that despises us, will we defend the worth of our lives, establish our own authentic integrity, and, at last, achieve our freedom?' (War, 202), but this is all very problematic, not least the reduction of all oppression to sexuality and pornography, which is more than offensive to those feminists who regard pornography as a minor diversion in the grand scheme of things, far inferior as a topic of controversy compared to, say, racism, or world poverty, but, no, Dworkin goes on with it, in articles, speeches, lectures, books, novels, claiming in her declamatory fashion that 'pornography gives us no future; pornography robs us of hope as well as dignity' (War, 205) the trouble is, the Dworkin-MacKinnon leads, inevitably to that most problematic of socio-

84 Luc Irigaray: "How to define sexuate rights", in Irigaray, 1991, 208

politico-æsthetico-ideological notions, censorship, and then of course, who says what censorship shall be? who watches the watchdogs? because, as we know, watchdogs themselves are very dubious, as Pratibha Parmar writes: '[t]he Dworkin/MacKinnon ordinance, which seeks to enable anyone to bring a civil suit against anything deemed to be 'offensive' and hence 'pornographic', poses several problems. What puzzles me is how women who have defined all men as the enemy can ask the 'patriarchal state' to intervene on their behalf and pass laws in the interests of women. Expecting the state to behave in a benevolent manner is naive';[85] Elaine Showalter sees in Dworkin's analysis 'language strongly reminiscent of the 1890s purity campaigners',[86] but Dworkin maintains that her 'civil rights law undermines the subordination of women in society by confronting the pornography, which is the systematic sexualization of that subordination. Pornography is inequality' (War, 273), but the problems here multiply, for is not unequal pay also exploitation and inequality? why focus on sexual exploitation, why not include in a civil rights law of racial and economic and medical and educational exploitation? is any depiction of a sexual experience pornographic? this is a recurring question in the pornography debate, and one that Dworkin cannot answer straight on, she has to squirm a little, as this extract from "Pornography Is a Civil Rights Issue", an account of Dworkin's testimony 'before the Attorney General's Commission on Pornography on January 22, 1986, in New York City' (War, 276): Dworkin is asked a question by Dr Dietz: 'I would like to pose some hypotheticals, some specific images and ask you whether there is enough information here to tell me if that is subordination; and if there is, is it or isn't it? Is it subordination of women to depict naked – a woman on her knees, naked, a man standing, while the fellates the man, she on her knees, he standing. Ms Dworkin [replies]: I need to explain something to you about our law, which deserves a little more credit than you are giving it, which is that the definition itself isn't actionable. All right. There is nothing actionable about something meeting the definition. It has to be trafficked in,

85 Pratibha Parmar "Rage and Desire: Confronting Pornography", in Chester, 126
86 Showalter: *Sexual Anarchy*, 36

somebody has to be forced into it, it has to be forced on somebody or it has to be used in a specific kind of assault; so that the hypothetical question about whether I think that is subordination or not depends a great deal – has the woman been forced into it? I want to know. What is the sociology around it, is it being used on people, are women being forced to watch it and then do it' (War, 298-9), here Dworkin is floundering, here the problems of implementing the civil rights bill are apparent, for it is the 'sociology' of the sexual situation that is crucial, as Dworkin terms it, the context, and whether 'force' is present, here Dworkin cannot state straight whether a depiction of fellatio is pornographic, she cannot say for sure whether a woman sucking a man is pornography, is violence against women, because if the participants consent to do it, where is the violence? (can there be a 'politically correct blow job', as W. Dennis put it),[87] and in her next answer she admits that the fellatio scenario – woman naked kneeling, man standing – would not be a violation of civil/ women's rights, because the Dworkin-MacKinnon bill is 'violence-orientated' (War, 299); the Dworkin-MacKinnon Bill, says Dworkin, turns not upon *any* sexual depiction, but upon violent representations: the bill 'applies only to sexually explicit material that subordinates women in a way that is detrimental to our civil status, and *not to any sexually explicit material*' (my italics, War, 290), the anti-porn bill, then, targets violent pornography, although we know Dworkin is against most if not all pornography, from her other writings, yet she admits that consent and mutual agreement makes sexual acts non-pornographic: acceptable, non-obscene material would contain, Dworkin says, '[s]exually explicit, sexual equality, sexual reciprocity' (War, 290), Carole Vance, commenting on the way the Meese commission was handled, writes that 'witnesses provided by women's antipornography groups proved more useful than social scientists. They were eager to cast their personal experiences of incest, childhood, sexual abuse, rape and sexual coercion in terms of the 'harm' and 'degradation' caused by pornography. Some were wiling to understate, and most to omit

87 W. Dennis: *Hot and Bothered: Men and Women, Sex and Love in the 1990s*, HarperCollins, 1992

mentioning, their support for those cranky feminist demands so offensive to conservative ears: abortion, birth control, lesbian and gay rights. Other feminist groups, including COYOTE, the US Prostitutes collective, the ACLU Women's Rights Project and the Feminist Anti Censorship Task Force... criticized the panel's simple-minded attempt to link violence against women with sexual images';[88] basically, the links between pornography and violence are hotly debated, and we keep coming back to this issue, because Dworkin does, because people do, whenever they're discussing rating movies, or censorship, or the effects of 'video nasties', or violence on television, they always come back to this issue, this link between images and actions, between representation and 'real life', and there are many confusions, and assumptions, quite often simplistic assumptions, such as an uncritical over-simplification of what pornography actually is, and why people consume it in vast quantities, yet, despite this massive consumption of pornography, there is not a massive increase in sex crimes – or is there? – no one agrees here, because on the one side feminists say that there are no scientifically established links between pornography and violence, while on the other side there are those feminists, such as Dworkin, MacKinnon, Brownmiller, Millett, Griffin, who are anti-porn and who, in one way or another, believe in the porn-violence connection, but, as Sue George asks, is pornography really the *cause* of violence, or is it, rather, an *expression* or *manifestation* of desire and violence? '[a] film of continuous sexual activity, real or faked, may be boring, insulting to women, or a turn-on, but it does not *cause* women's oppression. Its continual reflection *may* reinforce it, but it cannot cause it on its own',[89] Julienne Dickey says that Dworkin's polemic is based 'on a theory, not on sound evidence' (in Chester, 165); Linda Williams says that Dworkin's books are pornography in themselves: 'the novels and the critiques written by Andrea Dworkin themselves qualify as pornography',[90] which is a very interesting twist to radical feminism, where the criticism becomes that which it is

88 Vance: "The Meese Commission On the Road", in Chester, 90
89 Sue George: Censorship and Hypocrisy", in Chester, 110
90 Linda Williams: "Second Thoughts on *Hard Core*: American Obscenity Law and the Scapegoating of Deviance", in Gibson, 48

criticizing, and then there is the question of race, which for so many feminists is more important than the pornography issue, although Dworkin and MacKinnon did tackle it,[91] in fact, much of the economics of the pornographic industry is founded on Black, non-white labour, so that feminists note that despite so-called 'improvements' in race relations, it is still Black people who are at the bottom of the societal pile, who do the menial jobs, such as cleaning, in other words, the economics of Black labour helps institutions such as pornography – and art, medicine, education, government, etc – to thrive.[92] When you come to the issue of race, the pornography issue is overshadowed; for feminists, the privileged person is white, middle class, First World, Anglo-Saxon, Protestant/ Christian – and male, so whoever it is who makes pornography, pornography privileges a white, middle class, Anglo-Saxon, North American and European male view-point; whoever the producers may be, pornography, as a text, is firmly located within white, middle class, Christian, masculine discourse, whoever the authors are, pornography ends up, textually, and contextually, as a white, middle class, Anglo-Saxon, Christian, male discourse; we must always remember, feminists say, the racial as well as the sexist implications of pornography: not only it is produced by and for men, it is produced by white, bourgeois, Anglo Saxon, Christian men, but is 'for' anybody who will buy it; as Barbara Smith writes: '[as] 'lesbian' pornography is not for or about lesbians and lesbian sexuality, so 'black' porn is not for black people, and 'kiddie' porn is not for children. Pornography does not describe sexuality, it describes sexual *acts*. It solidifies white, male, heterosexual fantasies, and then commoditises them';[93] perhaps Dworkin's books are really pornography in themselves, even as they tackle and criticize pornography, so that when Dworkin summarizes and rewrites

91 see Liz Goodman: *The Pornography Problem*, in Bonner, 274-5; E. Wilson: *What is To Be Done About Violence Against Women?*, Penguin 1983; Patricia Hill Collins: *Black Feminist Thought: knowledge, consciousness and the politics of empowerment*, Unwin Hyman, Boston 1990

92 see La Frances Rodgers, ed: *The Black Woman*, Sage, Beverly Hills 1989; G.T. Hull *et al*, eds: *All the Women Are White, All the Blacks Are Men, But Some of Us Are Brave: Black Women's Studies*, Feminist Press, New York 1982; B. Bryan *et al*, eds: *The Heart of the Race: Black Women's Lives in Britain*, Virago 1985; Anima Mama: "Black Women, the Economic Crisis and the British State", *Feminist Review*, 17, 1984

93 Barbara Smith: "Sappho Was a Right-*Off* Woman", in Chester, 179

pornographic literature, as she does in *Pornography*, paraphrasing books such as *The Story of the Eye*, *Whip Chick*, *Black Fashion Model*, de Sade; so that Dworkin's rewrites of pornographic texts remind Liz Kotz of Kathy Acker,[94] the 'post-punk' writer whom some critics call feminist, while others call her a pornographer; perhaps even speaking about pornography, no matter how viciously critical, is pornography too, as some feminists have noted, they have said that talking about pornography positions the critic in an ambivalent relation with pornography itself, because pornography breaks down distance and introduces a new, ambivalent kind of relationship and subjectivity, as Liz Kotz writes: 'pornography represents a place where distance breaks down, where subjectivity is insistently engaged, even uncomfortably so. Even its incorporation into a project of critique is notoriously unstable, since even the most determined efforts to reframe pornographic representations as objects of a politically motivated examination can go deeply awry, subverting authorial intention in fascinating if problematical ways',[95] perhaps any mention of pornography sets up an involvement and semantic circularity between critic and subject, so that there can never be a 'distanced', cool, detached, 'objective' reading of pornography, so that Dworkin's critiques of pornography are pornography itself, yet pornography remains a crucial issue with feminists, even though many feminists regard it as secondary to issues of power, race, class, economics and so on, yet even to speak of pornography is, for some feminists, to broach a still problematical issue, as the filmmaker Bette Gordon says: '[e]ven though I say pornography is not so much of an issue for me anymore, I recognise that indirectly it is. There is a need to be subversive in this culture that is becoming increasingly conservative. A culture that is becoming asexual demands sexuality',[96] and even to speak of sexuality is problematical, as is clear when the mainstream media tries to deal with the 'outrageous' sexuality of Madonna, who blissfully mixes the personas of pop star, movie star and porn star, the media simply

94 Liz Kotz, op.cit., 121

95 Liz Kotz, op.cit., 107

96 Bette Gordon & Karyn Kay: "Look Back/ Talk Back", in Gibson, 95

cannot deal with outspoken sexuality, they can't deal with it, as the filmmaker Karyn Kay says: '[t]o be sexual at all - particularly outside what we know as the nuclear family – seems to be a subversive act',[97] and certainly this is an extraordinary state of affairs, that, to be simply sexual is classed as subversive! that to exhibit or acknowledge sexuality is subversive! it's amazing, but then we live in a bizarre society, where, in Western culture, it is a *crime* to go naked, simply to be nude in public! a crime! and where pregnancy and images of pregnancy still disturbs people! pregnancy disturbs them! even though *everyone* slid out of that mythical/ mysterious space between a woman's legs, *everyone* was birthed from the vagina, science ain't simulated birth from seed to foetus yet, but pregnancy still upsets people! they don't like to see it! a survey for the Royal College of Midwives of November 1993 found that half of the men interviewed were opposed to breast-feeding, they don't want to see mothers breast-feeding in a restaurant, because it puts them off their food, they think it's 'embarrassing, unnecessary, exhibitionism, disgusting',[98] can you believe it, men think breast-feeding is 'unnecessary', like, 'unnecessary'! it's 'unnecessary' to feed children, it's OK for men to stuff their gobs in restaurants, but not for mothers to feed their children! men are 'disgusted' by breasts even though they adore them and make jokes about them, and put them in their newspapers and magazines, in *Mercy* Dworkin writes: 'what's so dirty to men about breasts so they put tassels on them and have them swirl around in circles and call them the ugliest names; as if they ain't attached to human beings' (298), when a movie star (Demi Moore) appeared on the cover of a glossy magazine, it created controversy, ditto with the French advert which featured a nude, pregnant woman, this goes to heart, in a different way, of the double standards of patriarchy, where, in the masculinist system, women are exalted as mothers, as they have been down the ages, it is the one 'function' or stereotype that the masculine system has let women have, as enshrined in thousands of *Madonna and Child* paintings, which was for centuries *the* prime image in the West, of any

97 Karyn Kay, in ib., 95
98 Chris Mihill: "Breast-feeding falls foul of men", *The Guardian*, 6 November 1993

image, it was always the *Madonna and Child*, yet, yet at the same time, images of motherhood *as it actually is*, with all the tensions, work and problems, is not shown, and, further, pregnancy is suppressed, and this suppression reached its height in the Victorian era, when, amazing though it seems now, *pregnancy could not be mentioned*, it was not permitted by the powers that be for pregnancy to be mentioned, thus, in *Tess of the d'Urbervilles*, Thomas Hardy had to take out the chapter where Tess nurtures her child, born from her rape; there is a sequence in Dworkin's *Pornography* where she investigates 'the pornography of pregnancy, a culture of pornography based on childbearing; she begins with a look at a magazine called *Mom: Big Bellied Mamas*, for Dworkin, the 'pornography of pregnancy' is where the masculinist system eroticizes motherhood, reducing it to genitals again, focusing on the body in that insidious, reductive way, she writes: '[t]he pornography of pregnancy, as of now, is right-wing pornography: kept secret, a hidden trade in the sluts who get knocked up... Women are not cleansed of purified or made good by pregnancy. Pregnancy is confirmation that the woman has been fucked: it is conformation that she is a cunt. In the male sexual system, the pregnant woman is a particular sexual object: she shows her sexuality through her pregnancy. The display marks her as a whore. Her belly is her sex. Her belly is proof that she has been used. Her belly is his phallic triumph... The pregnancy is punishment for her participation in sex. She will get sick, her body will go wrong in a thousand different ways, she will die... And now, the doctors have added more sex – to birth itself. *Vagina* means sheath. They cut directly into the uterus with a knife – a surgical fuck. She is tied down – literally cuffed and tied, immobilized by bondage, the bondage of birth, her legs spread; they pour drugs into her to induce labor; their bondage and their drugs cause intense and unbearable pain; she cannot have natural labor; she is drugged and sliced into, surgically fucked' (222-3); Dworkin's rage is understandable, for, confronted with the 'pornography of pregnancy', she is stunned by the violence, psychic and cultural as well as physical, of the male system; she continues: '[t]he epidemic of caesarean sections in this country is a sexual, not a medical, phenomenon. The doctors save the vagina – the birth canal of old – for the husband; they fuck the uterus directly, with a knife. Modern childbirth – surgical childbirth comes from the metaphysics of male sexual domination: she is a whore, there to be used, the uterus of the whore entered directly by the new rapist, the surgeon, the vagina saved to serve the husband' (223); this is powerful polemic, highly controversial in its way, for it aims for the heart of Western culture, which is the thoroughly masculinized institutions of medicine, science, education and politics, but at the same time, is Dworkin's reading of the medical profession believable, is it realistic? or is it simply reactionary and unreal, moving towards a reactionary politics, quite out of touch with societal realities, yet the rage against pornography continues to be central to Dworkin's polemic, and is central to feminists such as Susan Griffin and Mary Daly; for these radical feminists, we live in a 'rapist' culture, a 'sadospiritual' society, as Mary Daly called it,[99] using her new terms which she invented to described the phallocentric nature of Western society: '[t]he fact is,' writes Daly, 'that we live in a profoundly anti-female society, a misogynistic 'civilization' in which men collectively victimize women, attacking us as personifications of their own paranoid fears, as The Enemy';[100] many feminists concur with Mary Daly's view of the West as phallocentric and violent, but at the same time, it seems to be simplistic, reducing everything to us and them, always us and them, it seems to be always 'us and them', as Ann Snitow notes: 'the brotherhood of the oppressors, the sisterhood of the victims', [101] the problem with this view is that it ignores so much; Pratibha Parmar glosses Ann Snitow's comment thus: 'again this sisterhood of all women assumes that there are no significant differences between women, compared with the similarities of our experiences of pornography. I find such analysis both Eurocentric and nationalist. It is also insulting in its simplicity',[102] and as Audre Lorde, 'an Afro-American lesbian

99 Mary Daly: *Pure Lust: Elemental Feminist Philosophy*, Women's Press, 1984

100 Mary Daly: *Gyn/Ecology: The Metaphysics of Radical Feminism*, Women's Press 1978

101 Ann Snitow: "Retrenchment Verses Transformation: the Politics of the Anti-Pornography Movement", in Varda Burstyn, ed: *Feminists Against Censorship*, Douglas & McIntyre, Toronto 1985, 113

102 Pratibha Parmar: "Rage and Desire: Confronting Pornography", in Gail Chester & Julienne Dickey, eds, 123

poet and philosopher'[103] wrote: '[f]or then beyond sisterhood is still racism';[104] wonderful as Dworkin's polemic can be, it can so often backfire on her, as Clare Whatling writes of a 'violent' passage in *Mercy*, 'one of the questions raised by the book is, how do such description[s] differ from established violent porn? Namely, is Dworkin's conviction of the clarity of her own intentions enough to override the vagaries of reception in this instance?'[105] it is of course deeply ironic that Dworkin's work should be regarded as pornography, when so much of her life's work is a campaign against pornography, it's a confusion that is problematic, for one has to know of the author's intentions *before* one reads the book, that is, Dworkin's fiction trades on her position as a radical feminist in the world of non-fiction, because in Dworkin's fiction there are moments (in *Mercy*) when the ''reconstructed' heroine gains deep pleasure from her shockingly sadistic anti-male fantasies', as Clare Whatling put it,[106] in the fiction Dworkin is no more angry than in the non-fiction, both non-fiction and fiction offer a prose of rage, except in the novels Dworkin's protagonists target men specifically, and individually (and violently), and here's where the problems of confusion begin, for, while Dworkin may agree with Luce Irigaray that '[m]en always go further, exploit further, seize more, without really knowing where they are going',[107] it can't be simply a case of 'blaming' men for everything, as Simone de Beauvoir said – blame men, yes, but blame 'the system' (society) too; *Ice and Fire*, Dworkin's first novel, is an extremely painful account of the birth of a writer;[108] whatever happens, the narrator will win through; it is a helluva struggle, from the early years playing witch, to the maturity in an apartment writing writing writing; the book opens with a hard-hitting portrayal of an urban childhood, that is, it appears to be 'hard-hitting', or 'hard-boiled', in the Raymond Chandler sense, but Dworkin applies the direct prose of

103 Maggie Humm's description, in Maggie Humm, ed: *Feminisms: A Reader*, 137
104 Audre Lorde: "An Open Letter to Mary Daly", 1980, in *Sister Outsider*, Crossing Press, New York 1984
105 Clare Whatling, op.cit., 205
106 Whatling, ib, 196
107 Irigaray, 1994, 5
108 'Her novel, *Ice and Fire*, makes me weep whenever I read it.' Michael Moorcock, 1989, 167

crime fiction to an unsentimentalized vision of childhood; even so, in amongst the poetic evocation of the streets and the goings on in Brooklyn, Dworkin is didactic: she describes a game called 'witch', where the boys chase after the girls and emprison them in a wooden cage – the implication is that the games children play when young become the games adults play when 'grown up', for it is obvious to the writer that the term 'witch' equals 'whore' (in *Tess of the d'Urbervilles* Alec calls Tess a witch), so the girls in Dworkin's fictional American world become 'witches', and the boys are the hunters: '[e]veryone wanted to be caught and was terrified to be caught' (*Ice*, 11), and the scenario Dworkin portrays reflects the adult world, so that women wanted to be caught and are terrified to be caught, or, one could substitute the term fucked for caught: 'everyone wanted to be fucked and was terrified to be fucked', because, for Dworkin, women want to be part of the sexual economy, at the same time as they are scared of it, because the sexual economy, that is, in our culture, i.e., Western/ First World society, is a dual system, an economy of double standards, in which women are denigrated and men (generally) benefit, and this dichotomy is seen throughout Dworkin's work, so that, at the end of *Ice and Fire*, it is the woman, the narrator, who works like hell to become a writer, while her partner, 'the beautiful blond boy', simply sleeps, he sleeps and sleeps, while she works like a maniac, and she has to learn about loss, about having everything she once believed in smashed utterly, for, as artists know, much of art stems from a sense of loss, as Julia Kristeva notes: 'the creative act is released by an experience of depression without which we could not call into question the stability of meaning or the banality of expression. A writer must at one time or another have been in a situation of loss – of ties, of meaning – in order to write';[109] with a 'racing heart', the narrator of *Ice and Fire* becomes a witch, and a cowgirl, and it all starts from there, the breathlessness of life, the intensity of living, from the euphoria and fear of those early childhood games around the backstreets of Brooklyn, to the euphoria and fear of the writer, so that, wow, the witch becomes a writer; but Dworkin is not completely on the

109 Julia Kristeva, "A Question of Subjectivity", *Women's Review*, no. 12, in Philip Rice, 1992, 133

side of women and women only, because she does include moments of violence, either psychic or physical, perpetrated by women, sometimes against other women, sometimes against men, as when *Ice*'s narrator tortures a baby-sitter with her friend (*Ice*, 29), so it's not all one-sided in Dworkin's mythopœia; later, as *Ice*'s narrator grows up, there are archetypal evocations of a late 20th century city, descriptions of a city which we have read a million times – streets full of trash, smelling of piss, stinking apartments, sound of gunfire, tramps, bugs, the whole city bit, as found in any down and out fiction (Orwell, Miller, Durrell, Acker, Selby), but Dworkin adds some slants of her own on the typical urban hell: the apartment, for instance, is a storefront, so the front room is a wall of glass, with hardly anything in it, in these (and more) ways, Dworkin brings her themes to the fore, in this instance by putting her women characters almost right on the street, with nothing but a glass window between them and the scum that passes for humans outside, so the women who live in the New York apartment are always on display, in one way or another; the rest of the apartment is archetypally bohemian: a typewriter, jazz and blues records, a saxophone and bottles of vodka are placed around the apartment (40); from this down-at-heel launchpad the women characters lunge off into the adventurous world of counter-culture, fucking their way through hundreds of lovers, in order to obtain pills, money, meals, booze; as expected, Dworkin's narrator in *Ice and Fire* receives her share of knocks, and then some, so she is beaten by men she fucks, such as the old lover, Nikko that she runs into down St Mark's Place, one of the classic New York haunts, but the lover, after insisting on fucking the narrator with a condom, which she doesn't want, he hits her (43); the novel is full of descriptions of living the low-life, of hanging out with junkies, of jazz, of summers in New York, of talk-talk-talk, talking all night, walking the streets, then sitting in all-night joints (*Ice*, 52); and, by the sea, more sex, this time group sex, group sex with the narrator's friend N and some guy, called 'Mister', some guy with a knife, a man who fingers a knife in between bouts of violent sex, and this part of *Ice and Fire* is related in Hemingway-type machine-gun prose, the bang-bang prose of direct statement followed by direct statement: '[h]e pulls down his pants. He fucks me. I get dressed. N and I sit and watch the ocean' (54), this kind of prose recalls Dworkin's scathing summaries of the hard core pornography she surveyed in her book *Pornography*, where she condenses porn into bullet-like sentences: '[t]hey undress. Andy fucks Rod. Rod sucks George. Andy sucks Rod' (41), but this form of prose has a poetry, too, which Dworkin exploits to the full: '[h]ave you ever seen the moon, full, rising behind the head of a man fucking you on a dirty beach?' (*Ice*, 55), and there is much lesbian sex, because every bohemian down-on-the-streets avant garde novel features gay and lesbian fucking, so there are women lovers, 'there was just having the women: because you wanted them: because it was a piece of heaven right in the middle of hell: because they knew your name too: because you went mad with them in your mouth: and you went crazy thigh to thigh: and it was earth, sublime: and the skin, pearl: and the breasts: and coming, coming, coming' (*Ice*, 59), there are times in Dworkin's fiction where her characters are 'coming, coming, coming', yet it seems, from her sombre, didactic non-fiction, as if the last thing she desires is multiple orgasms all round, for one and all, yet this orgasmic hedonism lies behind her two novels, it's a central element in Dworkin's passion and radicalism, and more of *Ice and Fire* than you might imagine, as it's an Andrea Dworkin book, is taken up with sex, all kinds of sex, group sex, for instance, or sex for money, where N and the protagonist make love on a bed watched by men (76); there are plenty of moments of horror in *Ice and Fire*, for instance, when the protagonist goes to a 'junkie doctor in the Village for a prescription' he touches her, '[h]e rubs his hands up and down my arms and all over my breasts' (72); but one of the most horrible scenes is where the protagonist is on her own in the open-fronted apartment, the place open to the streets, and she barricades herself in, or wants to, and there's a bunch of men outside, who hang about, who bang on her door, yelling that they're going to smash the front window unless she opens the door, so, eventually, frightened, she opens the door, and the leader of the pack offers the protagonist a choice: 'you let me in and you take care of me real nice girl right now and we have a good time or you close the door girl and we come in all together and we get you good girl: you see girl you decide' (IF, 67), that is, she is being offered either gang rape or rape by an individual, and this is the fatal choice Dworkin's protagonists are offered through the fiction, whether to be raped by a gang or by one person, whether to give in to being raped, either physically or economically or spiritually or however by one or by a group; the 'leader of the pack' comes in, and chatters, brandishes a sharp knife, talking arrogantly, and then goes to the mattress – 'OK girl you come' (68) – but before the rape begins there is a knock at the door: it's a man called 'W', someone the protagonist and N know slightly, who saves the protagonist, as the 'leader of the pack' finds himself confronted by tall W, who is a drug dealer, and the 'leader of the pack' backs off, and the protagonist is grateful to W for saving her from being raped by the 'leader of the pack', and here Dworkin rubs in the terrible fate of women, the horrible situation women find themselves in, with violence on top of violence, of hidden, domestic violence, violence behind closed doors, not the bar brawl, not the public boxing match, not the public violence of war, but the hidden, locked-away violence that occurs everywhere, in homes, and Dworkin rubs the face of her protagonist in the horror, and the face of the reader into the horror, because, after escaping rape, the protagonist is raped, in one of those bleak, horrible moments associated with Kafka, Dostoievsky or Hardy at their bleakest, it's a moment of personal (therefore) total devastation: 'Joe fumbles and sweats. They talk smack. Joe is sloppy and scared. W is austere and serious. W shows Joe to the door. Then he comes back. I thank him. It isn't enough. He tears into me. He bites my clitoris and bites it and bites and until I wish I was dead. He fucks. He bites my clitoris more, over and over, for hours, I want to die. The pain is shooting through my brain. I am chewed and bitten and maimed. I am bleeding. He leaves. I hurt so bad I can't even crawl' (IF, 70), yes, sure, many writers have written terrifying, horrific scenes – they are a standard element in the crime novel, for instance, and every nearly every 'writer' has written ghastly, violent scenes – Sophocles and the blinding of Oedipus, Gloucester having his eyes cut out in *King Lear*, the pathetic hanging of Little Father Time in *Jude the Obscure*, and of course the grandest catalogue of horrors are to be found in the works of de Sade (which caused

Dworkin such pain when researching her book *Pornography)*, but Dworkin's use of horror or violence is made extra-powerful by the plain, straightforward prose style, a flat style, flat though passionate, polemical though straightforward, it's a prose style like a police report at times, it's a style of verbs, mainly, verbs such as '[i]t is W. He is invited in. I don't talk. I sit. N sits. He stands' (IF, 70), simple verbs, short sentences, short bursts of information, which, when describing simple actions such as sitting or smoking seem to fit in and pass by without comment, but when these short, simple sentences are aligned to violences such as rape, the effect can be startling, disturbing, difficult, because, coupled with a 'plain' prose style (it's not really 'simple' at all, but finely crafted, finely judged), Dworkin leads us into a powerful evocation of one person, the eternal 'I' or self of fiction, this is (partly) what makes Dworkin's fictions so powerful, this use of the first person to relate the horrors of what is actually 'everyday life', it's this first person subjectivity in the fiction which makes the works have the ring of authenticity, for Dworkin always writes from the first person, from her self, you find this powerfully evoked sense of self and subjectivity in all Dworkin's work, she does not use impersonations or personas in her work, she uses her own self, her own voice, so that the fiction and non-fiction are a continuum, so that one can move from extracts of *Pornography: Men Possessing Women* to *Ice and Fire* without needing to adjust very much, and this, too, is what, I think, upsets people about Dworkin, for she is very much *in* her books (or seems to be), that is, her speeches and lectures, collected in *Letters From a War Zone*, have such a powerful, polemical tone to them (Dworkin is a very good public speaker, one feminist said), and this powerful personal voice, which runs throughout the speeches, seems the product of a committed, serious (and eloquent) person, so that it is assumed that Dworkin herself is like this, and this committed, polemical voice gives all the works an added authenticity, for, while (some) other authors distance themselves from their works, by using jokes or self-deprecation, Dworkin is very serious about what she does, and it shows in all her works, so the serious, committed tone is found in the fiction, the non-fiction, the speeches and the lectures, and for some reason some people find this difficult to deal with, so that Dworkin is seen as someone threatening, perhaps because what she has to say is usually not said, or not said in quite the way Dworkin says it, or not said in the contexts in which Dworkin says it, or it could be something to do with Dworkin being a prominent personality, or perhaps because she is a woman, we come back to the same sort of problems again and again, and these problems – of being 'accepted' as a female writer, or listened to as a woman writer – are also the problems of Dworkin's protagonists in *Ice and Fire* and *Mercy*, for the whole fight of *Mercy* and *Ice and Fire* is to become a writer, it is this fight that is the central journey of the novels, and it's also the fight behind the non-fiction, behind *Woman Hating, Our Blood, Intercourse, Pornography, Right-Wing Women* and *Letters From a War Zone*, it's a fight that never ends, for, even though Dworkin has achieved success, and has found a 'voice' and is listened to, or at least heard, she knows that she and her companion feminists are very few, they are a tiny minority of voices in the media landscape, and the changes she wishes to see occur haven't yet occurred, so she must continue to write, so the journey described in her books, the burning ambition to become a writer, *to write*, is eternal, it's always there, it's a theme that will never go away, because one must always write, otherwise one gets written, or as Hélène Cixous says, in the famous, excellent article "The Laugh of the Medusa", '[a]nd why don't you write? Write! Writing is for you, you are for you... Write, let no one hold you back, let nothing stop you',[110] for Hélène Cixous (who is loved and loathed by feminists nearly as energetically as Andrea Dworkin) writing is absolutely crucial, and central, it is oxygen to her, she must write to live, as she writes: '[h]aving never been without writing, having writing in my body, at my throat, on my lips... to me my texts are elements of a whole which interweaves my own story';[111] and this sense of writing is central to the life of Dworkin's narrator in *Ice and Fire*: she says: 'I wanted to be a writer. I want to write. Everyday I write. I am alone and astonishingly happy' (IF, 118); she becomes a feminist, but 'not the fun kind' of feminist (90), because 'coitus is

110 Cixous, in Marks, 1981, 246-7
111 Cixous, "Preface", in Cixous, 1994, xv

punishment' (IF, 88), she becomes a tough feminist, 'in color, 3-D, fearsome feminista, ballbuster, woman who talks mean, queer arrogant piece' (91), and she writes, in 'that Northern city of Old Europe', she writes word by word, sentences, paragraphs, putting together her texts piece by piece, and she is alone, and she can concentrate, with no distractions, it's a passion, this kind of writing: 'I am not distracted, I am alone, I love solitude, this is passion too. I am intensely happy' (89), it is significant that the narrator calls herself happy when she is alone and writing, this is where happiness is for her (118), and the second half of *Ice and Fire* concerns the struggle to become a writer, the loneliness of the writer, the absolute solitude of the writer, working alone, during the day, or at night, working, working, in appalling conditions, in a disgusting apartment that the landlord won't fix, so it fills up with fumes, so the protagonist has to have all the windows open in winter to get rid of the fumes, so that she becomes acquainted with 'wind, rain, ice, fire' (IF, 100), and works, with the police sirens wailing, in numbing cold or stifling heat, either one or the other, this is the struggle to become a writer, to work with her fingers 'jammed stiff from the cold' (91); and sometimes there is music from the disco, music so loud it drowns the Mozart on the protagonist's radio (109); at other times, she dreams, dreams which, in a Rimbaudian sense 'were like a delirium' (122), and she has walks, baths, and all this caught up in 'a great, soft stream of solitude and concentration' (122), and in between the long hours of writing are the excursions into everyday life, into the life outside, into relationships with other people, and her blonde boy is always there, always asleep, 'sleeping, curled up in a ball, fetal, six feet, blond, muscled' (102), whatever happens, he sleeps, he knows how to sleep in all weathers (101), the blond boy's the most mysterious part of *Ice and Fire* – he hardly ever speaks, he sleeps all the time, yet he is, against all odds, the real lover of the protagonist, the one she comes back to, the one she invites into her private world, the one she lets step over the barriers she erects to keep out the horrors of the world, he's the softness at the heart of her life, he's where the tenderness lies (115), and sometimes the tenderness the protagonist feels overwhelms her, it's so acute: '[s]ometimes I feel the tenderness for this man now... sometimes I feel the tenderness so acutely' (116), she goes away from him, and then meets with him again, after spending months alone, because with him there is a different kind of relationship, where '[t]alking with him was different from anything else: the way the wind whispers through the tops of trees just brushed by sunset' (122), and when they make love the protagonist's private world is not 'betrayed': '[w]e were like women together on that narrow piece of foam rubber, and he, astonished by the sensuality of it, ongoing, the thick sweetness of it, came so many times, like a woman: and me too: over and over' (122), there are other people in the rebirthing writer's life, as she works in New York City, people she has affairs with, meetings which she calls 'brief piercing moments of sensation' (122), but these are not central, the writer's solitude is central, 'I came alive again: in solitude: concentrating: writing' (122), and everything else takes second place, even the boy, for, so burning with desire is the protagonist, she puts 'solitude first, before him' (124), and, gradually, over the weeks and months and years, the price of writing looms larger and larger, for writing, as D.H. Lawrence said, is its own reward, that is, writing for oneself, the act of it, and the second half of *Ice and Fire* concerns in part the flipside of the urge to become a writer, which is the desire (or need) to be published, this is where the real hurting comes in, for one can write *ad infinitum*, but it is not enough, it should be enough, but writing without publication is not enough, and the protagonist begins to realize this, she realizes that 'the written word does not sell: some is published, but it is not embraced, it offends, it does not make money' (124), and although she will not stop writing, and nothing will prevent her from writing, writing will also kill her, because she comes to loathe it as well as love it: one carries on, 'endures the continuing, worsening poverty' (123), writing, once thought of a refuge from the world, becomes something much bleaker: Dworkin turns up a terrible realization for the writer, a truth which affects the creative person directly, and acutely: '[e]ach book makes you poorer: not just blood: money: food, shelter: the more time you use writing but not making money, the poorer you are. Each book makes you poorer' (IF, 125), this turns out to the bleakest view in Dworkin's *œuvre*, perhaps, that art, for the individual, is a slow death, it kills the self, slowly, like a glacier crushing life underneath it, or as the narrator of *Ice and Fire* puts it: '[w]riting is your slow, inexorable suicide' (125), it's a terrible realization, the opposite of Dworkin's idealism, the flipside to her utopian visions; finally, the bleakest part of *Ice and Fire*, and the longest sustained theme, is the double-edge sword of being a writer, the love and the loathing, the writing and the need to be published, the loneliness and the craving to be loved: on the one hand, there is the joy of writing, in a bliss of being alone and listening to Bach and Mozart, and of relaxing with one's lover: 'I listen to music: Bach, Chopin, Mahler, Mozart. They and the ocean are renewal, the will to live. So is the boy, sleeping on the beach' (IF, 128), but, on the other hand, there is the writing itself, back in New York City, cold, always cold, and headachey from the fumes in the apartment, feeling like a refugee, 'profoundly despondent and tired enough to die' (IF, 127), for such enthusiastic idealism and radicalism is immensely exhausting, and the protagonist veers from elation to exhaustion, from passion to poverty, always living on the edge, always going to extremes, swooping from rage to resignation, one week raging ('I raged. I bellowed. I howled. I was delirious with pain', 104) the next, trying to work amidst the sirens, screams, cars, guns and clubs of New York City; more humiliating, more despairing and more painful than the rapes the protagonist endures, more humiliating and painful than the moment of violence and rape, is the protracted involvement with the publisher, who embodies the downside of the protagonist's (and Dworkin's) idealism and radicalism, the publisher represents all that is loathed in the establishment, all that the protagonists of *Ice and Fire* and *Mercy* kick against, all that they and their fellow radicals campaign against, the publisher is the Devil, he is the one who has the keys to Heaven, he can make her name, he can create a writer's sense of authenticity and acceptance, he has the power, by publishing the protagonist's work, to make her accepted, to make her heard, to make people listen to what she has to say, so she must do a deal with the publisher, she must sell her book, her soul, to him; from the first the publisher or editor is described as 'a subtle piece of slime' (91), and, though all the time she fundamentally loathes him, she has to bow low before him, she has to appear humble, she has to admire his intelligence, his taste, his seriousness; significantly, they meet in a 'wet, smelly, crowded' coffeehouse (92), and discuss literature and being published, and, for the narrator, it's all so horrible, the slimy publisher, the dirty, damp tables, the grey air and rain, everything damp and grey, like soggy cardboard, the colour grey here clearly describing a kind of spiritual death, for grey symbolizes death, like some kinds of brown, and this grey-on-greyness signifies a horrible bland world, a world of deathly banality, and this is in the nowhere-zone that the writer and the publisher meet, and the sequences with the publisher are where Dworkin puts into fiction what she has been saying throughout her essays and lectures, about the horrors of patriarchy, about the way men do all the talking and women have to listen ('he talked, I listened', 93), about the way men manipulate women, about the way men make decisions for women, about the way men are sweet and intelligent and courteous when in fact they are scheming and sly, about the way men talk women into silence; these meetings with the editor are the most incisive Dworkin has written: they are not explosive, searing scenes, or dogmatically polemic, rather, they show the insidious nature of male culture, or masculinity and patriarchy, they show how institutions such as publishing favour masculine culture and men, how these institutions (literature, media, finance, law, government) are biased towards a masculine economy, how these institutions downgrade women, and this downgrading operates in subtle ways, not in loud, blatant ways, and this is why Dworkin's scenes with the publisher are so effective, because they are not 'racy' depictions of violence, they are not rapes or drug busts; rather, they show the lengthy and slow and subtle seduction and exploitation of women, they show how sly the seduction is, how it starts with men talking to women, with men offering certain things to women on certain conditions, for the first few meetings with the publisher involve him talking and the protagonist listening, him outlining the breadth of his intellectual knowledge, and her having to admire him, with her silent nods and grimaces, she must be the mirror, as Virginia Woolf put it, to reflect his intellectual prowess, she must glorify him; so, when the man starts talking about the great names of literature, it is music to the protagonist's ears, after all the suffering she has had to endure, to hear about these names is bliss to the protagonist, it is the opposite of the horrible grey world outside: '[h]e does the canon, my heart. Dostoyevsky, Rimbaud, Homer, Euripides, Kafka my love, Conrad, Eliot, Mann, Proust. His courtesy is sublime. Dickinson, the Brontës, Woolf, Cather, Wharton, O'Connor, McCullers, Welty. Oh, I love them but I have ambition like a man. I am curt, quiet, tender, bleeding, especially quiet, but lit up from inside. He seduces' (96), and the seduction goes on and on, over hours: '[h]ours more of the canon, my heart. Except that we had reached the end hours before, but still he went on' (98), the intellectual seduction, though, leaves the protagonist at once exhausted and elated, for there is a hollowness at the heart of it all, there is something not quite right about the deal, although the publisher wants to publish her book, the protagonist remains suspicious, why her? she wonders, why me?, it does not fit, it cannot work like that, something must be wrong, what does he really want? but the protagonist burns to be published, so that, when she returns to her blond lover she is fired up, and expresses her desire to be a writer and to be published in the following extract, one of Dworkin's best sequences, which recalls the compacted poetry of Gertrude Stein: 'I want, I say, I want, I say, to be this human being, and I want, I say, I want, to have somebody publish my book, I say, this simple thing, I say, I want, I want, I say, to be treated just like a human being, I say... I want, I say, to be treated, I say, I want, I say, to be treated with respect, I say, as if, I say, I have, I say, a right, I say, to do what I want to do, I say, because, I say, I am smart, and I have written, and I am good, and I do good work, and I am a good writer' (105); the protagonist fights, and keeps fighting, and doesn't stop fighting, but, for a time, though she rages, she submerges her personality and desire when she meets the publisher, she rages, but when she is confronted by men, she softens, her subordination to the publisher is horrible to witness, but the protagonist is also subordinate, in a different way, to her blond lover: '[h]e is gentle, I am the time bomb' (IF, 115), the blond lover advocates gentleness and quietness, while the protagonist bellows and rages; the coming-into-birth writer must eat dirt and go to the publisher, in order to get her book published, he is too abrupt, so her friend, an agent, tells her what to say, how to conduct herself during the interviews, the agent offers things to say, but the protagonist goes over the text and crosses out the adjectives (130), because she thinks that the publisher will think her stupid, because she's so grateful to him for deciding to publish her book, because she wants to be seem grateful but she does not wish to appear gushing, so she crosses out the adjectives, and this is part of women's self-silencing, women's self-censorship and self-effacement, this silence in the face of men's talk, this self-effacement which the narrator calls 'woman's slow death, the familiar silence, the choking, the breathy death' (131); and then comes the final sequence of *Ice and Fire*, which is a short novel (144 pages), though it seems long, so long, because so much happens to the protagonist, the final sequence of the meeting with the publisher, where the protagonist walks through the cold cold streets of New York City to reach the publisher's apartment, his place is always warm, and cosy, and full of good things, high culture, exquisite music, and fantastic books, and she has to walk, not drive or take a taxi, to his apartment, she walks through cold streets where a man thinks she is a prostitute and offers her $50, and when she gets there, the editor is in bare feet, as the place is so warm, and all the time the narrator exaggerates the differences between the two of them, the radical, visionary feminist and the smarmy, cool editor; while the feminist has a fumy, chilly apartment with a pockmarked foam mattress for a bed, the editor has a big round table, three comfy sofas, a fantastic four-speaker music system, and the record collection is 'sublime', the narrator is transported by the music, each piece of music he puts on its better than the last, and the narrator is still wary, she eyes this seduction from a distance, although she can't escape, because he plays records, and rushes to show her books and this or that, and he has cooked steaks for them, and over the meal he confesses he was gang-raped, and the confession numbs the protagonist, numbs her, and now, after the confession, she wants to escape, but he won't let her, she doesn't know what the editor wants, he doesn't want to fuck her, she knows that, and she knows what she wants: 'I know what I want: a publisher, not a lover; a publisher, not a barter' (137); the editor, she's sure, doesn't want *that*, surely not *that*, 'he can't want *that*. I don't believe it really, but others say he can't want *that*' (138), no, he's gay, isn't he? he tells the narrator that 'he picked up a baseball team and brought them all back here and got fucked by all of them' (137); she meets the editor later, over a period of time, he buys her gifts, books, kisses her, invites her out to dinner, while she remains 'formal', shaking his hand, definitely not kissing him, always keeping her distance, he talks to her on the telephone, '[h]is voice slithers' (140), he is very much the snake, the serpent, the Devil, and when, finally, the book is published, it is savaged (141), but there is a contracted second book, but this book is put out to die, it sinks without a trace, the editor lets it sink, and all the promises from the editor/publisher come to nothing, absolutely nothing, it is devastating to the protagonist but not devastating at all, because she is a survivor, she has survived, so that, by the end of *Ice and Fire* she is still alive, which is the thing, the thing to cling onto, and the thing she is is a writer, which is how she survives, she says 'I am a writer, not a woman', and she says, in the last sentence of the novel: '[d]id I remember to say that I always wanted to be a writer, since I was a little girl?' (144); in *Ice and Fire* the sense of life is feverish, and the fervour of being alive is intense, there are no half measures for Dworkin's protagonist, she cannot rest in an indeterminate zone, she will have all or nothing, so the atmospheres of *Ice and Fire* are either very hot or very cold, very light or very dark, and *both* hurt, the heat as much as the cold, the ice and the fire, so, when it's hot in Dworkin's fiction, it's blisteringly hot, 'it burns like Africa' (37), and when it's cold, it's cruel, this is the way of post-Petrarchan conceits, the ice and fire of the title referring, among other things, to the Petrarchan conceit, where, in Petrarch's early Renaissance *Rime Sparse* the poet-lover would burn with love but be cold; in Dworkin's novel the intensity of being alive never lets up for a moment, which makes it a difficult novel to read, or not difficult, but intense, the novel is about some great catastrophe that's occurring now, that's extended, that is expanded, elastically, so the intensity is stretched over pages and pages, so the reading experience is itself like being trapped in an inhospitably cold/ hot city, so the novel is a disaster prolonged over a hundred and forty pages, *Ice and Fire* is a kind of holocaust in its own way, it's a holocaust of love, desire, pain, violence, as well as referring to the Nazi holocaust, to the Jewish holocaust, which is more explicitly referred to in *Mercy*; the lessons that have to be learnt by the end of *Ice and Fire* are that life is incredibly horrible and hard and yet one must go on, or not 'must', but one *does* go on, even though, as Samuel Beckett's narrator says at the end of *The Unnamable*, 'I can't go on' he then says 'I'll go on', it's a similar situation here, that, though life has horrors, though it has a 'thousand natural shocks', as Hamlet put it, and a million unnatural (human-made) shocks, one still 'goes on', people still go on, struggling through, and the way forward for the narrator is by writing, the very act of it, the stitching together of word and word, to make sentence after sentence, page after page, just as, in life, one lives from heartbeat to heartbeat, from one moment to the next, stitching them together, with blood and breaths, so that one day becomes the next, until years have gone by, so that writing becomes not only a parallel for life, it becomes life itself, so that writing *is* life, or as the narrator puts it in *Ice and Fire*, twisting Kafka's epigram about, '[s]lowly I saw: coitus is the punishment for being a writer afraid of the cold passion of the task. There is no being together, just the slow learning of solitude. It is the discipline, the art. I began to learn it' (88), so, for Dworkin's feverish, intense protagonist, the skill to learn is the art of being alone, and not just alone, but *writing*, because, she says, she wants, she says, she wants, she says, to be published, she says, a simple thing, but so difficult, it seems, or other people make it difficult, so that writing is only one part of the matrix of 'being a writer', but the narrator doesn't really want to 'be a writer', she wants *to write*, or rather, *she writes*, that is, by the end of the novel, she is writing, but it's not a question of becoming 'a writer', but of *writing*, for, on the one hand, the story of *Ice and Fire*, as of *Mercy*, is the growth of a person into being a writer, much as, after one of the tumultuous orgasms in *Lady Chatterley's Lover*, Lawrence's narrator states, so awfully, that Connie has become 'a woman', it's such a stupid thing to say, but Lawrence says it: after piling on the poetics, the descriptive words and the metaphors ('[s]he was an ocean rolling its dark, dumb mass'), Lawrence ends the orgasmic paragraph by writing: '[s]he was gone, she was not, and she was born a woman',[112] but it would be quite wrong for Dworkin to end her piquant, frequently searing book by writing 'I was born a writer', or 'I was become a writer', and one can see how different Dworkin is from D.H. Lawrence: Connie Chatterley's rebirth comes from a sexual encounter, whereas Dworkin's protagonist's rebirth as an artist is in opposition to sexuality, in spite of sexuality; for Connie, bliss and transformation come from being anally fucked by a gamekeeper, while for Dworkin's protagonist, transformation comes from a steely determination to win through despite being abused, attacked and raped, despite poverty, despite numerable setbacks; in *Lady Chatterley's Lover*, despite its discourses of materialism, work, class and family, salvation is sexual, and Connie is 'awoken' sexually by Mellors; in *Ice and Fire*, salvation comes not from the state or society, nor from sex or money, but from an individual's rebellion and determination; unfair, perhaps, to compare *Ice and Fire* with *Lady Chatterley's Lover* – far better to compare *Ice and Fire* and *Mercy* with *The Rainbow* and *Women in Love* among Lawrence's books, or with other *Bildungsroman*-type novels, or not D.H. Lawrence at all, but Virginia Woolf, Emily Bronte, Adrienne Rich, Sylvia Plath, Alice Walker, Toni Morrison, for Dworkin knows, as many female writers know, that it is much more difficult for women writers to become successful, to break through the many thresholds of silence; *Ice and Fire* is about the birth of a writer against all the odds; *Mercy* is indeed Dworkin's most virulent and violent text, *Mercy* is an attempt, in a sense, to write the book that can never be written, an 'ultimate' book, a book to end all books, because it tells the 'truth' as it is, as Hélène Cixous writes '[a]ll the books that I could write revolve around the book that I shall never write, which allows all the others to be written, and this book of books is the book of You';[113] *Mercy* is Dworkin's 'book of books', an *Ur*-text, an attempt at the book that can never be written; *Mercy*

112 Lawrence, *Lady Chatterley's Lover*, 181
113 Cixous, "The Art of Innocence", Cixous, 1994, 96

covers much the same ground as *Ice and Fire*, describing, like *Ice and Fire*, a woman growing up in New York, from childhood on the streets with friends, through the traumas of teenage, to the idealism and fervour of political activity, being involved with activists and radicals, to, finally, at the end of *Ice and Fire*, the 'birth' of the writer; the journey – critics call it 'rites of passage' – described in *Ice and Fire* and *Mercy* is extremely painful, extraordinarily awful, verily the experience of the concentration camps, but set in contemporary New York, so that the horror and pain of the worst moment of many in the 20th century, Auschwitz and Dachau, is seen to occur everywhere in history, and, especially, here, in Camden, New York City; of all the many depictions of journeys into the horrific underbelly of angst-ridden 20th century life – *Tropic of Cancer* by Henry Miller, *The Story of the Eye* by Georges Bataille, *Blood and Guts in High School* by Kathy Acker, *The Naked Lunch* by William Burroughs, *The Atrocity Exhibition* by J.G. Ballard, *Last Exit From Brooklyn* by Hubert Selby, etc, Dworkin's *Mercy* goes further and deeper; for depictions of depravity, perversion, pestilence, horror, trauma, pain, suffering, vice and sin, she goes further than Mailer, Miller, Acker, Burroughs, Selby, Amis, name anyone you like; at the same time, *Mercy* is a problematic text; at the outset, Dworkin tries to tackle the issue of the Author and of subjectivity, she prints a prologue entitled 'Not Andrea: Prologue', and an epilogue, entitled 'Not Andrea: Epilogue', these pieces aim to shift distance and subjectivity, the creation of the authorial self, which is complicated because the main character is called Andrea, and has a similar lifestory to Andrea Dworkin (born in Camden, NYC, etc), so that *Mercy* consciously creates self-consciousness, but Dworkin is not a postmodern writer, her philosophy is humanist, it believes that authors mean what they say, that they are present in their texts, whereas cultural theorists, such as Barthes say that the author is dead,[114] and the text is all there is, or, rather, texts and readers and fields of floating signifieds, changing continually, there is no 'fixed' reading, nothing is fixed and certain, everything changes, and

114 Roland Barthes: "The death of the Author", *Image-Music-Text*, Hill & Wang, New York 1977

continually, as Catherine Belsey writes: 'meanings circulate between text, ideology and reader' (144), Barthes wrote that '[a]ll images are polysemous... they imply, underlying their signifiers, a floating chain of signifieds', and the consumer has the ability to 'choose some and ignore others';[115] for Barthes, the link between text and 'real world' is not direct, but is a convention: thus, 'reality too, like the literary text, was itself inseparable from the language and discourse which shaped it', writes Leslie Hill,[116] so Dworkin's clinging onto the author and the authorial self, and the singular meaning of pornography, is fraught with problems, and, further, as *Mercy* progresses with its colloquial first-person voice, the problems multiply, as with *Ice and Fire*, for there are many passages in *Mercy* that could come from Dworkin's polemical non-fiction, and, vice versa, passages from *Pornography* or *Letters From a War Zone* that could be put into *Mercy* or *Ice and Fire* without anyone noticing, yet this is true also of, say, D.H. Lawrence, who, like Dworkin, wrote passionately and polemically of sexual politics, and who freely stuck polemical attacks into the midst of his novels, passages which sometimes stand out dramatically from the rest of the work (think of *Kangaroo* or *The Rainbow*); *Mercy* is about the atrocities of rape and torture that happen to an American Jew living in NYC, and it opens with a girl aged nine being sexually abused in a cinema by some 'uncle' character, and the 'uncle' or 'father' haunts the novel, dogging the protagonist, for the epigraphs of the novel are from *Isaiah* and from Sylvia Plath's anti-patriarchy poem 'Daddy': '[d]addy, daddy, you bastard, I'm through', and Plath is one of those writers who is a heroine for feminists, like Virginia Woolf or Emily Dickinson or Sappho; Plath was a poet whose rage came out of psychic disorder, so patriarchal critics say, but women know the experience as hysteria, a 'womb-madness', if you like, a rage bound up with biology, with the vagaries of the body, with self-image and so on, but also, ultimately, Plath was a poet who took on the hypocrisy and violence of patriarchy and won, as did Virginia Woolf, or Simone de Beauvoir, and, as Dworkin does, for

115 Roland Barthes: *Image-Music-Text*, Hill & Wang, New York 1977, 39
116 Leslie Hill: "Julia Kristeva: Theorizing the Avant-Garde?", in Fletcher & Benjamin, 141

Dworkin wins, she's a winner, she's victorious, despite the backlash, the polemics that go wrong, she is still one of our most exciting critics, who is not afraid, who dares, who is not afraid to dare, who dares not be afraid, witness the opening of *Intercourse*, where she relates the pain Sonia Tolstoy, wife and whore of the 'great' Russian novelist; the style of Dworkin's fiction is that of the Great American Voice, the great Amerikan narrator, like Mailer, Hemingway, Miller, Faulkner, Whitman, a big voice, not scared to bring in all manner of colloquialisms, slang, 'street talk', her language is that of the streetwise but also of course highly intellectual and well-read person, a person at home on the street, and a soul in the thick of life but also in the thick of fictionalizing her life, so that she lives it but also relates it, using that ubiquitous novelistic 'I', that huge, all-encompassing voice that we are so familiar with in the works of Whitman or Henry Miller, in fact, one of the funniest sections of *Mercy* is where the narrator takes on the 'great' writers, the pantheon of macho males with their phallic aggression who toured the world looking for the 'Land of Fuck', as that old Crazy Cock, Henry Miller, called it: '[t]here's writers being assholes about outlaws; outlaw this, outlaw that, I'm bad, I'm sitting here writing my book and I'm bad, I'm typing and I'm bad, my secretary's typing and I'm bad, I got laid, the boys say, like their novels are letters home to mama, well, hell's bells, the boys got laid: more than once. It's something to write home about, all right; costs fifty bucks, too; they found dirty women they did it to, dirty women too fucking poor to have a typewriter to stuff up bad boy writer's ass. Shit. You follow his cock around the big, bad city: New York, Paris, Rome – same city, same cock. Big, bad cock. Wiping themselves on dirty women, then writing home to mama by way of Grove Press, saying what trash the dirty women are; how brave the bad boys are, writing about it, doing it, putting their cocks in the big, bad, dirty hole where all the other big, brave boys were' oh they say dirty words about dirty women good. I read the books... The men writers make it as nasty as they can, it's like they're using a machine gun on her; they type with their fucking cocks – as Mailer admitted, right? Except he said balls, always a romancer... When I read the big writers I'm them;

careening around like they do; never paying a fucking price; days are long, their books are short compared to an hour on the street; but if you think about a book just saying I'm prick the books are pretty long; my cock, my cock, three volumes. They should just say: *I Can Fuck,* Norman Mailer's new novel. *I Can Be Fucked,* Jean Genet's new novel. *I'm Waiting To Be Fucked Or To Fuck, I Don't Know.* Samuel Beckett's new novel. *She Shit.* James Joyce's masterpiece. *Fuck Me, Fuck Her, Fuck It.* The Living Theater's new play. *Paradise Fucked.* The sequel. *Mama, I Fucked a Jewish Girl.* The new Philip Roth. *Mama, I Fucked a Shiksa.* The new, new Philip Roth. It was a bad day they wouldn't let the little boys say that word. I got to tell you, they got laid. They're up and down these streets, taking what they want; two hundred million little Henry Miller's with hard pricks and a mean prose style; Pulitzer prizewinning assholes using cash... they stick the famous Steel Rod into any Fleshy Hole they can find and they Ram the Rod In when they can manage it which thank God often enough they can't. The prose gets real purple then. You can't put it down to impotence though because they get laid and they had women and they fucked a lot; they just never seem to get over the miracle that it's them in a big man's body doing all the damage; Look, ma, it's me. Volume Twelve' (M, 111-3); when Dworkin rants, she rants just like the big bad macho American writers she detests because, despite her reservations, she employs the big, sweeping Walt Whitman approach, the impressive generalization, indeed, much of her polemic is generalization – 'all men do this, all men think that' – which is rubbish, on one level, because it's simply generalizations, and no one can say how other people feel, without asking them, and even then it's difficult getting a decent answer, partly because of the inarticulate nature of language in the first place, so no one can say how other people feel, for sure, but Dworkin says it, she is thoroughly outspoken, a little like another loud feminist, Camille Paglia, of whom Nicci Gerrard writes: 'she brings herself to orgasms of hatred for the 'endlessly complaining', 'glum' feminists, locked in their 'little mental cells', calls Kate Millett a poisonous beanbag... spits on a left-right divide, and strides into the date-rape debate with all the sensitivity of Arnold Schwarzenegger at a teadance',[117] you could say that Dworkin too works herself up into 'orgasms of hatred', although Dworkin would dislike the Reichian terminology of the phrase, and, like Paglia, Dworkin confuses a lot of people with her virulent condemnations of rape and patriarchal power and her exaltation of erotic feeling and wildness, but Dworkin is at no point pro-pornography, as Paglia is, but Dworkin's polemic, like Paglia's is often simplistic, founded on the 'us and them' philosophy, a polarization of society, a hierarchy of power thoroughly stereotypical in its gender orientation, but Dworkin reaches her targets via generalizations, it's part of her poetics, which in *Mercy* are allowed to be as wild as possible, so she kicks out against everything: against the city, which is horrible, and cold, and stark, and bleak, and harsh with its grey concrete and red bricks, its alleys, and Nature is harsh when it intrudes, in the form of rain, for instance, '[r]ain is so hard' she writes in *Mercy*, '[i]t stops but you stay wet for so long after and you get cold always no matter what the weather' (137), so she goes on, she is not very good on natural events, she – the narrator of *Mercy* and *Ice and Fire* – complains about rain, but rain is essential to human life, if it didn't rain there wouldn't be any human life anyway, and then the narrator complains about the cold, it's always cold in Dworkin's Big Apple, always cold, and snowy, and there's always a wind, and it's always blowing at 15 miles an hour, how does she know the wind speed? it's always 15 miles an hour, a steady wind, a disabling wind, cold, harsh, difficult, always blowing, so the *mise-en-scène* of Dworkin's fiction is always harsh, it's always horrible in her world, her characters always have a terrible time, and Nature too is terrible to them, it snows, it rains, it blows, its wets them and exhausts them, and even the sun, when it shines, is harsh, because it is too bright, or too hot, or just horrible, in the sequence in Greece in *Mercy*, for instance, where the sun is burning, her poetic world is that of an urban nightmare, strip lit, at night, or in the bleary-eyed daytime, windy, always windy, cold in the canyons between the skyscrapers, a postwar post-atomic post-holocaust world,

117 Nicci Gerrard: "'I'm a cartoon figure, an Italian opera [interview with Camille Paglia]", *The Observer*, 9 January 1994, *Review*, 14

apocalyptical, catastrophic, disastrous, a terrible city where everyone is harsh, harsh, harsh, no one has any time, it's cruel, the city is cruel, we've heard all this before, in Henry Miller, or William Burroughs, or Hubert Selby, it's familiar territory – *London Kills Me*, as that ridiculous title by Kureschi puts it – the city kills you, it's rubbish but these writers cling to it, the 'city' does it, it beats you down, but what is a city but humanity, don't they mean, then, always that New York is a hellhole because people are hell, don't these writers really mean that London kills you because people kill you, it's people that are hell, hell is other people said another macho writer, Jean-Paul Sartre, and so Dworkin's awful city, with its cement, stone and concrete, is hell, a living hell, a constant hell, except at times it can be wonderful, for a while, for a few moments, not on drugs, not mainlining, not shooting up, not dropping acid, but a spectral splendour that comes from being alive, as after rain, then, after rain, the splendour comes, one of those 'magic nights', as Dworkin calls them in *Mercy*, when everything shines: '[i]t's one of them magic nights where the rain glows and the neon is dull next to it; like God lit a silver flame in the water, it's a warm, silver, glassy shine, it sparkles, it's at night but it ain't dark because it's a slick light you could skate on and everything looks translucent and as if it's moving, it slides, it shines. It's beckoning to me as if God took a paint brush and covered the world in crystal and champagne. It's wet diamonds out there, lush and liquid, I never could pass up the sparkle, it's a wet, shimmering night, a wet, dazzling night; but warm, as if it's breathing all over you, as if it's wrapped around, a cocoon, that wispy stuff' (22-3); these are the (few) moments when Dworkin's texts ooze idealism and poetry, rare they are, rare because a book about being successively raped can't have silly bits of nature lyricism, it don't fit, and anyway, there ain't much Nature in New York anyway, not in Dworkin's New York, with its cement and sidewalks and cold wind, there's no place for Nature, except Nature as annoying stuff that gets in the way of the urban machine, for example Woody Allen never travels from New York, and, like Julie Burchill, regards Nature with distaste, the countryside, folks, is that 'green stuff', out there, beyond the city, and people don't go there, not city dwellers, it's as if they're astronauts living in some spaceship, or hippies living in some dome on a planet, never venturing beyond the confines of their city, because an influx of Nature would ruin Dworkin's polemic, because *Mercy* and *Ice and Fire* are about being raped, continually raped, living from one rape to the next, in essence, that's plot, the women grow up, gradually, or quickly, and they get raped, gradually or quickly, usually quickly, there's a build-up, then the rape occurs, so, in *Mercy*, the narrative is one woman's journey from abuse to abuse, and she gets raped all the time, she's a child and she gets raped, then she meets the activists, and it all seems to go well for her, but soon, she gets raped, it has to happen, her hopes are raised, she gets emotionally involved, she begins to like the people she's involved with, then, then it happens, the wonderful man she was with rapes her, and her world falls apart again, except, she goes on, she continues to live, she struggles on, like Hardy's Tess, then, with the boy or young radical in Greece, and travelling around Europe – it's a boy, any boy, an idealistic boy, she doesn't give them names, it's a boy, called M – she gets raped, at first it goes swimmingly, they enjoy a passionate love affair, fucking high on a ledge, on the Venetian walls, over the sea: '[a]ll night we fucked with the wind trying to push us down to death and I tore my fingers against the stone trying to hold on, the skin got stripped off my hands, and sometimes he was against the wall and my head fell backwards going down toward the sea and on the Roman walls we fucked for who was braver and who was stronger and who wasn't afraid to die. He wanted to find fear in me so he could leave me. He was desperate for freedom from love. On the Roman wall we fucked so far past fear that I knew there was only me, it didn't matter where he went or what he did, it didn't matter who with or how many or how hard he tried' (93); but it all goes wrong, this exhilarating mix of pleasure and danger, the usual concoction of occidental fear and desire, or love and death, or sex and pain, call it what you like, it's the metaphysics of love and religion in the West, this love and pain, and it goes wrong, the narrator fucks various people, Michel, who sodomizes her, nearly murdering her, and G, a 'teenage boy, Greek, maybe, fifteen' (M, 92), but M fucks other women, and leaves her, and she moves back to the US, and falls in with the hippies, and the 'peace boys', as she calls them, and she fucks them, takes drugs, the usual stuff, but the hippies expect her to be their housewife: 'peace, flowers, love, clean my house, bake my bread' they tell her (118), and it goes wrong, all the time, every time, every relationship winds up crap, first there is hope and idealism, high expectations, and then every illusion is shattered, mercilessly shattered, violently shattered, brutally, aggressively, physically, so, in *Ice and Fire*, the hopeful writer goes to a publisher's apartment, she's heard he's gay from friends, she doesn't think anything bad will happen, she walks through the streets, of course it's night, of course it's dark and cold and mean and harsh, and of course she's so broke she can't afford a taxi, and of course she spends hours getting there, trying to find, and it's so warm inside, once she gets there, and he's talking to her, and it's all so strange, to her, because she's so poor, and she's a struggling writer, and it seems strange that this gay publisher should be interested in her, and he seems genuinely interested in her work, her writing, not in her body, but then, of course he rapes her, it always turns out like that in Dworkin's fiction, he rapes her, and everything is fucked up, fucked down, fucked sideways all ways every which way so she's back down on the streets again, fucked senseless, raped senseless, and like a cat she licks her wounds and *goes on*, like Beckett's protagonists *go on*, there's nothing to be done, Beckett's people say, but go on, so they go on, and Dworkin's protagonists do the same, so in *Mercy* she goes to a painter, a highly respected New York artist, and it all seems good, and he gives her things, 'cos she's poor, she can't afford the sort of luxuries he has in his studio and apartment, but he fucks her, brutalizes her, rapes her, and it's the same pattern of misogyny and rape again with a taxi driver, a nice English man, quiet, well-spoken, he's kind, he seems to be kind, he offers a lift home, it's night, she's feeling awful, it's night and the taxi man says he'll take her home, and she accepts, what else can she do, it's a long way home, and it all seems good, and he comes to her place, and he's talking to her, and, eventually, sex manifests itself: 'I want to make real love, arduous, infatuated love touched by his grace, and I'm wondering what he will be like, naked and fine, intense, first slow, now; and I reach for him and he pulls me up so I'm on my knees in front of him and he's standing on the mattress and he takes his cock out and I'm thinking I'll hold it and he wants it in my mouth and I'm thinking I will kiss it and lick it and hold it in my mouth and undress him as I do it and I'm thinking how happy and fine this will be, slow, how stopped in time and tender, he holds my head still by my hair and he pushes his cock to the bottom of my throat, rams it in, past my throat, under it, deeper than the bottom, I felt this fracturing pain as if my neck shattered from inside and my muscles were torn apart ragged and fast, an explosion that ripped them like a bomb went off or someone pushed a fist down my throat but fast, just rammed it down' (268-9), so it all turns out to be rape again, and the crucial connection is made between radical, political protest, and radical, feminist protest, embodied in the figure of the burning Buddhist monk; for the narrator, Andrea, the Buddhists who burnt themselves as a protest for the Vietnam war are heroes, because of their calm, their use of fire, which she feels burning through, the fire of rage, of political anger, which she burns with constantly towards the end of the novel, where all the threads are drawn together, tighter and tighter, for 'Andrea' begins to burn with rage, saying 'I will rage on these streets a lifetime and I will build fires from garbage in buildings and I will hurt men' (268), her pain gets worse and worse, because 'Daddy', as in the Sylvia Plath poem, is not merciful, he is the brother, lover, husband, father, senator and Lord, God: 'He loves you with pain, by inflicting it in you, a slow, ardent lover, and you love back with suffering because you are helpless and human, an imprisoned child of him caged in the world of His making; it's a worshipful response, filled with awe and fear and dread, bewildered, why men, why now, why this, why aren't You merciful, why aren't You kind' (274), but He isn't kind or merciful, Daddy is the rapist posing as the kind avuncular figure, as described in Elizabeth Ward's powerful book *Father-Daughter Rape*: '[f]ather-Daughter sexual union is implicitly sanctioned, from the Bible to the latest movie-star marriage. When this is integrated with the fact that an enormous proportion of girl-children are raped by men within their own families, then the reality of existence for

The Daughter becomes plain. To be born female is to be a (potential) rape victim, from that moment on. Girl babies are raped. Girl toddlers are raped. Girl children are raped. And grown women are raped' (4) Ward's polemic is fully in tune with Dworkin's – for them, the enemy is male, and the abused is female, it is men attacking women, it is 'us and them', 'us against them', 'us against them because they attack us', and so on, an overly-simplistic dichotomy, over-simplistic because it reduces a very complex arena of experience to two poles, men versus women, and can it ever be that simple? just the two poles? men against women, women against men? can life ever be reduced to these sorts of simplicities? Elizabeth Ward continues with her analysis: '[t]he Father to The Daughter: My little princess. My little girlie, Lass, Blossom, Flossie, Dolly, Sweetheart, mine. Bring Daddy his paper, Blossom. My little girl's not old enough to go out with boys yet! Why were you late home from school? Who were you talking to? Who were you talking to? The Father to The Daughter: lollies, lacy dresses, rides in the car, special cuddles, rape' (4), the agony is here, in this outrageous movement, from 'special cuddles' and 'lollies' to that word, 'rape', you can see the rage in Dworkin's writing, the way she moves from the list of lovely things daddy gives his daughter – lollies, lacy dresses, special cuddles – to that awful, intolerable reality, rape; here is the agony of the feminist's position, in this emphasis on the hideous act, something no one would dwell on if it could be helped, but it can't be helped, because, as feminists say, time after time, men keep doing it, they don't stop, they keep on with it, keep on sexualizing situations, they keep on eroticizing people, turning them into sex objects, turning them into something they want to control, they must control, they must have what they want, like children, like angry babies must have what they desire, so men must rape, they must have sex, they must be allowed by the cosmic system to rape, they must be allowed by the social and political and psychological economy to have sex, they must rape, this is the reality feminists confront daily, and they would rather not, of course, they would rather not have to confront the horrors of rape, and torture, and violence, but they have to, because violence is there, in life, at the foundation of life, in the male system, it's still a mainly masculine system, it's largely men who make this violence; though, true, Nature is violent, earthquakes happen, tidal waves happen, there are electrical storms and animals tear each other apart, Nature, you could say, is vicious, sure it is, but people, now wait a minute, the viciousness and violences of Nature pale into insignificance compared to humanity's ability to create viciousness and violence, yes, a killer whale may be aggressive, of course it is, of course it's like that, but the violence of the killer whale, the praying mantis, the spider, the lion and the eagle is as nothing compared to the mass destruction of people, people who can burn down forests, who can dam up rivers and kill any animal on Earth, people who can drop bombs on cities and destroy them, *with one bomb*, with just one bomb, who have countless numbers of bombs and missiles dotted around the planet and *aimed at each other*!, they are aimed at other people, to smash them to pieces! so much for 'civilization', '*civilization*'! say the word in your lowest, fiercest, most bitter whisper, what hypocrisy! this 'civilization' of humanity! this psycho-social-political sophistication which allows billions of dollars to be spent annually and every day on weapons of mass destruction, that's what these weapons are for! to kill other humans! think of it! think of the praiseworthy refinement of such an organism that spends billions of petrodollars on nothing more sophisticated than a steel club, a club to bash the enemy!, a club made of steel and microchips and wires and nuclear material, a caveman club tipped with plutonium, for that's all these nuclear weapons are, really, just clubs, just iron phalluses, steel pricks, something with which to smash the opposition! it's incredible! and they call themselves 'civilized'! they sit in circles in European and American parliaments! they sit in *circles* to be '*democratic*'! they speak about the hi-falutin' ethics of democracy! yet at the same time they have armed themselves to the teeth with Minuteman III missiles, with Mark 12A warheads, 375kt yield – these are the 'fathers', the daddies and uncles, feminists claim, who have armed themselves with Tu22 M/26 Backfire medium-range aircraft, Mach 2.5 speed, with 7,927kg weapons payload, a 3,000 km combat range; watch out, because we live in a world of B52H strategic bombers, range l6,000 km, payload 70,000 pounds, SS-N-18 Mode 3 submarine-launched ballistic missiles, 7 MIRV, range 6,500km, total yield over 150 megatons, just 150 megatons, not much, really, just enough for breakfast, just enough to make sure you don't walk again, not after that, not after that delivery, of a ground burst, an air burst, an attack on Nagasaki or Hiroshima, New York, Washington, Seoul, Lima, Caracas, Delhi, Jerusalem, Cairo, Johannesburg, Santiago, Los Angeles, Chicago, Paris, Berlin, Mombasa, Bombay, Calcutta, Baghdad, Sydney, Hong Kong, Bangkok, Montreal, Oslo, Moscow, Toronto and Prague, these are just some of the sites the fathers and daddies and uncles will target, don't worry, your town won't be left out, they'll make sure everyone gets invited to the Party, they'll make sure you get your fair share of megatons; you're on the guest list, you live on planet Earth so you must be invited, don't worry, these people are MAD, that is, they are assured of Mutually Assured Destruction, that is, self-destruction, the babies will be soiling their beds for the last time, though some critics will be moaning that all this nukepseak is out of date, because it is so much a part of the mid-1980s, when all the nuclear theology was at its height in the media and the political arena, and now we're ten or twenty or thirty years distant from the mid-1980s, and no, 'It' won't happen, the Big 'It', the be-all-and-end-all 'It', It can't happen, they wouldn't do It, but the world governments/ militia/ multinational industries haven't destroyed many (any?) of these nuclear weapons, because they cost *billions*, they ain't gonna destroy their so-expensive toys, are they? the most expensive toys ever created, and *ooooh*, men do have a lot of lovely toys, don't they? *listen*: Soviet Oscar Class, cruise-missile submarines fitted with SS-NX-19 antiship missiles, MX missiles, 95-ton 3-stage solid-propellant missiles with inertial guidance using gyroscopes and accelerometers, there is an excellent array of machinery in nuclear theology: A-bombs, H-bombs and neutron bombs which'll go off all around the planet like fireworks, these are the 'sins of the fathers', the nuclear missile as the ultimate phallus of male power, the rape doctrine made into metal: F-16s, Jaguars, Tornadoes, Mirages, F-4s, MiG 21s, Su-24s, Blinder and Badger jets; AGM-86B, SS-20, SSBS-S3, Polaris A-3, Minuteman

III, SS-NX-17 missiles; and the missile launchers and tanks: Pershing 1A, Lance Honest John, M-110 howitzer, Frog 7, SS-C-16, and the lovely submarines, bristling with warheads: Delta-Class, Yankee-Class, Lafayette-Class, each submarine delivering more explosive than all that dropped in the Second World War, and this is not all the fathers and daddies (and, as Dworkin would say, the rapists) are doing, right now, for the atmosphere, the very air we breathe, is buzzing with commands, counter-commands, decisions, arguments, prayers, from every radar base, jet, ship, satellite, submarine and Command Centre; computerized commands and codes fly even now from military centres to Pershing II missiles – W84, SSM, airburst, 40-kiloton yield – and out of the window soon you'll see the flights of Tu95 Bear jets coming in for another dropload, and you'll hear the scream of towns burning after a W78 Minuteman III ICBM 330-kiloton yield attack; you'll hear this and other floccinaucinihilipilifications, for, terrifying though it is to contemplate, there are men in anoraks who dream of LGM-30G Minuteman III missiles, with their Triple MIRV warhead with penaids, Mark 12A with 335-kiloton thermonuclear warheads, length: 18.2 metres, speed at burnt-out: 15,000 mph, range: 7,000 kilometres; and there are people who think about, design and construct and control MSBS M-4 missiles, 150-kiloton yield, which are ready for impact, their primary targets are: Bristol, Singapore, Buenos Aires, Melbourne, Tehran, Tripoli, St Petersburg, Tashkent, Lisbon, Dakar, Dallas and Mexico City, among other cities; the jargon of the defence package on the radio has a sinister edge: C3, SAC, DCS, BMEWS, COCNAADC, Green Pine and Giant Talk radio networks; the Soviets had/ have gigantic radar ships – big liners and cruisers fitted with enormous spheres and dishes as wide as the ships themselves; since 1945 there have been over 2,500 nuclear detonations; DEW, AWACS, NORAD, ASM, CEP, TEL, TNF – the whole war machine lumbers along, and there are men who dream of another mechanical phallus, the Vought Corporation's Miniature Homing Vehicle – a cylinder 12 inches in diameter, 13 inches long which is ejected from an F-15 fighter at a speed of 17,5000 mph, sensors home in on the target and the onboard computer guides the cylinder to its target using mini-rockets, it destroys the target not with explosives but by simply smashing into it at 17,500 mph, it is the sheer speed and force which destroys the target, how beautiful that would seem to a rapist culture, no need for explosives or messy chemicals, just pure brute force, slamming into a target at 17,500 miles per hour, how *luscious,* it's the ultimate penetration, the ultimate fuck, penetrating the love object at 17,500 miles per hour, what bliss, and there are men who not only dream about but also control the military satellites, locked in their geostationary orbits like technological guardian angels, whispering to command centres about secret manœuvres, with their atomic clocks that lose only one second in 30,000 years, the world may be on Panic Alert, Attack Warning Red, and we wouldn't know, we don't really know what goes on at this level, there are forty thousand megatons ready to go, these people are, in Dworkin's terminology, the nuclear rapists, rapists who are dubbed scientists and politicians, and these scientists and politicians, they'll sort you out, and you probably know some of them, you've probably sat next to nuclear scientists or atomic chiefs on the train, or in cinemas, bars, cafes, for the rapists, as Elizabeth Ward, Mary Daly, Susan Griffin and Luce Irigaray remind us, are all around us, as Elizabeth Ward writes: '[t]he fact that Daddy is The Stranger to all the other little girls is one of the mindbinds of patriarchy. As little girls, we never quite see other girls (our friends) seeing Daddy as the Stranger. But he is. And some are raped by The Stranger who is her friend's father. The daughter-rapers, child molesters, dirty old men, creepy uncles, and sticky-fingered grandfathers, are men who are in our families, next door, across the street, in grandma's house. The myth that there is a difference between the Father and The Stranger helps create the passivity of Daughter-victims. No one tells The Daughters (all girl-children) to beware of The Fathers (all male relatives, and male adult friends, trusted by the family). No one tells The Daughters how to say No to The Fathers' (5) and Ward is right, they are all around us, we are surrounded by these people, as Dworkin says in her speech "The Lie" (1979): '[f]or centuries men have consumed pornography in secret – yes, the lawyers and legislators and the doctors and the artists and the writers and the scientists and the theologians and the philosophers' (War, 11), these are the people who surround us, Dworkin says, even now, even as we speak, even as we breathe, they speak of arms escalation, ground shock, detonation, air burst, broken arrows, ground zero, maximum yield, deterrence, the sanctuary theory, overkill, overpressure, time-sensitive targets, stealth, fratricide, launch-under-attack, single-shot kill probability, first strike, AEW, CIWS, HEAT, SOSUS, MAW, WPO, NATO, ICBM, SS-20, Pershing II, BGM-1099 – these are the wonders of nukespeak and nuclear theology, the whole arms industry, which costs 1,000,000 dollars per minute (1982 figures), it's bigger than the pornographic industry, even though, as Andrea Dworkin reminds us, the porn business is bigger than the music and film industry combined, that's what she says, but the arms business, *wow*, it's even bigger than pornography, for 100,000,000 people work in the military forces worldwide or in back-up services, and arms are second only to oil as a money-making enterprise, and there are 30,000-plus tactical and intermediate-range nuclear weapons and 20,000 strategic weapons, and one Lance battlefield missile can deliver six Hiroshimas, while a submarine costs 1.5 billion dollars, and when 'It' does happen, you know, the Big 'It', the 'It' that ends all others, not Dworkin's 'it', not fucking, not that pornographic 'it', but the Big 'It' of global politics, when that apocalyptical and tumultuous End of the World occurs, maximum capability is about one strategic warhead hitting a target every twenty seconds; so, to illustrate what would actually happen in a nuclear strike, let's take a one megaton air-burst scenario: at ground zero, all buildings would be destroyed; there would be winds of 1,000 mph; all combustible stuff would ignite; flesh would melt; people would die in the suffocation from the firestorm; from two to five miles away, most buildings would be flattened; winds of 130 mph; clothing would ignite; radiation sickness is inevitable; at three miles away you'd feel a flash of light, then intense heat which chars to the bone (full-thickness burns), fifteen seconds later the windows would be blown in by the blast wave, and you'd be thrown around by the wind; most people would be permanently blinded by the light, fall-out is second-stage radiation, contaminating water, the food chain, everything, everywhere would be a 'Z Zone', a fallout zone; nuclear reactors will be hit with ground-bursts: the fallout from the cores will be deadly, not just cities but airfields, communications centres, military stores and camps will also be targets, a list of targets would include: submarines and bases, stockpiles, strategic command centres (Hawthorn, Whitehall, High Wycombe, etc, in the UK), communications links (including British Telecom centres and the microwave tower network), the very low frequency radio stations at Rugby and Criggon, used for talking to submerged submarines, missile and long range radar centres (such as Clee Hill, Fyllingdales, Bishopcourt in the UK), air defence missile and interceptor bases, nuclear production sites (such as Burghfield, Aldermaston, Sellafield, Cardiff), power stations, nuclear power stations (such as Dungeness, Dounreay, Wylfa, Heysham), the chemical industries, oil and gas terminals and ports, troop concentrations (Salisbury, Aldershot, Colchester, etc), fuel depots, ammunition stocks, ports, government administration centres, and finally the major urban and industrial centres: in the UK, London, Manchester, Hull, Birmingham, Leeds, Bradford, Sheffield, Bristol, Glasgow, Dundee, Newcastle, Huddersfield, Portsmouth, Swansea, Leicester, Southampton, Coventry, Liverpool, Cardiff, Nottingham, Derby and so on; if birds are killed insects might devastate crops; fires fanned by the winds will destroy much woodland; the UK 'Square Leg' operation of 1980 estimated 100 US military targets in Britain, including Upper Heyford, Boscombe Down, Greenham Common, Burtonwood, etc, as well as Birmingham, Sheffield, Liverpool, Swansea, Glasgow, etc, in the UK, a million dead, three million injured, or 35 million surviving, depending on which survey you read; towns such as Oxford, Cheltenham, Carlisle, Chester and Birmingham will have airburst attacks – the idea being to kill as many people as possible; places such as Liverpool, St Mawgan, Coningsbury, Bracknell and Farnborough will receive ground bursts to knock out machinery, ports, industries, ships and buildings; places like Felixstowe and Canvey Island will have ten times more bombers attacking them than, say, Swindon or Manchester; and don't forget chemical, biological and radiological warfare; we go into this nuclear scenario at length because this is precisely what Dworkin is kicking against – not simply what men *think*, or what they say, but what they *do*, for they really do build enormous and highly complex killing machines and systems, and they really do mean to murder millions of people in a nuclear war, if or when it happens, and soldiers have been shown pornographic movies before going into battle, this is what Dworkin is fighting against, this massive patriarchal system and machine, and in her fiction she makes the all-important connection – between the personal and the political – between the rape of one person and the rape of many people, she's doing 'atrocity work', as she says in a lecture of 8 April 1983 in upstate New York: 'I represent the woman with the shit, the real shit. Robin Morgan calls it "atrocity work." And that's pretty much what it is',[118] for the horrors never stop, in *Mercy* the horrors increase in Andrea's life, for she makes connections all over the place, connections in patriarchal power, so that the taxi driver who shoved his dick down her throat, choking her to coma, is connected with child abusers the world over, the child abusers who are fathers and 'uncles', who are everywhere, those people who are familiar and real: '[d]addy watches; a perpetual pornography; blood-and-guts scenes of pushing and hitting and humiliation, the girl on the bed, the girl on the floor, the girl in the kitchen... all colors, a rainbow of suffering, rich and poor, sick and well, young and old, infants even, a man sticks it in the mouths of infants, I know such a man; oh, he's real; an uncle of mine; an adult; look up to him, listen to him, obey him, love him, he's your uncle; he was born in Camden but he left, smart, a big man, he got rich and prominent, an outstanding citizen; five infants, in the throat, men like the throat, his own children, it was a daddy's love, he did that, a loving daddy in the dark, and God watched, they like the throat' (284), yet not all feminists agree with Dworkin in her utter hatred of 'deep throat', the kind of cock-sucking made notorious by Linda 'Lovelace' in the movie, about which Dworkin writes in a note at the end of *Mercy*, but Gayle Rubin writes: 'sadomasochism is not the only behaviour subjected to condescending and insulting judgements; for example, MacKinnon has also described porn in which someone was 'raped

118 Dworkin: "Feminism: An Agenda", War, 133

in the throat where a penis cannot go'; there are plenty of gay men, and even a good number of heterosexual women, who enjoy cock-sucking. There are even lesbians who relish going down on dildos. Obviously, oral penetration is not an activity for everyone, but it is presumptuous to assume that it is physically impossible or necessarily coercive in all circumstances',[119] in other words, what turns one person on is horrific to another, or, as Ellen Willis puts it: 'what I like is erotica, and what you like is pornographic',[120] Dworkin agrees with this, but what's clear is that there is no consensus at all among feminists on the issue of pornography, and many feminists have criticized Dworkin's simplistic 'us and them', biologist arguments; but Dworkin remains vociferous and vehement on the pornography issue ('[p]ornography is the sexualized subordination of women' she says in "Silence Means Dissent", War, 248), and her crusade against pornography and rape remain absolutely crucial, and central, to her life's work, for, in her view, fucked in the throat, people are silenced, they cannot breathe, let alone talk, and Dworkin, under the guise of her narrator in *Mercy*, 'Andrea', says this is worse than Auschwitz: 'five infants, uncle; it makes Auschwitz look small, uncle' (286), so for 'Andrea', all the pornographies of the world blend together – the hell of the Jews at Masada, the people in the death camps, black people brutalized by whites, the Klu Klux Klan, child abuse, rape, violence, the pornography of Times Square – all the horrors are blended together, all controlled by men, men are to blame, they are the controllers and instigators of this global pornography, Dworkin/Andrea says, the men control it, they're not in the frame, but they have the cameras, which manipulate the images of pornography, as Dworkin writes: 'if there's a camera there's a plan' (297), a brilliant summary of pornography, and of image-making in general: *if there's a camera there's a plan,* it perfectly describes the notion of *intention* in art and pornography, the intention of desire and longed-for gratification, which she enlarges upon, saying we are all stuck in the sex circus created by

119 Gayle Rubin: "Misguided, Dangerous and Wrong: an Analysis of Anti-Pornography Politics", in Assister & Carol, eds, 32

120 Ellen Willis: *Village Voice*, 15 October 1979, 8

men: 'when I see a woman under glass, I know the game, a sex animal trained for sex tricks; and the camera's ready; maybe Masta's not in the frame' (297), and she catalogues, towards the end of *Mercy*, the acts that men perpetrate which are real, real and fantasized, acts that are found throughout pornography: 'I know there's blood... Linda. They do all the things to her; glass in her vagina; from the front; from behind; all the things... they grabbed us off the streets in vans and gang-raped us and bashed us with baseball bats, smashing us not looking where, arms, head, chest, stomach, legs, and filmed it, and dumped us, some of us lived, some of us died, or before they set dogs on us to fuck us, and filmed it, or before they cut us open, to ejaculate on us, and filmed it, or before they started urinating on us, using us like common toilets, to film it...' (302, 326), she lists the atrocities that men commit and women suffer, from rapists who beat and sodomize and slice up women (329) to fathers who sexually abused their children and the judge gave them custody (330), the abuse becomes so horrible that, later on, it creates suicides; she writes: 'I know girls whose fathers fucked them; near to death; it's a deferred death sentence on her, she does it herself, later. I know girls who been banged by thousands of men; I am one such girl myself. I know girls who been cut open and fucked in the hole. I know a girl who was kidnapped by a bunch of college boys, a fraternity, and kept for days; used over and over; beat her to blood and pus; sliced her throat and dumped her; I know her and I know another woman raped the same way, wasn't sliced, she escaped; I know so many girls who been kidnapped and gang-raped you couldn't fit them into a ballroom; I know so many girls who been tortured as children you couldn't fit them into a ballroom; I know so many girls who was fucked by their daddies you couldn't fit them into a ballroom,' (330), and the result of all this cataloguing of horror is, of course, activism, an activism that uses the methods of political activism, but targets pornography, so that the protagonist of *Mercy* begins to attack the porn houses of Times Square, the establishments where sexism is offered, or displayed, or produced: '[n]o one cares; how many times can you say *raped*; it don't matter and no one stops them. I throw rocks through the windows of rape emporiums; I destroy business properties of men who rape; or men who beat women' (330-1), 'Andrea' goes out onto the streets and fights the sex war, the porn war, she dreams of a group of women sweeping through the streets, shock troops of an anti-porn organization, she says she's searched for the right words to describe the horror, but couldn't find any, she didn't want to use old words, she has tried to describe 'what he did' (332), but words were not enough for her, so she moved into action, as the terrorists do, when no one listens, so they get violent, because 'Andrea' is still idealistic, still in love with 'freedom' and 'love': 'I want love, freedom first, freedom now; rape rape rape; fucking O; I found the word, it's the right word; fucking O' (332), for Dworkin, men experience freedom and women do not: '[t]he truth is that men do experience freedom of movement and freedom in action and that women do not';[121] the Linda Lovelace phenomenon is an abomination to the narrator of *Mercy*, it crystallizes so much that she despises about men and their aggression, the utterly horrible practice of sticking their pricks down women's throats, and the fact that Linda Lovelace is shown *smiling*, it infuriates her, this lie of pornography, that the woman 'enjoys' being raped – 'he fucks her throat and she's in love with him because he's got this giant penis so he satisfies her, at last, completely, a romance, he fucks her throat, he is a cold creep, a sheet of ice descends over the screen' (302), and the sick thing, one of the many sick things, is that men *believe* all this is real, 'these men are crazy to think this is a woman moaning in sex' (302), 'why would anyone, even a man, think it's true – her all strung out, all painted, all glossy, proclaiming being peed on is what she wants' (306), and the end result is that 'Andrea' makes the connection between sex and politics, between radical politics and radical feminism, so that she enacts the Buddhist self-immolation outside the cinema where *Deep Throat* is showing in Times Square, she puts up signs saying *Porn Is Rape* and *Free Linda*, and sets light to herself like the Buddhist ascetics, but this is not the end of the novel, this is not the most shocking thing about this, 'Andrea's' suicide outside the porn cinema, no, because in the final chapter, entitled "April 30, 1974 (Age 27)", she joins a martial arts group presided over by a powerful lesbian, Sensei, who trains her to be able to defend

121 Dworkin: "The Night and Danger", 1979, War, 16

herself, but, finally, 'Andrea' cannot afford to continue with the classes, but she continues to fight, in her own way, by writing a plan of action, by terrorizing porn makers and consumers, she becomes a Che Guevara of anti-porn activism: 'I have clear priorities... number one is that I am writing a plan for revenge, a justice plan, a justice poem, a justice map, a geography of justice; I am martial in my heart and military in my mind; I think in strategy and in poems, a daughter of Guevara and Whitman ready to take to the hills with a cosmic vision of what's crawling around down on the ground; a daughter with an overview; the big view; a daughter with a new practice of righteous rage, against what ain't named and ain't spoken so it can't be prosecuted except by the one it was done to who knows it, knows him; I'm inventing a new practice of random self-defense; I take their habits and characteristics seriously, as enemy, and I plan to outsmart them and win; they want to stay anonymous, monster shadows, brutes, king pricks, they want to be sadistic ghosts in the dark with penises that slice us open' (316), so she takes on male methods, male systems, male ways of action and rebellion, something some feminists are suspicious of, or doubtful of, this taking on of masculinist methodologies, but that's 'Andrea's' way, to use violence, aggression, karate kicks and self-defense, because she isn't dead, she has survived all the abuse men have heaped on her, he has survived, and one of the most poignant sentences in the book is 'I am not dead' (317), she is not dead, they have not succeeded in killing her, she still lives, lives to attack men, and thus we arrive at the most shocking message of the book, but it's the logical conclusion, enunciated twice, first when a woman she's not met before says to her: 'Andrea... it is very important for women to kill men' (328), this is the endpoint of *Mercy*, of the long battle against men, it ends with a crusade against men that turns to violence, it takes the biologist or essentialist argument of feminism to its logical conclusion, the murder of men, the male genocide, the endpoint of a feminism turned into fascism: 'I enunciated a political principle, which went as follows: It is very important for women to kill men. His death, of course, is unbearable. His death is intolerable, unspeakable, unfair, insufferable; I agree; I learned it since the day I was born;

terrible; is death is terrible; are you crazy; are you stupid; are you cruel? He can't be killed; for what he did to you? It's absurd; it's silly; it's unjustified; uncivilized; crazed' (328-9); fucked to near-death, 'Andrea' becomes a night creature, going into all the dark places, and murdering men, she and her sisters, it's a sisterhood of assassination, the men are shocked, utterly surprised to be confronted by her, and she picks on the big ones, the big men, they don't believe it when she approaches them, she says 'what I appreciate is their surprise, which is absolute, their astonishment, which invigorates me; how easy it is to make them eat shit' (324), and what does our 'Andrea' do when she meets these drunks and bums by night, in the dark corners of the city? she beats the shit out of them, the fuck out of them, as she says, as men say in movies, I'll beat the shit out of you, they say, I'll beat you to fuck, men say in the movies, in thousands of movies that pour out of LA, in 'Andrea's' words this is what she does to the men she finds on the streets: 'I fucking smash their faces in; I kick them; I hit them; I kick them blind; I like smashing their faces in with one kick, I like dancing on their chests, their rheumy old chests... I like smashing the bottles into their fucking faces' (324), this is the endpoint of *Mercy*, while, at the end of *Ice and Fire*, the narrator became a writer, that was the final result of her journey through the hell of contemporary life, to become a writer, to win through to being an artist despite all the shit society could throw at her, but at the end of *Mercy*, she becomes a porn terrorist, a feminist-activist who believes that 'I don't fucking care about fair. It is obscene for a girl to think about fair' (324), for, ultimately, in men's eyes women are simply 'cunt', 'Andrea' claims, as does Dworkin in her non-fiction, 'cunt' is the bottom line, the fundamental material of pornography, where men like to put women, or as Dworkin says in *Pornography*: '[f]or the fuck to exist, the cunt must exist: and abuse to enhance the cuntiness of a cunt' (112), while in her fiction writes 'cunt is cunt is cunt', says the narrator of *Mercy* (325), echoing Dworkin in *Pornography* and *Intercourse*, but Dworkin/'Andrea' is not a 'cunt' who is going to be fucked into silence, for she has a will to live, to shout, to scream, she will *not* be silenced, even though pricks have been shoved down her throat, she will not shut up, she will not choke and die, she will fight, because she knows that '[t]here's not one human gesture [in pornography]; not one. There's not one woman in the world likes to be hung or shit on or have her breasts tied up so the rope cuts in and the flesh bulges out' (M, 29); the mission of 'Andrea' in *Mercy* is to break the silence, to name names, to name the men that raped her, to turn the tide, the tables, the aggression, to turn men's tactics onto themselves, so that women will stop being mere' cunt', the 'hole' into which they stick their penises; the rage is against pornography in all realms of culture; the French feminist Benoîte Groult describes the 'intellectual' books of high-class pornography – by Miller, Bataille, de Sade: '[n]o matter what book it is, we always find the same male hero who, with the same arrogance, takes his pleasure in some creature who for him is reduced to two holes in the bottom of her body, plus a third on the bottom of her face';[122] Dworkin brings the pornography of fellatio to the fore in *Mercy*, so that the link between sex and speaking, having sex and not being able to speak, between pornography and silence is foregrounded, she makes the connection, continually, between the imagery of pornography and the actuality of violence, an extremely contentious issue, where pornography is the theory and social power is the reality, or as Robin Morgan put it: 'pornography is the theory and rape is the practice';[123] Morgan writes: '[a]nd what a practice. The violation of an individual woman is the metaphor for man's forcing himself on whole nations (rape as the crux of war), on nonhuman creatures (rape as the lust behind hunting and related carnage), and on the planet itself (reflected even in our language – carving up "virgin territory", with strip mining often referred to as a "rape of the land")' (Morgan, 88); for Dworkin, as for other radical feminists, such as Susan Griffin, Kate Millett and Susan Brownmiller, rape

122 Groult: "Les portiers de nuit", in *Ainsi soit-elle*, Grasset, Paris, 1975, and in Marks & Courtivron, 71
123 see L. Lederer, ed: *Take Back the Night: Woman on Pornography*, William Morrow, New York 1980

is sanctioned and sanctified in patriarchy,[124] and pornography helps to legitimize rape, to make it appear the norm so that feminists see marriage as sanctified rape,[125] Dominique Poggi writes: 'one of the principal functions of pornography: the purveying of an ideology of pleasure and enjoyment which urges rapelike relations, exalts rapists',[126] or as Catherine MacKinnon puts it: '[m]an fucks woman; subject verb object',[127] but some people might think that Dworkin, Griffin, Poggi, Brownmillr, Millett, Groult and Morgan are exaggerating about rape, but they are not, for rape surrounds us, all the time, in the newspapers we read that an unnamed Dublin man raped his daughter, made her pregnant, 'hit her fingers with a hammer and slashed her stomach with a knife in separate incidents over a 16-year period';[128] men are indeed strange creatures – five 'homosexual sadomasochists' were convicted in 1990 of inflicting 'injuries on each another's genitals during ritual sex' which involved 'cutting each other's genitals with surgical scalpels, sandpapering scrotums and pushing hooks into penises';[129] rape is so horrible, so painful, it'll kill you, they'll kill you – who's 'they'? – 'they' is men – 'They'll kill me,' says Andrea in *Mercy*, 'fuck me dead or kill me after', and she hopes to simply be able to get through it – through what? – through life: 'if I can just get through it; minimum damage, minimum pain, the goal of all women all the time' (M, 126), while in her book *Right-Wing Women*, Dworkin notes that rape as a phenomenon is eternally sidelined and suppressed in our culture, so that it doesn't seem to exist: '[t]he accounts of rape, wife beating, forced childbearing, medical butchering, sex-motivated murder, forced prostitution, physical

124 Susan Griffin: *Rape: the Power of Consciousness*, Harper & Row, New York 1979; Susan Brownmiller: *Against Our Will: Men, Women and Rape*, Simon & Schuster, New York 1975; D. Rhodes & S. McNeil, eds: *Women Against Violence Against Women*, Onlywomen Press 1985; J. Hammer & M. Maynard, eds: *Women, Violence and Social Control*, Macmillan 1987
125 see C. Kramarae & P. A. Treichler, eds: *A Feminist Dictionary*, Pandora Press 1985
126 Dominique Poggi: "Une apologie des rapports de domination", *La quinzaine littéraire*, August 1976, in Marks, 77
127 Catherine MacKinnon: "Feminism, Marxism, Method and the State: An Agenda for Theory", *Signs*, vol. 7, no. 3, Spring 1982
128 Joe Joyce: "Dublin acts after rapist father jailed for 7 years", *The Guardian*, 6 March 1993
129 Ian MacKinnon: "Lords reject appeals by sado-masochists", *The Independent*, 12 March 1993

mutilation, sadistic psychological abuse, and the other commonplaces of female experience that are excavated from the past or given by contemporary survivors should leave the heart seared, the mind in anguish, the conscience in upheaval. But they do not. No matter how often these stories are told, with whatever clarity or eloquence, bitterness or sorrow, they might as well have been whispered in wind or written in sand: they disappear, as if they were nothing. The tellers and the stories are ignored or ridiculed, threatened back into silence or destroyed, and the experience of female suffering is buried in cultural invisibility and contempt' (RWW, 20), but perhaps Dworkin, Griffin, Daly, Morgan, Millett, Groult and Irigaray have got it wrong about men, perhaps it's not men who're to blame after all, perhaps 'blaming' itself is wrong, perhaps it's the 'system' of patriarchy, a system which 'favours' men, gives them more opportunities than women, a system which favours male ideas and values and attitudes above those of women, perhaps it's the patriarchal culture, not men as individuals, who are the problem, that is, it's not individuals, but 'society', or 'culture', or 'education', i.e., something bigger than men, far huger than mere men or boys, far more difficult to assess and manipulate, yet, yet, Dworkin is not convinced, she is convinced of the opposite, that one can 'blame' men, than men should be the targets of feminist attacks; others agree with Dworkin, and not just committed, active, published feminists, but also the 'general public', that is, people in general, such as Christine Jackson, who writes: '[b]oys, not girls, are filling remand centres. Men, not women, batter their partners, abuse children and fight on the football terraces';[130] and of course, when a battered woman kicks back against her tormentor, the press pounce and do the dirt, shrieking that 'men can get raped too', an idea which is an obscenity to Andrea Dworkin, the idea that men can be raped by women; true, men get raped by men far more frequently than men are raped by women, but when a woman murders her husband, society hounds her, as in *Tess of the D'Urbervilles,* where Tess does the deed to counter being raped by Alec, and it is Tess who is punished, not Alec, while Angel looks on, unable to do anything constructive about her predicament; the

130 Christine Jackson, letter to *The Guardian*, 6 March 1993

hypocrisy of this double standard is explored by Dworkin in *Pornography,* but perhaps there is too much emphasis in feminism on the importance of the victimization that rape produces? more controversially, Jenny Diski suggests that a rape 'victim's' life need not be utterly shattered after the rape, because it means we put too much emphasis on sexuality: '[e]very act of physical violence will have traumatic effects but what do we mean when we tell a young woman that her sense of self-esteem can be destroyed by an act of enforced penetration? Are we really meaning to say that a woman's central identity resides in her genitals?'[131] the genitals have replaced the soul as the site of a person's core or essence, and pornography – and art – adds to this emphasis on the genitals, as if people are nothing but genitals these days, just a cock and cunt squirming in bliss, or not, as the case may be, but the Freudian reduction to genitals is part of the patriarchal or pornographic worldview which Dworkin so violently detests, and it is very much a lingual or æsthetic or cultural problem, as well as a psychological or physical one, for there is an immense *violence* in language, just as there is immense violence in the things people do, as Dworkin notes, time after time, in each of her books, always drawing attention to the violences of lingual expression, drawing attention to those particular ways which people use to control and categorize other people, as she writes in *Right-Wing Women,* '[t]here is a spectrum of insult. Lesbians, intellectuals, and uppity women are hated for their presumption, their arrogance, their masculine ambition. Prudes, spinsters, and celibates may not want to be like men but they seem able to live without them; so they are treated with contempt and disdain. Sluts, "nymphos," and tarts are hated because they are cheap, not expensive, and because they are sex raw or sex itself. These epithets (often in ruder form) directed against a woman are intended to malign her own relationship to her own gender or to sexuality as men define and enforce it. The epithets are situational: chosen and applied not to show what she is in her essential self but to intimidate her in a particular situation. For instance, if she does not want sex, she

131 Jenny Diski: "Double jeopardy of the victim victim", *The Guardian*, 27 August 1993

may be called – by the very same observer – a slut' (RWW, 198), you see Dworkin here working up her analysis step by step, slowly and carefully, and she is not done yet, for she continues: '[e]pithets as sex-based insults are like machine-gun rounds, fired off, bringing down whatever gets hit – anything female around... Every time this use of a lexicon of hatred passes unremarked, every time the hate is expressed and there is no visible rebellion, no discernible resistance, some part of the woman to whom it happens dies and some part of any woman who watches dies too. Each time the use of such an epithet or its evocation passes without retaliation, something in women dies' (200), and she continues: 'each time contempt is expressed for the dyke, the prude, the slut, hatred is being expressed toward all women. Whether the insults are accepted in society, tolerated, encouraged, the main stuff of humor, or merely passively acquiesced in, the devaluing of women is perpetuated, the intimidation of women is furthered' (201), and Dworkin does not stop with her analysis, she keeps on developing it, turning it this way and that, trying new slants or 'takes' on the basic premise of women-hating: '[w]oman hating is the passion; anti-feminism is its ideological defense; in the sex-based insult passion and ideology are united in an act of denigration and intimidation' (201), for Dworkin language can be violence, as religion or politics can be violence – for 'violence' in Dworkin's metaphysics read 'violence against women', as she puts it in *Pornography*: '[s]ome men will renounce violence in theory, and practice in secrecy against women and children. Some men will become icons in male culture, able to discipline and focus their commitment to violence by learning a violent skill: boxing, shooting, hunting, hockey, football, soldiering, policing. Some men will use language as violence, or money as violence, or religion as violence, or science as violence, or influence over others as violence. Some men will commit violence against the minds of others and some against the bodies of others. Most men, in their life histories, have done both' (52), for feminists such as Dale Spender, language is male-made: '[t]he English language has been literally man-made and... it is still primarily under male control',[132] for Spender, language is a

132 Spender, *Man-Made Language*, 12

product of patriarchal power and control, and all of language can be violence against women, and Dworkin believes whole-heartedly in the power of words, she really does believe that language can influence, persuade and corrupt, that words can be weapons, she says in her speech "The Power of Words": '[w]ords can be used to educate, to clarify, to inform, to illuminate. Words can also be be used to intimidate, to threaten, to insult, to coerce, to incite hatred, to encourage ignorance. Words can make us better or worse people, more compassionate or more prejudiced, more generous or more cruel. Words matter because words significantly determine how and what we do. Words change us or keep us the same. Women, deprived of words, are deprived of life';[133] men can use the whole of language as violence against women, not just the harsh or 'dirty' words, such as fuck and cunt, it's not only these words that are verbal violence, for even the 'soft' words, like 'soft' or 'gentle' can be violence against women if employed in certain ways in certain contexts, for all words can be strung together to form violence against women, a kind of linguistic or verbal rape, so that any words, not just the 'dirty words', can be seen as æsthetic rape, but the 'dirty words' themselves are *very* violent for some feminists, the word 'fuck' is very hurtful to some feminists, while the word 'cunt' is not used by even radical and trendy feminists, the word 'cunt' frightens and annoys them, they won't use it, 'fuck' is OK, but not 'cunt' because, simply, the word 'cunt' is the ultimate verbal violence against women, it is the one word that is absolutely outlawed and forbidden, no one may use it, and even otherwise violent and aggressive films do not use it, they use fucking, fuck, fuck off, and that favourite, motherfucker, but not cunt, somehow they steer clear of cunt, for the reason, perhaps, that it's much more 'offensive' than 'fuck', 'cos 'fuck' is OK, but 'cunt' is not, saying 'cunt' is going just a little too far, perhaps; Dworkin knows all the subtleties of the 'dirty words', how they are used in vernacular, in slang, in 'high art' and 'low art' contexts, and, of course, throughout pornography, where the word fuck is used so much it loses its original meaning, of having sex, and becomes a word meaning 'doing', as in, 'he fucked her'. 'he did her', so that any word it seems can be substituted for the

133 Dworkin: "The Power of Words", 1978, War, 30

word fuck in pornography, and the word fuck is as far from being 'shocking' as is possible for a word, and no one can get 'uptight' or 'hot under the collar' about the word fuck, 'cos you hear it everywhere anyway, I mean, *everyone* uses it, some people can't communicate without saying fuck or fucking, there are some people who can't speak to other people without saying fucking this or fucking that, they use the word 'fucking' as the all-purpose adjective, adverb, anything word, as in: *I went down the fucking street and bought a fucking newspaper and someone had fucking broken into my fucking car, fucking bastards,* or as Dworkin says in *Mercy*: 'Every other word is nigger or cunt or fucking' (82), for right-wing guardians of society, such as Mary Whitehouse, using the word fuck is going over the edge: when you use the word fuck where can go after that? Whitehouse asks, meaning, you've used the 'ultimate' in verbal violence, but the word 'fuck' is everywhere anyway, so what the hell is all the fuss about, or, rather, to use the proper contemporary phrasing here: *what the fuck is all the fucking fuss about with the word fuck?* D.H. Lawrence got well stuck into this 'dirty words' debate with his novel of religious transformation via a good bout of sodomy (or 'ass fucking' as the pop singer Madonna calls it), for Lawrence hated pornography, because it made sex 'dirty', it 'did the dirt' on sex, which he viewed as holy, but he used the 'obscene' four-letter words to try to reclaim their power, because fuck, cunt and shit had been degraded, as Dworkin writes: 'Lawrence believed that the use of sexual euphemism created the dirty connotation of the more direct language... The *phallic reality* he intended was ecstatic, not dirty, a sacrament of fucking, human worship of a pure masculinity and a pure femininity embodied in, respectively, the penis and the cunt (another word favored by Lawrence). Lawrence himself was forced to recognize 'how strong is the will in ordinary, vulgar people, to do dirt on sex' (I, 201-2); Dworkin's view is that these words can never be redeemed from pornography: 'words stay dirty because they express a contempt for women, or for women and sex, often synonyms, that is real, embedded in hostile practices that devalue and hurt women... Dirty words stay dirty because they express a hate for women as inferiors, that hate inextricably, it seems, is part of sex – a hate for women's genitals, a hate for women's bodies, a hate for the insides of women in fucking. Dirty words stay dirty because they express a true dimension of women's inferiority, a forced inferiority, the dirty words part of the ongoing force; the penis itself signifying power over women, that power expressed most directly, most eloquently, in fucking women. Lawrence's *phallic reality* meant *power over*, and his "ordinary, vulgar people" had the same religion. Women stayed dirty because women stayed inferior' (I, 202); and Dworkin is right, because there is just about no way now that fuck or cunt can be redeemed from being pornographic words, and no amount of faecal or anal mysticism can turn the word shit into something sublime, like God or love, and we see this pornographic power relation clearly in *Lady Chatterley's Lover*, where Mellors wields the 'obscene words' to gain 'power over' Connie, for she is subdued by his words, his penis, his aggression, his sexuality; Mellors uses language in very much the way which Dworkin describes, as a way of exerting power over Lady Chatterley, and, again, in *Mercy*, the narrator describes some young America men she meets on Crete: '[t]hey are pale, anemic boys with crew cuts'; slight and tall and banal; filled with foul language that they fire at the natives instead of using guns. The words were dirty when they said them; mean words. I didn't believe any words were dirty until I heard the white boys say cunt' (81-82), that's powerful, that statement, it focuses a lot of Dworkin's feminist polemic: 'I didn't believe any words were dirty until I heard the white boys say cunt', this is so accurate, really, this remark, although it's just one amongst so many in Dworkin's *œuvre* which get to the crux of the matter so swiftly and succulently, but, really, isn't Dworkin's linguistic analysis all too reductive and simplistic, isn't she over-simplifying a more complex problem, for her analysis is always to be reduced to simple notions of 'masculine' and 'feminine', and so it's men who use words to exert power over and above women, it's women who are the 'victims' of men's ability to wield language as a weapon, but isn't this too simplified? is language really that simple? after all, language mutates continually, and even one sentence or one word changes in different contexts, as Jacques Derrida has noted;[134] texts are open, not closed or fixed, and thus pornography, like any literature, like any series of words, can be read in multiple ways, so that there is no single, fixed and sexist reading of pornographic films or magazines, but many readings; notions of 'masculinity' and 'femininity' Dworkin regards as fixed categories, whereas other feminists acknowledge the fragility and flux of sexual identities;[135] indeed, the notion of sex difference in language is fraught with problems: it 'is not only a theoretical impossibility, but a political error' suggests Toril Moi;[136] and Cheris Kramer, Barrie Thorne and Nancy Henley conclude: '[w]hat is notable is how few expected sex differences have been firmly substantiated by empirical studies of actual speech';[137] the notion of sexism in language, it seems, is founded on flimsy evidence, according to some feminists; of course, when Dworkin uses words such as fuck, cunt and slut as an example of male violence in language, she's used the most brutal words in the English language, yet, is there really a conspiracy on the part of men to imbue the language with sexism and violence against women? is there really a secret plot by which men seek to subordinate women? Toril Moi is sensible on this point, as she is on most other points: she writes: '[t]he crudely conspiratorial theory of language as 'man-made', or as a male plot against women, posits an *origin* (men's plotting) to language, a kind of non-linguistic transcendental signifier for which it is impossible to find any kind of theoretical support';[138] feminists such as Mary Daly fight vigorously for new terms to be introduced into the language: Daly's rejuvenation of language is exhilarating: in *Gyn/Ecology* we hear of Journeying, Enspiriting, Fury, Gynergy, Crone-power, A-mazing Process, Positively Revolting Hags, Re-sister, Meta-living, Totaled Woman, Unpainting, Rite of Unravelling and Re-versing; it's great stuff, this new wild Dalian vocabulary, in fact, is there a writer around who has

134 Derrida: *Eperons: Les styles de Nietzsche*, Flammarion, Paris 1978

135 see Toril Moi: *Sexual/Textual Politics*, 154f; Shirley Ardener, ed: *Perceiving Women*, Malaby Press 1975

136 Moi, in ib., 153

137 Cheris Kramer, Barrie Thorne and Nancy Henley: "Perspectives on language and communication", *Signs*, 3, 3, 640

138 Moi, ib., 157

rebirthed language so optimistically, positively and humorously as Mary Daly? her sexual politics may be in the Anglo-American vein, like Dworkin's, firmly humanist and dualist, setting men against women and 'masculine' against 'feminine', but at least Daly seems to be putting something back, creating something instead of just criticizing all the time, for Daly's books (*Gyn/Ecology, Pure Lust, Beyond God the Father* and *Webster's First New Intergalactic Wickedary of the English Language*) are exuberant and positive additions to the feminist canon: take this, from the end of her book *Gyn/Ecology*: '[t]he play is part of our work of unweaving and of our weaving work. It whirls us into another frame of reference. We use the visitation of demons to come more deeply into touch with our own powers/virtues. Unweaving their deceptions, we name our Truth. Defying their professions we discover our Female Pride, our sinister Wisdom. Escaping their possession we find our Enspiriting Selves. Overcoming their aggression we uncover our Creative Anger and Brilliant Bravery. Demystifying/demythifying their obsession we remember our Woman-loving Love. Refusing their assimilation we experience our Autonomy and Strength. Avoiding their elimination we find our original Be-ing. Mending their imposed fragmentation we Spin our original Integrity' (423), Daly's vivacious respinning of language is an ingenious effort at rewriting language, she cuts words up ('be-ing', 're-membering') and uses those delicious, seemingly old-fashioned capitalizations which are so much a part of her new poetry ('Enspiriting', 'Female Pride', 'Spinsters'); it is a witchy, wild poetry, which aims to be more than mere wordplay; she continues: '[a]s we feel the empowerment of our own Naming we hear more deeply our call of the wild. Raising pairs of arms into the air we expand them into shells, sails. Splashing our legs in the water we move our oars. Our beautiful, spiral-like designs are the designs/purposes of our bodies/minds. We communicate these through our force-fields, our auras, our O-Zones. We move backward over the water, over the Background. We gain speed. Argonauts move apart and together, forming and re-forming our Amazon Argosy. In the rising and setting of our sister the sun, we seek the gold of our desire. In the light of our sisters the moon and stars we rekindle the Fore-Crones' fire. In its searing light we see through the father's lies of genesis and demise; we burn through the snarls of the Nothing-lovers' (423-4); Mary Daly's poesie builds on the language of religion, mysticism, witchcraft, occultism, politics, sociology and radical feminism, but it employs the traditional, dualism of humanist feminism, the 'us and them' tactics which so severely simplifies a complex area of experience and politics; high-spirited and polemical as Mary Daly's philosophy of language is, like Dworkin, she employs assumptions of a seemingly child-like nature at times; for Toril Moi, the very fact that Daly can conjure up, magically, new, non-sexist terms means that language is in essence not sexist: '[t]he fact that feminists have managed to fight back,' Moi writes, 'have already made many people feel uncomfortable in using the generic 'he' or 'man', have questioned the use of words like 'chairman' and 'spokesman' and vindicated 'witch' and 'shrew' as positive terms surely proves the point: there is no inherent sexist essence in the English language, since it shows itself appropriable, through struggle, for feminist purposes';[139] in *Mercy* and *Ice and Fire* Dworkin tackles the problem of the relation between a reader, the text, a narrator and the author; the prologues and epilogues of *Mercy* simultaneously associate and dissociate Andrea Dworkin the actual person with 'Andrea' the narrator: in a piece that relates directly to the problems of Dworkin's *Mercy*, Shoshana Felman has criticized Luce Irigaray's writings on 'women's' art and 'feminist' æsthetics: 'Is [Irigaray] speaking *as* a woman, or *in the place of* the (silent) woman, *for* the woman, *in the name of* the woman? Is 'speaking as a woman' a fact determined by some biological *condition* or by a strategic, theoretical *position*, by anatomy or by culture? What if 'speaking as a woman' were not a simple 'natural' fact, could not be taken for granted?';[140] certainly, Dworkin's polemics and fiction is based on these sorts of assumptions, that it is enough to 'speak as a woman', that being a woman is enough, and so on, these are some of the assumptions that infuse Dworkin's writing, for she is always talking about 'women' and 'woman' as if these are fixed things, as if 'women'

139 Moi, in ib., 158

140 Shoshana Felman: "The critical phallacy", *Diacritics*, Winter 1975, 3

are unchanging notions in writing, whereas the French feminists know that notions of 'woman' and 'women' and 'femininity' are not only always changing, they are also to be abandoned, at times, or maybe all the time, because they are not fixed things, and, further, the very words 'women' and 'femininity' have an ambiguous and confused relationship with the things they purport to describe, so that, at one extreme, some of the French feminists claim that the idea of 'woman' does not exist, the 'she' is 'elsewhere', rather as Andre Breton, darling of the Surrealists, said that 'existence is elsewhere', for these French feminists, you cannot speak of 'woman' in a simplistic fashion, whereas Toril Moi reckons that 'to define 'woman' is necessarily to essentialize her' (ib., 139), that is, for the French feminists, to speak of 'woman' is to rely on essentialist and biologist philosophies which are not, finally, useful, because they reveal only the constructs of patriarchy, and have little to do with authentic notions of 'femininity' or 'woman'; indeed, for Luce Irigaray, women are elsewhere, unrepresentable in patriarchal art, all we get in patriarchy is the reflection of patriarchal negativity, in Irigaray's feminist notion of specularization;[141] for Luce Irigaray, 'woman' exists in some forbidden space, an in-between space, 'in between signs, between the realized meanings, between the lines',[142] she writes; the hope is that there is still a truly 'feminine' space, the 'wild zone' of feminists such as Elaine Showalter and Jeanne Roberts, for there is a male 'wild zone' which we know about, that masculine version of wild zone eroticism which Hélène Cixous calls 'glorious phallic monosexuality';[143] the female 'wild zone' is beyond patriarchal space, beyond patriarchal representations; Julia Kristeva and Luce Irigaray have spoken of something in 'women' or the 'feminine' that is 'unrepresentable', beyond art, beyond male culture; Victor Burgin, describing Julia Kristeva's philosophy,[144] says that she positions 'the woman in society... in the patriarchal scheme, as perpetually at the boundary, the

141 Irigaray: *Speculum de l'autre femme*, Minuit, Paris 1974
142 Irigaray, in ib.
143 Cixous, "The Laugh of the Medusa", in Marks, 254
144 Victor Burgin: "Geometry and Abjection", in John Fletcher and Andrew Benjamin, eds, 115-6

borderline, the edge, the 'outer limit' – the place where order shades into chaos, light into darkness. This peripheral and ambivalent position allocated to woman, says Kristeva, had led to that familiar division of the field of representation in which women are viewed as either saintly or demonic – according to whether they are seen as bringing the darkness, or as keeping it out'; we know about these stereotypes or archetypes, these saintly women (the Virgin Mary is a typical example) who keep the amazing energy of the female wild zone out of men's lives; the demonic woman (Mary Magdalene, the *femme fatale*, vampire, 'devil woman') is the one who brings the wildness with her, and is, of course, feared (and desired) and suppressed by patriarchy, for patriarchy of course prefers bland, mute, passive door-stops in women, people who will stop the darkness from coming in, who will sit there and say nothing and get on with society's housework; '['woman'] is indefinitely other in herself,' writes Luce Irigaray, maintaining that women 'are already elsewhere than in the discursive machinery where you claim to take them by surprise. They have turned back within themselves, which does not mean the same thing as 'within yourself'. They do not experience the same interiority that you do and which perhaps you mistakenly presume they share';[145] Luce Irigaray also spoke in spatial terms of idealist feminism: '[w]e need both space and time. And perhaps we are living in an age when *time must re-deploy space*. Could this be the dawning of a new world? Immanence and transcendence are being recast, notably by that *threshold* which has never been examined in itself: the female sex. It is a threshold unto *mucosity*. Beyond the classic opposites of love and hate, liquid and ice lies this perpetually *half-open* threshold, consisting of *lips* that are strangers to dichotomy. Pressed against one another, but without any possibility of suture, at least of a real kind, they do not absorb the world either into themselves or through themselves, provided they are not abused or reduced to a mere consummating or consuming structure. Instead their shape welcomes without assimilating or reducing or devouring. A sort of door unto voluptuousness, then? Not that, either: their useful function is to designate a *place*: the very place

145 Irigaray: *Ce sexe qui n'en est pas un*, Minuit, Paris 1977, 28-9

of uses, at least on a habitual plane. Strictly speaking, they serve neither conception nor *jouissance*. Is this, then, the mystery of female identity, of its self-contemplation, of that strange word of silence; both the threshold and reception of exchange, the sealed-up secret of wisdom, belief and faith in every truth?';[146] Irigaray's essentialist/ biologist form of sexuality reckons that female eroticism is in some ways 'superior' to male eroticism, even though Irigaray's great feminist ethic is sexual *difference*, i.e., not 'better than', but simply 'different', that is, not equal, but different; female sexuality is an all-over eroticism, not just concentrated in the dick, says Irigaray; her famous description of women's sexuality is of a total body sensuality, where the whole of the skin is alive to touches: '[t]he whole of my body is sexuate. My sexuality isn't restricted to my sex and to the sexual act (in the narrow sense)' writes Luce Irigaray;[147] and Dworkin too suggests that female sexuality is in some way superior to male sexuality – she does not say so, not directly, but it is implied, more in the two novels than in the non-fiction, but Irigaray's sense of female eroticism has been criticized by feminists because it reduces women to their sexuality, it concentrates far too much on the vulva (but not the clitoris), rather than on the other, infinite aspects of 'woman', and the concentration on sexuality obscures debate on other issues, ('[p]orn is a sexier topic than the more intractable problems of unequal pay, job discrimination, sexual violence and harassment, the unequal burdens of child-care and housework, increasing right-wing infringements on hard-won feminist gains, and several millennia of unrelenting male privilege *vis-à-vis* the labour, love, personal service and possession of women' writes Gayle Rubin),[148] and anyway, the emphasis is always on what people *do* sexually, rather than what they are, for '[e]roticism itself is increasingly being defined less as a fixed identity dependent on the gender of one's partner, and more as a dynamic mode based on the sum of one's erotic *practice*';[149] a good critique of Luce Irigaray's theory of female

146 Luce Irigaray: "La différence sexuelle", *Ethiope de la différence sexuelle*, Minuit, Paris, 1984, and in Toril Moi, ed: *French Feminist Thought*,128

147 *Je, tu, nous*, 53

148 in Assister, 38

149 Valerie Traub: "Desire and the Difference It Makes", in Valerie Wayne, 88

eroticism, of Irigaray's view of women's eroticism as two lips continually embracing which could also apply to Andrea Dworkin, comes from Monique Plaza, who says: '[a]ll that 'is' woman comes to [Irigaray] in the last instances from her anatomical sex, which touches itself all the time. Poor woman';[150] even as Irigaray argues for a metaphysically non-representable form of female eroticism she also concentrates very much on the physicalities of female eroticism, on vaginal lips, her stance is eternally contradictory and paradoxical,[151] and it is the same with Andrea Dworkin, who simultaneously despises just about *any* form of sexual writing, for it must all be pornography, in her view, yet she also discusses sexuality positively and at length in her novels, so there is always this paradox in her work, always this hatred of pornographic representations of sex though she herself writes in detail of sex, so that all her depictions of sex must be ironic, yet they aren't, they clearly aren't ironic, not all of them, for in *Mercy* she describes an exuberant, idealistic, visionary and revolutionary form of sexuality, where sex is 'joy and risk and fun and orgasm' (M, 171); the insistence on biology and sexuality in French feminism, as in Dworkin's worldview, is, some feminists think, a drawback, because it too often speaks of only one kind of sexuality: '[i]f we define female subjectivity through universal biological/ libidinal givens [writes Ann Rosalind Jones], what happens to the project of changing the world in feminist directions? Further, is women's sexuality so monolithic that shared, typical femininity does justice to it? What about variations in class, in race, and in culture among women? About changes over time in *one* woman's sexuality? (with men, with women, by herself?) How can one libidinal voice – or the two vulval lips so startlingly presented by Irigaray – speak for all women?';[152] female sexuality is, as Anais Nin maintained, multiple, or, as Xavière Gauthier says: 'witches [women] are bursting; their entire bodies are desire; their gestures are caresses;

150 Monique Plaza: ""Phallomorphic power" and the psychology of "woman"", *Ideology and Consciousness*, 4, Autumn 1978, 32
151 other feminists who have crticized the 'vagino-centric' nature of French feminism include Janet Sayers,*Biological Politics*, 131; Donna C. Stanton in Miller, 1986, 157-182; Jane Gallop, in Miller, 1986,140; Still & Worton,1993, 60
152 Jones: "Writing the Body", in Showalter, ed, 369

their smell, taste, hearing are all sensual. Their pleasure is so violent, so transgressive, so open, so fatal, that men have not yet recovered... Female eroticism is terrifying; it is an earthquake, a volcanic eruption, a tidal wave. It is disquieting and so is mystified. It is made a mystery';[153] for the French feminists, this transgressive, terrifying eroticism has not yet really been depicted in art or pornography, and maybe Dworkin would agree here, for she maintains that what we get is men's version of female eroticism, those male ideas of what wild female eroticism would be like, which is usually reduced to the stylized, style-conscious, pseudo-intellectual hash violence of Georges Bataille and Donatien-Alphonse-François de Sade; yet many feminists suggest that women's eroticism cannot be represented, much as women themselves cannot be represented; Julia Kristeva writes: '[i]n "woman" I see something that cannot be represented, something that is not said, something above and beyond nomenclatures and ideologies;'[154] other feminists echo this idea, that women cannot be fully represented in the traditional media of patriarchy, as Hélène Cixous writes: '[i]t is at the level of sexual pleasure in my opinion that the difference makes itself most clearly apparent in as far as woman's libidinal economy is neither identifiable by a man nor referrable to the masculine economy';[155] the unrepresentable in art and pornography, according to some feminists, is women's eroticism, their *jouissance*, that 'explosive, blossoming, sane and inexhaustible *jouissance* of the woman', as Julia Kristeva describes it;[156] and it is this incredible, fateful, explosive orgasmic sexuality that Dworkin aims to describe in her books, because her protagonists love sex even though are beaten to shit by it, they are raped yet they continue to fuck, they are beaten and violated yet they continue to be idealistic and orgasmic, this is the amazing thing about Dworkin's work, which makes it, ultimately, not pessimistic but optimistic, not cynical but idealistic, even though her books are written out of utter despair and utter rage, for she feels so

153 Xavière Gauthier: "Pourquoi Sorcières?", in *Sorcières*,1, 1976, in Marks & Courtivron, 201-2

154 Kristeva: "La femme, ce n'est jamais ça", *Tel Quel*, Autumn 1974, in Marks, 135

155 Hélène Cixous: "Sorties", in Marks, 95

156 Kristeva: *About Chinese Women*, Marion Boyars 1977, 63

passionately about basic facts, such as, why are so many women *still* raped?, and why are women *still* not paid equally for the same jobs as men?, and why are women *still* second class citizens, when compared to men, for in this respect Dworkin is not being essentialist or biologist, she is merely relating the facts, on these issues Dworkin is passionate, and, again, we find Luce Irigaray voicing the same concerns, for Irigaray does seem to be like a French counterpart to Dworkin: Irigaray writes, so simply yet so effectively: 'there are no grounds for paying less for one body's work than for another's',[157] and as Dworkin writes: '[w]omen who work earn fifty-six to fifty-nine cents on the dollar to what men get for comparable work... women get 100 per cent of the pregnancies, but only half the dollar' (War, 145); but Irigaray does not believe in full 'equality', the only sort of equality she deems possible is economic, otherwise she argues for difference, while acknowledging that '[w]hatever may be the inequalities between women, they all suffer, even unconsciously, the same oppression, the same exploitation of their body, the same denial of their desire',[158] all feminists agree that there is inequality and injustice in so many areas of life, for it's pointless always attacking men, because that is not the whole problem, and it's pointless always attacking sexuality, for sexuality is only one part of human experience, yet it is always overemphasized (and Dworkin is as guilty of emphasizing sexuality above, say, racism or economy, as other feminists); Irigaray is on to something when she argues for a 'culture of difference', for if you always resort to patriarchy and men you are always defining yourself and your concerns in terms of patriarchy and men, so that women's sexuality is always compared to, contrasted with, – and defined in terms of – male sexuality, which is clearly limiting, because you'll always be using masculinist or patriarchal terms, which is, of course, exactly what Andrea Dworkin does in her fiction, she employs the 'fuck this fuck that' terminology of masculine writers, her narrator says 'I could be the Zen master of fuck you' (M, 228), Dworkin employs terms such as 'he fucked me', just as Henry Miller, Norman Mailer, Martin Amis, J.P. Donleavy,

157 Irigaray: *Je, tu, nous*, 120
158 Luce Irigaray, "Women's Exile", in Cameron, 1990, 83

Leslie Thomas, Philip Roth, and Samuel Beckett wrote 'I fucked her', so that all Dworkin seems to be doing, at times, is switching the genders around, which is simply turning sexism on its head, which is simply being reactionary, swinging from one pole to the other, and is not that creative, really, though sure, it's fun to turn the tables round, to give men some of the lies and double standards they've fed to women for months, for years, for decades, for centuries, for millennia, for, perhaps, millions of years, it's fun to turn these things around, but it's not that creative, really, it just means that men will complain about being raped by women, which has happened, it's sick, it's really sick, but it happens, when someone, like Lorena Bobbitt cuts off her husband's penis, or when a woman murders her husband, yes, it's fun, there's a shout that echoes around the planet from many women, who shout 'YES!', for at last a woman has *hit back* and given the man a taste of his own medicine; the case of Lorena Bobbitt is a good one, for it is a case of a woman hitting back at a man, and attacking him, a case which Dworkin might discuss in detail in a future book, for it is something one of her protagonists might have done in a wilder moment, especially 'Andrea' in *Mercy* after she's been fucked in the throat, then, one thinks, she might take up the knife and make the final cut, murdering her attacker; this extract is from the biggest selling Sunday newspaper in the UK, *The Sunday Times*: '[i]n the early hours of June 23, 1993, the 5ft, six-and-a-half stone [*sic*] Mrs John Wayne Bobbitt [*sic*] claims that "an irresistible impulse" – or temporary insanity [*sic*] drove her to sever her husband's penis. Years of physical abuse by her husband, a US marine, led the slightly built manicurist [*sic*] to commit the act. On the night in question, she says, he raped her. At the time, she called the police from a pay-phone to say she had been raped and had fled the apartment in a panic. It was only while driving that she realised she was still clutching the penis in her hand. She then flung it out of the driver's window and went to the same hospital where her husband was having surgery, to be treated as a rape victim'; the dick-chopping case caught the imagination of America: the newspaper report goes on to describe the merchandize that people cooked up to cash in on the incident: '[o]ther T-shirts were for sale among the satellite trucks and live cameras set up from around the world. If you wanted a commemorative slogan you could choose from "You snooze, you lose", "He lost that loving feeling", "Hung jury", "What's up with you?" and "Clean-cut kind of guy". One enterprising vendor was hawking $10 gift packs of chocolate penises complete with knife. A prospective purchaser complained that the penises were broken. 'They're not broken, sir, they're sliced," was the reply. [...] Inside court, the debate boiled down to its essence. "A sleeping man's penis was amputated," stated the state persecutor (a man). "What we have, ladies and gentlemen," claimed the defence lawyer (a woman), "is Lorena Bobbitt's life juxtaposed against John Wayne Bobbitt's penis." The husband was the first witness to take the stand and his penis was an early exhibit. A photograph of what the police described as "the appendage" was quickly produced (prompting cheers, applause and roars of approval among reporters watching the trial in a nearby room). The photograph was not shown in close-up on national television. "It was just too gross," said Stephen Johnson, executive producer of Court TV',[159] what's interesting, and what Andrea Dworkin would surely comment on, is *how* the case was reported, how people discussed the case, how, for instance, they concentrated on the comical aspect of someone having their dick chopped off, ha ha, how hilarious it is, really, yet how many men would utterly hate it happening them, for the Bobbitt dick-topping case centres around docking the dick, whereas the case is really about rape and domestic violence, about a woman being brutalized over years, not just in one incident, of course it makes great copy for the media; but as in so many other similar cases of women hitting back at men, it is blown out of proportion, and over-sensationalized, with male critics and reporters drawing ridiculous conclusions about men being 'harassed' by women, which is typical of male critics or reporters, but quite ridiculous, for the numbers of men fucking over women, to use Dworkin's language, compared to women fucking men, is huge, 1,000:1, or more, in other words, hardly any women, in actual cases reported in the media, 'harass' men, whereas the number of men, in cases

159 Emma Gilbey, "Carving her name with pride", *The Sunday Times*, 16 January 1994

reported in the media, 'harassing' women is huge, really huge, for a large portion of domestic violence goes unreported, for women are silenced in so many ways, as we know, so the statistics of women being battered and humiliated and manipulated and oppressed by men must be far greater than those reported in the media, for the media, as we know, distorts information continually, as we see in reported cases of women murdering men, 'fifty percent of married women have perhaps been battered at some point in a marriage. That's war. That's not life, that's war' writes Dworkin (War, 141); yet, yet there are some experiences for which there are no words, as Dworkin knows: '[w]e all of us got the consolation that nobody remembers the worst things. They're gone; brain just burns them away. And there's no words for the worst things so ain't no one going to tell you the worst things; they can't. You can pick up any book and know for sure the worst things ain't in it... I am telling you you have never read the worst. It has never been uttered by anyone ever' (M, 157-8), for Dworkin there is a limit to words, there must be a scream, or animal sounds, instead of words, for words are limited, finally, as many poets have known: Paul Valéry, Samuel Beckett, Lawrence Durrell and T.S. Eliot, among many others, have written of the limitations of language, those limits of language which become the limits of the actual world, according to Ludwig Wittgenstein, in his *Tractatus Logico-Philosophicus*, Wittgenstein wrote: '[t]he world is *my* world; this is manifest in the fact that the limits of *language...* mean the limits of *my* world',[160] T.S. Eliot spoke of the 'raid on the inarticulate', while Samuel Beckett made a famous statement in the 1930s about language: 'B[eckett]: – The situation is that of him [*sic*} who is helpless, cannot act, in the event cannot paint, since he is obliged to paint. The act is of him who, helpless, unable to act, acts, in the event paints, since he is obliged to paint. D [Georges Dutuit]: – why is he obliged to paint? B. – I don't know. D. – Why is he helpless to paint? B. – Because there is nothing to paint and nothing to paint with',[161] this is the problem of all Beckett's anti-heroes: to speak without having anything to say;

160 Wittgenstein: *Tractatus Logico-Philosophicus*, tr D.F. Pears & B.F. McGuinness, Routledge & Kegan Paul 1961
161 *Disjecta: Miscellaneous Writings*, ed Ruby Cohn, Calder 1983, 142

to write without having the means, and it is also the problem of Dworkin's narrators, though Dworkin is never as nihilistic as Beckett, Dworkin always retains a certain fundamental idealism or utopian vision which lies behind or underneath her works, and Dworkin's, too, do have things to say, their problem is, rather, *how* to say these things, how to say the unsayable; in *Dialogues*, Beckett says: '[t]he expression that there is nothing to express, nothing with which to express, nothing from which to express, no power to express, no desire to express, together with the obligation to express' (ib, 139), but this is not Dworkin's view of writing, not at all, for Dworkin's protagonists have a lot to express, and they have great rage from which to express, it is this rage that powers their polemical outpourings, and Dworkin's narrators have a powerful desire to express themselves, and so they do, even if there are no words for the worst things, even if there is no one listening, even if they seem incoherent and bilious, Dworkin's narrators still write, and they fight to write, fight to have their say, fight to have the time to be able to work out what they want to say, what they are trying to say, they carve out time and space in the harsh cities, it hurts, it hurts all the time being a writer, for Dworkin, but her narrators still fight for time and space in which to write, it's heroic, you might say, but just as well you might see Dworkin's protagonists as martyrs, as victims, as well as freedom fighters or terrorists, for in *Ice and Fire* and *Mercy* they are both victims and fighters, both martyrs and heroines, it all hurts, and the writing or telling comes out of the hurt, the pain powers the art, for Dworkin, while for her protagonists the pain is thoroughly sexualized, a crucifixion of sex, sex as Christ's Cross, the bed as the Cross, fucking as the Crucifixion, as the narrator, Andrea, says in *Mercy* after being raped again: 'I didn't move because there is an anguish that can stop you from moving and I couldn't kill him because there is an anguish that can stop you from killing. Something awful came, a suffering bigger than my life or your life or any life or God's life, the crucifixion God; the nails are hammered in but you don't get to die. It's the cross for ladies, a bed, and you don't get to die; the lucky boy, the favourite child, gets to die. You've been mowed down inside, slaughtered inside, a genocide happened in you, but you don't get to die' (98), this is another example of Dworkin's very powerful polemic, for here she goes the whole way, and compares rape to genocide, she compares the rape of one person to the slaughter of many many people, this is a powerful comparison, the most powerful there is, really, for Dworkin reckons that being raped is as horrible as the crucifixion of Our Lord, a blasphemous comparison for religionists and the faithful, for no one suffered, they say, more than Christ, but Dworkin says that everyone/ anyone can suffer as much as Christ, and, further, that each rape is a crucifixion, that in each rape something dies in the woman, and so horrible is rape and male violence, that it can be like mass murder, it can be, further, like genocide, a genocide happening inside you, she writes in *Mercy*, and, finally, she makes the ultimate comparison between the sex act and violence, by making the link between rape and the concentration camps, that most massive of all human 'crimes', the killing of six million people, for in Dworkin's two novels she develops her narrative from personal/ individual horrors, of rape, upwards through Pearl Harbour, Vichy, the peace movement, Saigon and Vietnam – 'the fucking killers' she calls them (M, 254) – to, finally, the Nazis and concentration camps, it is an inevitable escalation of rage, it seems, for the narrator of *Mercy* is Jewish, and her 'true point of origin', she says, is Birkenau, which she describes thus in *Mercy*: 'I always knew what Birkenau was like from the parts of it I have in my mind. I know it was gray and isolated and I knew there were low, gray huts, and I knew the ground was gray and flat, and it was winter, and I knew there were pine trees and birch trees, I see them in the distance, upright, indifferent, a monstrous provocation, God's beauty, he spits in your face, and there were huge piles of things, so big you thought they were hills of earth but they were shoes...' (165), and 'Andrea', the narrator, goes on to explain how Birkenau, 'Auschwitz II or The Women's Camp' (164), is lodged deep in her soul, and out of this spiritual birthplace comes an incredible rage, a rage not only against nazis, but against all manner of oppressors, as she writes: '[j]ustice pushed you into a new womb and outrage, a blind fury, pushed you out of it onto this earth, this place, this zoo of sickies and sadists' (166), and so, our Andrea has a debt to settle, an agonized ghost to lay to rest, which never goes away, which haunts her eternally, which she can never kill, though she tries so many times; she writes: 'I burst out, I was looking for trouble and ready for pain, I wanted to kill Nazis, I was born to kill Nazis' (166), but then she gets confused, and finds it's Nazism not the Nazis themselves she wants to kill, as she puts it: 'killing killed the one doing the killing and that killing killed something precious and good at the center of life itself' (168), yet, however she wants to kill oppression, she is held back, her parents, her friends, everyone seems to stops her from attacking her targets, she is stopped from doing things from the year dot, she is not allowed to kill, or to write, the boys can do all that, but not the girls, the girls have to look passive and meek and helpful and nurturing, for they are mothers, while the boys and the men are active, aggressive, and oppressive: '[a]nd mother, handmaiden of the Lord, says wear this, do that, don't do that, don't say that, sit, close your legs, wear white gloves and don't get them dirty, girls don't climb trees, girls don't run, girls don't, girls don't, girls don't' (167), Sue Bridehead in Hardy's novel *Jude the Obscure* had also found out (the hard way) that there is some great voice from above which says '[d]on't, Don't' Don't': '[t]hen another silence, till she was seized with another uncontrollable fit of grief. 'There is something external to us which says, "You shan't!" First it said, "You shan't learn!" Then it said, "You shan't labour!" Now it says, "You shan't love!"';[162] *Jude the Obscure* is easily Hardy's most bitter and angry book, in which he rages against institutions such as marriage, education and the Church; Hardy's anger is focussed in his characters Sue and Jude, but particularly in Sue, where she reacts so piquantly to the oppression of the late Victorian age and its intolerance of other ways of living; Sue says '"[d]omestic laws should be made according to temperaments, which should be classified. If people are at all peculiar in character they have to suffer from the very rules that produce comfort in others!"' (233), here Sue puts her finger on the way society seems to collude with itself to subtly (or not so subtly) ostracize people that 'don't fit in', which is also the case with Dworkin's protagonists in *Ice and Fire* and *Mercy*, so

162 Hardy: *Jude the Obscure*, Oxford University Press 1985, 356

that the horror of the life of Sue and Jude is partially imposed on them from outside, by their society, by the people who are their 'neighbours', their 'fellow human beings': Sue again: '"I can't *bear* that they, and everybody, should think people wicked because they may have chosen to live their own way! It is really these opinions that make the best intentioned people reckless' (318); *Jude the Obscure* records the violence of societal intolerance: it is a novel of rage, in a similar manner to Dworkin's *Ice and Fire* and *Mercy*, but Hardy keeps his distance, using a third-person narrative form, while Dworkin rages on in the first person, always lively and fluid, colloquial and subjective, but the rage in both *Mercy* and *Jude the Obscure* is directed against similar things, such as patriarchal power, hypocrisy, sexism, and intolerance; *Jude the Obscure* is Hardy's most bitter book, full of barely restrained bile, *Ice and Fire* and *Mercy* come from a similar tradition of humanism, but Dworkin, though she seems to go further and deeper, remains full of hope, whereas Hardy's view is, seemingly, bleaker, though he would maintain that his philosophy is merely realistic, reflecting what goes on in society all the time; Hardy was, like Dworkin, censored ('edited' is the term critics use), and he felt he couldn't say things the way he would have liked to, and, similarly, Dworkin is from time to time misrepresented, or silenced, through omissions; but Sue never says 'fuck life', though she wants to say it, very often, like the old woman in Samuel Beckett's *Rockaby* says 'fuck life' at the end of the play, while Dworkin's protagonists say fuck life often, but they don't mean kill life or fuck off life, they mean that life hurts and what should be fucked are the people or maybe not the people but certainly the systems and institutions made by the people which so severely limit and ruin life, and how close Dworkin is to Hardy at times, even though she might disapprove of the comparison, for she is wary of any of the DWM (dead white males), those writers termed 'greats' by the lit crit establishment (Shakespeare, Dickens, Hardy, Lawrence, Goethe, Rimbaud, Hugo, Dante, Homer, Petrarch, Whitman, Melville, Thoreau, Emerson, Hesse, Miller), she dislikes those writers, often attacks them (she has levelled Tolstoy, de Sade, Lawrence, Tennessee Williams, Flaubert, Stoker, Augustine, Bataille,

Sartre, Mailer, Tillich, among others); but her analysis of rape fits so well at times with *Tess of the d'Urbervilles* and *Jude the Obscure,* such as this passage from *Right-Wing Women*: '[t]he propaganda stresses that intercourse can give a woman pleasure if she does it right: specially if she has the right attitude toward it and toward the man. The right attitude is to want it. The right attitude is to desire men *because* they engage in phallic penetration. The right attitude is to want intercourse because men want it. The right attitude is not to be selfish: especially about orgasm' (RWW, 81), how accurately this describes the state of so many female characters in so many 'classic' novels, by George Eliot or Charles Dickens or William Faulkner or Jane Austen or Emily Bronte or Virginia Woolf, you only have to think of those heroines of 'classic' novels – Clarissa, Tess, Catherine Earnshaw, Connie Chatterley – when reading Dworkin's analyses of women's sexual economy: '[i]n marriage a man has the sexual right to his wife: he can fuck her at will by right of law. The law articulates and defends this right. The state articulates and defends this right. This means that the state defines the intimate uses of a woman's body in marriage; so that a man acts with the protection of the state when he fucks his wife, regardless of the degree of force surrounding or intrinsic to the act... But even where marital rape is illegal, the husband has at his disposal the ordinary means of sexual coercion, including threat of physical violence, punitive economic measures, sexual or verbal humiliation in private or in public, violence against inanimate objects, and threats against children. In other words, eliminating the legal sanctioning of rape does not in itself eliminate sexual coercion in marriage; but the continued legal sanctioning of rape underlines the coercive character and purpose of marriage. Marriage law is irrefutable proof that women are not equal to men' (RWW, 77-78); and again, in "Pornography and Male Supremacy", Dworkin writes: that '[k]idnapping, or rape, is also the first known form of marriage – called "marriage by capture"' (War, 229); Dworkin's concern, like Hardy's and other politically/ socially committed writers, is oppression, and she has no doubts as to who is the oppressor, and what arguments the oppressor uses to further the cause of oppression: '[t]he oppressor, the one who perpetrates the wrongs for his own pleasure or profit, is the master inventor of justification. He is the magician who, out of thin air, fabricates wondrous, imposing, seemingly irrefutable intellectual reasons which explain why one group must be degraded at the hands of another' (War, 198), for Dworkin, the oppressor is male, it couldn't be otherwise – at no point in her non-fiction does Dworkin identify women as oppressors, but only as victims, the downtrodden and raped, but never oppressors, and only rarely does Dworkin call women colluders or conspirators in male power, rather, she sees women as having one choice – 'lie or die' – not a conspiracy but a forced pretense, because '[w]omen are still basically viewed as sexual chattel – socially, legally, culturally, and in practice' (War, 229); the difference between Dworkin and most other writers is that she has a passionately-felt political-ideological agenda in her work which is not at all buried, but is right on the surface, and it runs all the way through her work, from top to bottom – the agenda is women's oppression, and Dworkin never loses sight of her obsession, so that she is not, like, say, George Orwell, who writes of politics but couches his political discourse in metaphor or allegory, as in *Animal Farm*, and Dworkin is not like, say, Sartre or Camus, who write of existential themes, but put the existentialism under a cloak of a (relatively conventional) narrative, nor is Dworkin like Graham Greene, Evelyn Waugh, Lawrence Durrell or Somerset Maugham, writers who may have had quite strongly-felt political attitudes, but kept a distance from them in their novels; rather, Dworkin is like D.H. Lawrence, who could not stop himself from being polemical and political, in a very personal way, right in the middle of otherwise conventional narratives, that is, in the midst of *The Rainbow* or *Aaron's Rod*, Lawrence started writing in a political fashion quite out of keeping with the flow of the narrative; Lawrence would start going on about war, using the authorial voice to suddenly impinge directly on the text, so that, if Lorenzo felt like talking about religion for a moment, he would, and if he found some pet hatred, such as 'cocksure women' or ugly architecture, rest assured he would go about that pet hatred until his fury abated; and it's the same with Andrea Dworkin, in a sense: she has various things that she despises, and she won't let up – in her fiction as much in her non-fiction – with telling us; Dworkin is different from most writers, too, in another (related) respect: *she is not afraid of naming who the oppressors are*, that is, she points her finger at men, and lays into them; while other writers might inveigh against something through a character, Dworkin, like Lawrence, doesn't bother with personifications and distancing devices, she gets right in there; she says the oppressors are men, whereas Thomas Hardy would say that no one in particular is responsible for the awfulness of life, and Hardy contrives to create an interplay of characters who affect each other in deliberate, accidental or perhaps 'fated' ways, so that, if there is any one person that Hardy directs his anger at, it is 'God', or 'Chance', or 'Fate', or, (in)famously at the end of *Tess of the d'Urbervilles*, the 'President of the Immortals'; in traditional literature – Shakespeare, Homer, Catullus, Tolstoy, Austen – characters curse Fate, Time, Life, God, Chance, the gods, but Dworkin curses men, and again, men, and after thirty essays and speeches, men; of course, there is a blurring between the various personas in Dworkin's fiction – there is the author, the authorial voice, and the character, all of whom are called 'Andrea' in the novels, while the 'I' in the essays and speeches is clearly identified with the 'real' Andrea Dworkin (at least, that is how she wants us to read it), whereas, from the postmodern point of view, the 'I' in a text is directly the person who wrote the 'I'; in Dworkin's work, though, the autobiographical self is very much to the fore, and, as we read the speeches and essays, we see the construction of an 'I' or self that is meant to be the 'real' Andrea Dworkin, so that when Dworkin writes 'I have seen a lot [of horror/ pornography, etc]' (War, 5) we are meant to think, ah, yes, the 'real' Andrea Dworkin has 'seen a lot', whereas we know that the self in literature has a very ambiguous relation with the 'real' self, the flesh-and-blood person; and again, in *Intercourse*: '[i]n Christianity, attitude is everything; in Judaism, simple compliance is. In each faith, the man's authority means that he has a right supported by law – divine law – to fuck his wife; her legal duty to submit; and intercourse itself is a legally defined hierarchy in which the one who fucks has sovereignty over the one who submits' (193); Dworkin's views on rape are extreme in feminism, but she has feminists who agree with her – Catherine MacKinnon, for instance, with whom Dworkin organized the anti-porn Bill; MacKinnon says: '[p]olitically, I call it rape whenever the woman feels violated',[163] and feminists such as Robin Morgan and Michael Moorcock concur with this view, but other feminists, such as Camille Paglia, Naomi Wolf and Katie Roiphe disagree vehemently, claiming that not all violent sex is rape: 'I don't feel that whenever a woman feels violated it is rape' says Katie Roiphe, continuing: 'everybody has been date-raped according to these definitions – namely verbal coercion, manipulation and pressure. Most people I know have had sex with somebody they didn't want to', for Roiphe, bad sex ain't rape: 'we need to separate bad sexual experience from rape' she says,[164] but Dworkin, Adrienne Rich, Susan Griffin, Daly, Robin Morgan and Susan Brownmiller cannot agree with this; for them rape is a deeply serious problem at the heart of patriarchy and patriarchal institutions such as marriage, education and politics, and while feminists such as Rosalind Coward ask key questions, such as: does male sexuality always have a violent component? '[i]s it true that *any* public representation of sex is *only* for male sexuality and therefore male domination? Is it true that pornography is about violence against women or *necessarily* sustains violence against women?';[165] we return to this confusion of what is *represented* in pornography, and 'actual life', which Dworkin perpetrates time and time again, when, in "Pornography and Male Supremacy", she asks in a pleading tone: '[w]here is the visceral recognition, the *humanist* recognition, that it is impossible and inconceivable to tolerate – let alone to sanction or to apologize for – the tying and hanging and chaining and bruising and beating of women?' (War, 232); and feminists such as Gayle Rubin have questioned Dworkin's and MacKinnon's definition of pornography, and how pornography relates to violence – this is, as ever, the most contentious aspect of the pornography debate, this relation of porn (the 'theory', in Robin Morgan's terms) and violence or rape (the 'practice'), this is where feminists disagree

163 MacKinnon, quoted in John Cassidy: "[The] author who took on the feminists [interview with Katie Roiphe]", *The Sunday Times*, 9 January 1994

164 Katie Roiphe, in ib.

165 Rosalind Coward: "Sexual Violence and Sexuality", in *Feminist Review*, eds, 309

vehemently, for is, then, *all* 'violence' bad, is sadomasochism 'bad'? is painful sex 'wrong'? is S/M wrong because it's 'violent', and what is the definition of S/M 'violence'? these are some of the questions that feminists pose, as Gayle Rubin writes of Dworkin's civil rights bill: '[t]he notion of harm embodied in the MacKinnon/ Dworkin approach is based on a fundamental confusion between the content of an image and the conditions of its production. The fact that an image does not appeal to a viewer does not mean that the actors or models experienced revulsion while making it. The fact that an image depicts coercion does not mean that the action or models were forced into making it',[166] for the feminists who are against censorship (though not always pro-pornography), working in pornography is not *automatically* 'degrading' or 'wrong'; indeed, some feminists say that any menial, low-paid job is as 'degrading' as being photographed for a porn magazine: the Feminists Against Censorship write: '[t]he working-class women who make up a substantial part of the sex industry are not deeply moved by the suggestion that being pushed around and demoralized for 40 hours a week is so much better than posing for pornography for a few hours and making a lot more money at it. Nor are they thrilled to hear that feminists want to make them criminals and throw them in jail. Do anti-pornography feminists really imagine that sexual harassment happens *only* in relation to porn, or never occurs in any other industry? Do they think that working in a factory, or standing at a counter, is so much more desirable than being a 'page three' girl?',[167] these are good questions, which hit to the heart of the pornography debate: for Dworkin, anyone working in the pornography industry is colluding with the enemy – literally 'sleeping with the enemy', or fucking the enemy – men – as some feminists would put it, yet as a mode of labour, working in pornography is perhaps not as 'degrading' or 'demeaning' as working at a supermarket check-out for hours on end – now that really is slavery – but *all* labour is slavery, for the woman working at a check-out is literally, physically, *there,* she cannot

166 Gayle Rubin: "Misguided, Dangerous and Wrong: an Analysis of Anti-Pornography Politics", in Assister & Carol, eds, 32
167 Feminists Against Censorship: "The Wages of Anti-censorship Campaigning", in Assister & Carol, eds, 148

move, her *body* is *there*, she is being paid, like the prostitute, for her body, for her 'manual' labour, for her body being there, so, finally, *all* labour is prostitution, on one level, on a very simplistic level, perhaps, but all labour is about working with one's body for someone else; as Claudia, 'author of *I, Claudia, Love Lies Bleeding* and other Class Whore Productions' writes on this issue of working in pornography as unfeminist and morally 'wrong': '[i]t is apparently 'OK' for a woman to get a job as a waitress or a secretary, however. Work is an exchange of degradation for money... Anti-pornography feminists are quite comfortable with the degradation of the female (and male) labour force; many are employers themselves. They remain as millions of women wear out their mental and physical health – that is 'OK' so long as there are no topless calendars on the canteen walls';[168] the hypocrisy of the anti-pornography position is brought into focus on this issue of work and production, where it's OK for feminists to complain about the people who work in pornography, the anti-anti-pornography feminists suggest, but it's not OK for women to work in porn which may be not as 'degrading', finally, as other forms of work, including housework; the anti-censorship feminists would agree with the anti-pornography feminists, though, about the sexualized nature of labour, how much of labour is founded on sexual economies, as Sheila Jeffreys writes: '[t]he foundation of the family in which men are served emotionally, economically and through domestic labour, is sexual intercourse'[169] but the problem is, as the anti-pornography feminists put it, is, how can you be anti-pornography *and* anti-censorship, or, putting it another way, how can you be liberal or radical and for the non-censorship of all art, yet, at same time, you want to police pornography and set limits on what people can and cannot consume? this is the question that critics of Andrea Dworkin level at her, and both sides of the argument are very solid, and very eloquently argued, for these discussions go to the quick of our lives, to the quiddity of what we value in life, and what we value in art, and how art relates to life – and to love, for that matter – and to sexuality; Dworkin's

168 Claudia: "Fear of Pornography", in Assister & Carol, 136
169 Sheila Jeffreys: ""The Censoring of Revolutionary Feminism", in Chester, 138

stance is humanist, pro-women, pro-life, setting the anti-censorship liberals against the mutilated women in pornography: '[s]ociety, with the acquiescence of too many liberal-left feminists, says that pornographers must *not* be stopped because the freedom of everyone depends on the freedom of the pornographers to exercise speech. The woman gagged and hanging remains the speech they exercise. In liberal-left lingo, stopping them is called *censorship*' (War, 320) Dworkin's answer is that she is not pro-censorship, the goal of her Bill is not for censoring people; at times the anti-pornography lobby can seem to be ridiculously alarmist, and reactionary, for, after all, it's only sex, isn't it? after all, say some feminists, most of pornography is soft and merely depicts people having sex and so what is offensive about that? just because some piece of art or media shows people having sex, does that mean it should be banned? or as Julienne Dickey puts it: 'it *is* important that we distinguish between how pornographic material makes us (women) *feel* and how it makes them (men) *act*. There can be no doubt that many women *feel* offended by media sexism and pornography... But because we feel offended by certain material, is this sufficient reason to have it removed?',[170] why is lovemaking so offensive to some people, the anti-censorship feminists ask, for pornography just depicts people enjoying themselves, as Avedon Carol writes: 'most pornography is just about men and women enjoying sex together';[171] this is the liberal view that Dworkin abhors, for in her analysis women are systematically degraded in most pornography, yes, but, wait a minute, the anti-censorship feminists retort, that is not true, for women are shown as the ones who are largely in control of the sexual scenarios, they are the ones who have the juicy orgasms, they are ones who enjoy themselves the most, women are the ones who are empowered in (and by) pornography, claim some feminists; the anti-censorship feminists ask: surely, really, pornography is fantasy, and it's no use eternally mixing it up with reality, it is fantasy, dreaming, not about actual violence; the answer to this sort of argument from Dworkin, Daly, Griffin, Groult, MacKinnon and other anti-pornographers is: maybe, but

170 Dickey: "Snakes and Ladders", in Chester, 164
171 Carol: "Snuff: Believing the Worst", in Assister & Carol, 129

even the fantasy is harmful and degrading, even if pornography is fantasy, it is still abhorrent to most women; even the 'new women's pornography', made, supposedly, by and for women, is not truly liberating, but is ultimately patriarchal: for Catherine MacKinnon terms the new 'women's pornography' another strategy of the enemy, pornographers;[172] Elizabeth Carola, who describes herself as a 'radical feminist lesbian', describes magazines such as *On Our Backs, Bad Attitude, OW! – Outrageous Women: A Journal of Woman-to-Woman SM, Yellow Silk, The Power Exchange*: [l]ike all porn, this new 'woman's' porn is neither about nor for women. Like all porn it is, in a most basic sense, *against* women and *about* male fantasy – the basic male fantasy of Woman as Wholly Sexual Object whose Purpose is To Be Fucked – which feeds men's egos, fuels their violence';[173] according to Elizabeth Carola, lesbian pornographic magazines are full of images and themes usually associated with male pornography: '*On Our Backs*, in particular, is full of adverts for phalluses and endless verbiage about (and imagery of) extremely masculine 'Butches' introducing large objects – fists, bottles, phalluses – into the bodies of 'Femmes'... *On Our Backs* represents the 'middle range' of lesbian porn. The harder core publications like *The Power Exchange* feature half page adverts for surgical scalpels for 'unparalleled cutting and piercing' interspersed with litanies of young women being violently fist fucked, whipped and pierced and, of course, gratefully licking their 'mistresses' boots in return' (in ib.); Dworkin, one knows, would be very much against 'lesbian porn' or the 'new women's porn', for it is perhaps patriarchal, despite its new ways of representing sex, and it is to be despised, then, Dworkin would think; writers such as Pat Califa, Lisa Henderson and Sheila Jeffreys argue that sadomasochistic pornography operating inside lesbian practice

172 Lesley White: "A porn fighter", *The Sunday Times*, 12 June 1994, section 9, 7
173 Elizabeth Carola: "Women, Erotica, Pornography: – Learning to Play the Game", in Chester, 169-171; see S. Jeffreys: "Butch and femme: now and then", *Gossip*, 5, 1987

can be enriching;[174] for men it is clearly threatening, because it excludes them; it is made by women, for women: 'it is no longer for men alone to decide what is, or is not, exciting in pornography' as Linda Williams writes in her book *Hard Core*;[175] men are excluded from lesbian pornography: 'Pornography for lesbians is unique in that it presumes a *female* gaze, and a lesbian one at that,' writes Barbara Smith, but although 'lesbian' and 'women's' pornography is for made for and by women, it cannot escape from patriarchy or male-made structures and attitudes, just as lesbianism itself, according to some feminists, is not truly 'outside' of heterosexuality and patriarchy, the view is that '[l]esbians who engage in consensual S/M are thus merely imitating and even colluding in patriarchal structures,' writes Clare Whatling;[176] Sheila Jeffreys claims that 'Sm practice comes from nowhere more mysterious than the history of our very real oppression';[177] Clare Whatling suggests that lesbian S/M practice can parody and subvert patriarchal values and systems; she writes: 'S/M is never *intrinsically* revolutionary. Like all sexual practice, it is a product of its time and context. As with other sexual practices, it may be oppositional under certain conditions, but it is never always so... S/M is constructed in relation to the society in which it is played out and cannot be understood without reference to the structures that exist there... Where S/M does perhaps differ from more conventional sexual practices is in the self-consciousness it brings to encounters. For S/M as a practice does much to foreground

174 Pat Califa: "Feminism and Sadomasochism", *Heresies*, 12, 1981, *The Lesbian S/M Safety Manual*, Alyson, Boston 1990, and "Unravelling the Sexual Fringe: A Secret Side of Lesbian Sexuality", *The Advocate*, 27 December 1979; also: Lisa Henderson: "Lesbian Pornography: Cultural Transgression and Sexual Demystification", in Sally Munt, ed, 173-191; Sheila Jeffreys: "Sadomasochism: the erotic cult of fascism", in *Lesbian Ethics*, 2, 1, 65-82; M. Sulter: "Reviewing lesbian erotica", *Spare Rib*, no. 219, 1990-1, 42-4; see also, on sadomasochism: R.R. Linden *et al*, eds: *Against Sadomasochism*, Frog in the Well, East Palo Alto, California 1982; Justine Jones: "Why I liked screwing? Or, is heterosexual enjoyment based on sexual violence?", in Onlywomen, eds: *Love your Enemy?*, Onlywomen Press 1981; Katherine Davis *et al*, eds: *Coming to Power, Writings and Graphics on Lesbian S/M*, Alyson Publications, Boston 1983

175 Linda Williams: *Hard Core: Power, Pleasure, and the 'Frenzy of the Visible'*, Pandora, 1990, 264; see also Andrew Ross: "The Popularity of Pornography", in *No Respect: Intellectuals and Popular Culture*, Routledge 1989, 171-208

176 Clare Whatling: "Who's read *Macho Sluts?*", in Judith Still & Michael Worton, eds, 193

177 Sheila Jeffreys: "Sado-masochism", op.cit., 68

the constructedness of all sexuality';[178] as Barbara Smith writes: '[i]f heterosexual women fuck the enemy, then SM dykes fuck *like* the enemy';[179] other women writers are disappointed by the 'new women's pornography', such as the anti-censorship and liberal Tuppy Owens, who is the author of *The Sex Maniac's Diary* and organizer of The Sex Maniac's Ball, where there is 'a playpen for adult babies, and a tearoom for people who like messy cake fights',[180] and who participated in swinging orgies where she was 'in the middle of eleven bisexual men with everything being penetrated everywhere (heaven!...)' (ib., 117); Tuppy Owens writes: 'You may be curious to know what I think of porn, after all this time. Well, I still like it, but I'm disappointed that it hasn't moved very far. I really don't bother to look at it much. I think that porno is really only of interest when it deals with impossible things. It's rather like fantasy – no point in fantasizing about something if you can actually do it... It's been very interesting working on these new sex mags for women. I don't think that they've got the formula right and I hope that the magazines I'm about to edit will smash barriers, turn everything on its head and open up a new world' (ib., 124), but if pornography is a contentious issue among feminists, then lesbian or 'women's' pornography is extremely controversial, and feminists are very divided about it,[181] because, as Sue George notes: '[f]or a feminist... to enjoy pornography is to feel doubly guilty';[182] indeed, even to mention sex seems to be pornographic in itself, so that the idea of people actually *enjoying* sex becomes part of the disinformation surrounding the pornography debate; for women to say they enjoy sex, for women to speak freely about sex, gets them labelled as 'dirty', as prostitutes, as pornographic – the anti-censorship feminists are in agreement with the anti-pornography feminists on this point – that, for women to speak openly and positively

178 Clare Whatling, op.cit., 194

179 Barbara Smith: "Sappho Was a Right-*Off* Woman', in Chester, 182-4. On sadomasochism, see Thomas S. Weinberg & G.W. Levi Kamel: *S and M: Studies in Sadomasochism*, Prometheus Books, Buffalo, New York 1983

180 Tuppy Owens: "Sex On My Mind", in Assister & Carol, 121

181 see: the essays in Sally Munt's book; A. Koedt: *Radical Feminism*, Quadrangle, New York 1973

182 Sue George, in Chester, op. cit., 111

about sex gets them branded negatively, because sex is something to be hidden, to be suppressed, as our Judaeo-Christian society commands, and those women that openly display their sexuality are called whores, sluts, tarts – like Mary Magdalene; the stereotyping is either that of the obedient, passive, nurturing mother (Virgin Mary), or the voracious, 'dirty' (less sacred) prostitute (Mary Magdalene) or as Dworkin says: '[w]omen mistakenly think that pornography is largely built on the good girl/ bad girl or the Madonna/ whore theme. With rare exceptions, it is not. It is built on the whore/ whore theme' (War, 239); as Christobel Mackenzie writes: '[w]e aren't supposed to be really sexual, and we are discouraged from admitting we have positive feelings about being sexual. We are somehow seen as 'dirty' or 'bad' if we have sexual experience or if we admit we like sex';[183] what happens is the women who use their sexuality openly and positively are regarded as 'dirty', as whores – we see this in the media time and time again (in the figures of, say, Marilyn Monroe and Madonna, or 'mistresses' of ministers and presidents); Christobel Mackenzie writes: '[a]nd 'respectable' women [non-prostitutes] (again, including feminists), hate the women who say they like sex – especially the women who like sex with men... It is frightening to see so many feminists who want so desperately to believe that women can't enjoy sex, that every time we have sex with men, we are being victims. Why is it so necessary to see ourselves as poor little put-upon sufferers? ... Why do we need to think that when men want to be with us, they only want to 'take advantage' of us?';[184] these are good questions that Mackenzie poses, but Andrea Dworkin is not anti-sex, as we have said earlier, she is anti-bad sex, anti-rape, anti-victimization, for there is much sex in her fiction, a searing and orgasmic kind of lovemaking which, in *Mercy,* is merged with the protagonist's revolutionary idealism: '[w]e planned the political acts there, the chaos we delivered to the status quo, the acts of disruption, rebellion. We hid out there, kept low, kept out of sight; you turn where you are into a friendly darkness that hides

183 Christobel Mackenzie: "The Anti-sexism Campaign Invites you to fight Sexism, Not Sex", in Assister & Carol, 140

184 Mackenzie, in ib., 141-3

you. We embraced there, a carnal embrace – after an action or during the long weeks of planning or in the interstices where we drenched ourselves in hashish and opium until a paralysis overtook us and the smoke stopped at the time. I liked that; how everything slowed down; and I liked fucking after a strike, a proper climax to the real act – I liked how everything got fast and urgent; fast, hard, life or death; I liked bed then, after, when we was drenched in perspiration from what came before; I liked revolution as foreplay; I liked how it made you supersensitive so the hairs on your skin were standing up and hurt before you touched them, could feel a breeze a mile away, it hurt, there was this reddish pain, a soreness parallel to your skin before anything touched you; I liked how you was tired before you began, a fatigue that came because the danger was over, a strained, taut fatigue, an ache from discipline and attentiveness and from the imposition of a superhuman quietness on the body; I liked it. I liked it when the embrace was quiet like the strike itself, a subterranean quiet, disciplined, with exposed nerve endings that hurt but you don't say nothing. Then you sleep. Then you fuck more; hardy; rowdy; long; slow; now side by side or with me on top and then side by side; I liked to be on top and I moved real slow, real deliberate, using every muscle in me, so I could feel him hurting – you know that melancholy ache inside that deepens into a frisson of pain? – and I could tease every bone in his body until it was ready to break open, split and the marrow'd spread like semen. I could split him open inside and he never had enough' (M, 143-4); powerful indeed are Dworkin's descriptions of fucking in her fiction, but in her non-fiction, it seems as if she hates sex, at times, as if she can't imagine lovemaking without being a part of subordination to men and patriarchy, as she writes in *Right-Wing Women*: '[i]ntercourse is synonymous with sex because intercourse is the most systematic expression of male power over women's bodies, both concrete and emblematic, and as such it is upheld as a male right by law (divine and secular), custom, practice, culture, and force. Because intercourse so consistently expresses illegitimate power, unjust power, wrongful power, it is intrinsically an expression of the female's subordinate status, sometimes a celebration of that status. The shame that women feel on being fucked and simultaneously experiencing pleasure in being possessed is the shame of having acknowledged, physically and emotionally, the extent to which one has internalized and eroticized the subordination' (84); what a horror this is, that Dworkin describes, this view of sexual intercourse as *always* being an expression of masculine domination and feminine subordination, of constant female subservience and pain; is it really like this? Dworkin's problem, for some feminists, is that she is too simplistic in her analysis; it seems people can't help lumping everything together, so that any talk of sex must be 'dirty', so that any talk of pornography means *violent* sexuality, so that feminists who discuss sex are really nymphomaniacs who are obsessed with sex, or they are lesbians (the nympho/ tart and the lesbian are the two female extremes for men – one always voracious for sex with men, the other the opposite, hated by men because they don't want to fuck men; as Dworkin says in "The Power of Words": 'the contempt for lesbians is distinct. It is directly rooted in the abhorrence of the self-defined woman, the self-determining woman, the woman who is not controlled by male need, imperative or manipulation' [War, 28]); as Avedon Carol writes in her essay on the notorious 'snuff' movies: '[f]eminist hyperbole about the violence of pornography, along with an insistence from some that there is no difference between consensual sex and rape, reached such a peak by the mid-1970s that it had nearly become impossible, in discussion, to distinguish real violence from ordinary sex',[185] clearly, not all sex is violent in pornography by any means – but Dworkin's point is that sex in pornography contains hidden violences even when there is no violence on show; the links between pornography and violence that Dworkin constantly upholds are questioned by many feminists; they ask, well, what pornography shows *may* be violent, but in whose opinion? further, how can you say that no women at all enjoy the acts portrayed in pornography? certainly, you might say, men have strange fetishes – to be tied up, dressed as babies with nappies on, to be humiliated, to lick shoes, to be shat on, to be chained, etc, but these are not exclusively the province of lusty males, and it is not the acts themselves that are

185 Carol: "Snuff: Believing the Worst", in Assister & Carol, 126

to be despised, as Gayle Rubin notes, but the fact that men think they can make these demands of people: 'it is the fact that men feel entitled to make these demands which is disgusting – not what they desire sexually. This is not caused by the depiction of sex acts in pornography, but by a sexist society that does not afford women full human or sexual status';[186] Dworkin has the wrong target, the anti-censorship pro-sex feminists claim: pornography is not the problem, but pornography *may* be the manifestation of sexism, but it is not the root *cause*, as Christobel Mackenzie writes; '[w]e can't waste any more time arguing over symptoms of sexism and attacking the wrong targets – like sexual fantasy, pornography or bisexuality',[187] and Gayle Rubin agrees: '[i]nstead of fighting porn, feminism should oppose censorship, support the decriminalization of prostitution, call for the abolition of all obscenity laws, support the rights of sex workers, support women in management positions in the sex industry, support the availability of sexually explicit materials, support sex education for the young, affirm the rights of sexual minorities and affirm the legitimacy of human sexual diversity';[188] as for the actual, physical links between pornography and violence, Alison King has some useful observations to make in her survey of the pornography-violence surveys: '[a]lmost every major researcher has found that soft-core pornography can *inhibit* aggression in individuals',[189] and King concludes her survey: '[t]ime and time again, soft-core pornography far more explicit than that

186 Rubin, in Assister & Carol, 38

187 Mackenzie, op.cit., 145

188 Rubin, op.cit., 40

189 Alison King: "Mystery and Imagination: the Case of Pornography Effects Studies", in Assister & Carol, 73, referring to: R.A. Baron: "The Aggression-Inhibiting Influences of Heightened Sexual Arousal", *Journal of Personality and Social Psychology*, 30, 3, 1974; R.A. Baron & P.A. Bell: "Effects of Heightened Sexual Arousal on Physical Aggression", *American Psychological Association, Proceedings*, 8, 1973; E. Donnerstein *et al*: "Erotic Stimuli and Aggression Facilitation or inhabitation?", *Journal of Personality and Social Psychology*, 32, 1975; L.A. White: "Erotica and Aggression: the Influence of Sexual Arousal, Positive Effects and Negative Effects on Aggressive Behavior", *Journal of Personality and Social Psychology*, 34, 1979; A. Frodi: "Sexual Arousal, Situational Restrictiveness and Aggressive Behaviour", *Journal of Research in Personality*, 11, 1977; D. Zillmann & B. Sapolsky: "What Mediates the Effect of Mild Erotica on Annoyance and Hostile Behavior in Males?", *Journal of Personality and Social Psychology*, 35, 1977

available in Britain has been shown to lower aggression levels';[190] but, at times, it does seem as if Dworkin hates any kind of sexual expression – certainly in written form she finds few if any texts which are not pornographic; for her, erotica is simply high class porn, so all those people critics regard as writers of good, sensitive sexual moments – Anais Nin, D.H. Lawrence, Edna O'Brien, Alice Walker, Susan Griffin – are in fact peddling pornography just like everyone else, that is, their writing, no matter what their intentions might have been, turns out as pornography in the end; pornography, it seems, is inescapable when sex and art meet – this seems to be Dworkin's position, critically, when she looks at authors and books: all discussions of eroticism, it seems, end up as pornography, in Dworkin's view, so that there are no true 'erotic' writers, in Dworkin's view, much as Hélène Cixous reckoned there were three writers who wrote truly 'feminine' texts, only three 'inscriptions of femininity' written this century: Colette, Duras and Genet;[191] Dworkin and other feminists do not have any doubts – Dworkin has not shifted her basic position, which she has been pursuing for years, that men create cultures of violence which oppress women in many spheres, from the physical to the psychological, from the societal to the ideological, and when questions such as this are asked: is all pornography an incitement to violence? Dworkin replies, yes, pornography incites violence, although this was not the main issue of her Bill of Rights, which was, rather, that the very existence of pornography was an infringement of women's civil rights, although Gillian Rodgerson and Linda Semple defined the Dworkin-MacKinnon Ordinance against pornography as being based on a view that 'basically any depiction of women in a sexual situation' was wrong or bad,[192] but Dworkin and MacKinnon are not against *every* depiction of women as sexual beings, Anne Snitow writes that 'we need to be able to reject the sexism in porn without having to reject the realm of pornographic sexual fantasy as if that entire kingdom were without meaning or resonance for

190 King, ib., 86
191 Cixous: "The Laugh of the Medusa", *Signs*, Summer 1976, in Marks, 249
192 Gillian Rodgerson and Linda Semple: "Who watches the watchwomen?: Feminists against censorship", *Feminist Review*, no 36, Autumn 1990

women'[193] and Dworkin is not against sexual feelings, rather, she despises those representations that damage, terrorize, debase and exploit women, but, again, who is being exploited in pornography? surely pornography implicates everyone who comes into contact with it – not just the 'victims' of pornography, in Dworkin's sense, women, not just the models, but also the photographers, designers and pornography publishers, and also the consumers, and, because so much of pornography is 'hidden', then also the rest of society, everyone else, they're all embroiled in pornography, because, directly or not, overtly or covertly, pornography touches everyone's lives, no one can 'escape' the effects of pornography, in Dworkin's view, but all this depends on the real effects of pornography as consumption, as Carol Avedon and Nettie Pollard write: 'many hard-core porn models can be perceived as laying a particularly exploited role only if the viewer assumes that only men can enjoy sexual activity. However, that pernicious assumption pervades society to the extent that even some feminists claim that all pornography shows women performing acts that we could never enjoy': Carol and Pollard continue their discussion, and they could be describing Dworkin's *Pornography: Men Possessing Women* here: '[s]ome feminist authors have written whole books to this effect, maintaining that every aspect of the sexual acts portrayed in pornography represents sexual interests and approaches that are unique to male psychology and contradict the true female personality, in which all such acts are unpleasant and abhorrent. Dworkin asserted that all pornography is made by force or coercion, as no woman would willingly perform these acts',[194] Avedon and Pollard surely have Dworkin in mind in this critique, for Dworkin often maintains that women do not enjoy themselves in pornography, either as models or consumers, and that (most) pornography is produced 'by force or coercion': Dworkin writes, in "Women Lawyers and Pornography", a 1980 speech at Yale University Law School: '[p]ornography originates in a real social system in which women are sexually colonialized and have been

193 Snitow: "Retrenchment Versus Transformation: The Politics of the Anti-Pornography Movement", in *Women Against Censorship*, 117
194 Avedon and Pollard, in Assister, 55

for hundreds of centuries. Pornography – whether as genre or as industry or as aid to masturbation – originates in that system, flourishes in that system, and has no meaning or existence outside that system. Pornography is inseparable from the undeniable brutality of commonplace male usage of the female' (War, 237), but here, as elsewhere, but particularly in this speech, Dworkin goes too far: she states that pornography has 'no meaning or existence' outside of the 'real social system in which women are sexually colonialized', which is not true, for pornography has many meanings, and not all of them founded on sexual colonialization, yet Dworkin won't let go of this insistence on sexual colonialization: '[h]e owns you; he fucks you. The fucking conveys the quality of the ownership: he owns you inside out. The fucking conveys the passion of his dominance: it requires access to every hidden inch' writes Dworkin of the primal heterosexual 'act' in *Intercourse* (76); and, again, in "Sexual Economics: The Terrible Truth" (1976), she says that '[e]verywhere, then, the female is kept in captivity by the male'(122), which, again, is simply not true, it's too sweeping a statement, it's a statement founded on rage, which is right, but not on accuracy, it's an opinion, but a personal view made into a universal one, which is OK again, in one sense, because isn't most (all?) religion and art founded on individual views and individual revelations – after all, Christianity flows from the central, individual experience of one person, Christ, but it does not apply to all women, or does it? or in this statement, Dworkin says: '[w]omen have two choices: lie or die. Feminists are trying to open the options up a bit' ("Nervous Interview", War, 60); for Dworkin, women have to lie to get by, to pretend that women really do like being hurt during or not during sex; she writes: '[o]ne simply cannot be both for and against the exploitation of women' (RWW, 197); Dworkin is probably right when she suggests that American politics is largely a male creation: '[t]he Constitution of the United States was written exclusively by white men who owned land. Some owned black slaves, male and female. More men owned white women who were also chattel' ("For Men, Freedom of Speech; For Women, Silence Please", War, 222-3); Catherine MacKinnon suggests that pornography helps to encode power relations between men and women by making the power relations seem 'sexy': 'male and female are created through the eroticization of submission and dominance',[195] the submission is made 'sexy', as is the objectification of women that occurs in pornography; so much of Western, modern culture follows on from this eroticization; the world of fashion and 'style', for instance, comes straight out of the eroticization of women in pornography, as Dworkin has noted in most of her non-fiction books: '"[w]omen's fashion" is a euphemism for fashion created by men for women' writes Dworkin (P, 126), and as Kathy Myers notes, writing that, though 'the fashion image and the pornographic image are in the first instance produced within quite distinct sets of social and economic circumstances', 'notions of hard-core pornography as mediated through auteuristic eroticism affect the form and presentation of certain upmarket fashion images',[196] Myers is referring to those *auteurs* of high fashion photography, David Bailey and Helmut Newton and their ilk, whose sadomasochistic and highly fetishized motifs and pornographic images appear in the high fashion spreads of the glossy fashion magazines, where 'high art' clearly is pornography; this 'high art', fetishized photography is exploitation, Dworkin and MacKinnon claim, the exploitation of people, ideas, resources, of everything, in short, as Ann Snitow writes that pornography 'is exploitation of *everything*'[197] and this pornographic exploitation of everything is everywhere, even if one never consumes pornography, even if one never has sex, one is still being exploited pornographically, one still lives in a pornographic and patriarchal world, it's inescapable, which is horrifying, but Dworkin rams home this point: '[e]very woman – no matter what her sexual orientation, personal sexual likes or dislikes, personal history, political ideology – lives inside this system of forced sex. This is true even if she has never personally experienced any sexual coercion, or if

195 Catherine MacKinnon: "Feminism, Marxism, Method and the State: towards feminist jurisprudence", in S. Harding, ed: *Feminism and Methodology*, Indiana University Press, Indiana 1987, 136
196 Kathy Myers: "Passion 'n' Fashion: A Working Paper", *Screen*, vol. 23, no. 3/4, 1983
197 Ann Snitow: "Mass market romance: pornography for women is different", in Snitow *et al*, eds: *Powers of Desire: the politics of sexuality*, Monthly Review Press, New York 1983, 1983, 269

she personally likes intercourse as a form of intimacy, or if she as an individual has experiences of intercourse that transcend, in her opinion, the dicta of gender and the institutions of force. This is true even if – for her – the force is eroticized, essential, central, sacred, meaningful, sublime. This is true even if – for her – she repudiates intercourse and forbids it: if she subjectively lives outside the laws of gravity, obviously the laws of gravity will intrude' (RWW, 83), which is all so depressing, so horribly depressing and desolate and desperate, because Dworkin sees patriarchal force invading ('penetrating') *every single aspect of life*, and there is no escape, Dworkin maintains, even if one never has sex, and lives utterly outside of society, which is impossible anyway, and this is the point of the French feminists – Cixous, Irigaray, Wittig, Kristeva – that one can't live *outside* of society, one is *always* in society, in it, up to the neck, to the skull, in up to the mind, and body, and everything, all the way in, one is soaked through, every cell in the body, it seems, is thoroughly enculturated, it's not about Darwin or DNA or natural selection, it's not about flesh and blood, it's not about the body, it's about all the many many forms of social, societal, psychological and ideological control, this is patriarchal power, this is the 'Sado-state' or 'Phallocracy', as Mary Daly calls it, it's *everywhere*, and one can *never* escape it, one is thoroughly and utterly enculturated or socialized, even if one lived on a desert island for seventy years, one would still be thoroughly embedded in patriarchal discourse, because of the first five years or whatever that one spent amongst humans; which means that the future is very bleak, for Dworkin, for, despite her idealism and utopianism, things would take millennia to change, not just a couple of years or three generations, but thousands of years, all that time for the patriarchal discourses to die away, for, as she continues: '[e]very woman is surrounded by this system of forced sex and is encapsulated by it. It acts on her, shapes her, defines her boundaries and her possibilities, tames her, domesticates her, determines the quality and nature of her privacy: it modifies her. She functions within it and with constant references to it. This same system that she is inside is inside her – metaphorically and literally delivered into her by intercourse, especially forced intercourse, especially deep thrusting. Intercourse violates the boundaries of her body, which is why intercourse is so often referred to as violation' (RWW, 83-4), you can see the rage in Dworkin as she writes thus, making these huge claims, these polemical statements, but is she going too far? is not putting food in one's mouth also a violation of the boundaries of a woman's body? isn't embracing a child in affection a violation of a woman's body? isn't, then, accidentally drinking in sea water as she goes swimming on holiday a violation of a woman's body? isn't the very air she breathes into her body a violation of a woman's body? why doesn't Dworkin extend her metaphors outwards, in all directions, to not just include fucking but all manner of body-based experiences, so that cutting one's toenails is a violation of a woman's body, or excreting is a violation of a woman's body, for, yes, intercourse does violate a woman's body, as Dworkin says, but so does washing one's face, or brushing one's hair, all these activities violate the 'natural' course of things, you can take Dworkin's arguments to extremes, you can go even further than she does, and they become silly; yet, how right she is, how right she is about the prevalence of pornography, which critics hate her for, they hate her bringing attention to pornography, which they consume, or which they deny consuming in public but consume in private, or they consume 'high art' which is in fact pornography: Titian's *Urbino Venus*, Manet's *Olympia*, Goya's *Maya*, Miller's *Tropic of Cancer*, Bertolucci's *Last Tango in Paris*, etc; whatever you think of Dworkin's analysis of pornography's links to physical violence, Dworkin is probably right about the unseen nature of pornography: 'the harm to women of pornography is invisible because most sexual abuse still occurs in private, even though we have this photographic documentation of it, called the pornography industry' ("Pornography Is a Civil Rights Issue", War, 283), whatever you think of Dworkin, you must agree on the relative invisibility of much of pornography – certainly soft core and hard core pornography is usually out of sight, certainly it is consumed, read and watched out of sight, you don't see pornography being consumed much in the open, in front of strangers, although the fact that people (usually men) consume pornography is admitted in sly references (by comedians, for instance, such as Woody Allen in that scene in the newsagents where he's trying to disguise the fact that he's looking for porn), and James Bond, in the 1969 film *On Her Majesty's Secret Service*, reads *Mayfair*, and in Federico Fellini's 1982 film *City of Women* a group of males masturbate under a white sheet while watching not pornography, but Hollywood movie stars in a cinema – but, generally, one doesn't see pornography, in the sense of magazines and videos, being consumed in public, it is, rather, a 'private' consumption, in the bedroom, in the lounge with the video, among friends in a small group, etc, situations where the boundaries of experience are understood, and transgressions can be handled amongst people who know and trust each other, it is in this 'private' world (there is a hard core magazine *Private*) that pornography in Dworkin's sense (videos and magazines) is consumed; Elizabeth Sidney offers the following facts as an indication of the mass consumption of pornography: '[i]n America, according to NAPCRO the (U.S.A.) National Anti-Pornography Civil Rights Organisation, over 2 million households now subscribe to cable pornography and the magazines *Playboy, Penthouse* and *Hustler* each have a larger readership than *Time* and *Newsweek* combined;[198] some male feminists, among them John Stoltenberg, one of Dworkin's companions in the feminist cause, have explored their sexuality, debunking 'myths' about male ejaculation, orgasm, lovemaking, etc[199] while other anti-sexist men have claimed that in pornography, men are shown, ultimately, in an inferior way to women: '[m]en might set the rules, but women are shown to come out 'enjoying it most'' writes Andy Moye,[200] though Dworkin would not go that far; she is sympathetic to men's cause, but she reckons, like Virginia Woolf, that we've heard enough from men, that men have had their say, and have had their say for the past ten thousand years – no, make that two million years – so, we

198 Elizabeth Sidney, writing in 1988, the early years of cable and satellite consumption, so the figures must be greater now, in Chester, 206

199 see John Stoltenberg: "Refusing to be a Man", in J. Snodgrass, ed: *A Book of Readings for Men Against Sexism*, Times Change Press, New York 1977; Jack Litewka: "The Socialised Penis", in Snodgrass, op. cit.; H. Brod, ed: *The Making of Masculinities*, Allen & Unwin 1987

200 Andy Moye, "Pornography", in A. Metcalf & M. Humphries, eds: *The Sexuality of Men*, Pluto Press 1985, 58

don't need to hear from men anymore (although some feminists reckon men could help feminism by talking about their own sexuality, their fears and desires, which might help women to understand male desire and the structures it creates, such as pornography and marriage); Andrea Dworkin is revered by some and vilified by others; Michael Moorcock, as we noted earlier, thinks very highly of Dworkin, he appears on the cover of her book *Intercourse* saying '[a]ny man who chooses to ignore what Dworkin has to say is refusing the possibility of a dramatically better world', while in one of the standard feminist dictionaries, Dworkin is described thus: '[a] radical American feminist who has made significant contributions to feminist theory in her analysis of the exploitative and discriminatory nature of patriarchy' (Maggie Humm),[201] but other feminists are not so generous: Dworkin, they say, has sensationalized some feminist issues, concentrating too much on pornography and rape at the expense of other equally urgent issues, such as race, or economy, or poverty, and while Dworkin's courage and stamina are acknowledged, her constant simplifying of complex issues aggravates some feminists, for instance, Gayle Rubin, 'a veteran of the feminist sex wars', who lives in San Francisco, finds Dworkin's depiction of prostitutes offensive: '[t]hroughout her book, *Pornography*, Dworkin uses the stigma of prostitution to convey her opprobrium and make her argument against pornography. She says, '[c]ontemporary pornography strictly and literally conforms to the word's root meaning: the graphic depiction of *vile whores*, or in our language, *sluts, cows* (as in: *sexual cattle, sexual chattel*), *cunts*' [page 200, Rubin's emphasis]; this is a degrading and insulting description of prostitutes. Feminists should be working to remove stigma from prostitution, not exploiting it for rhetorical gain';[202] Rubin is opposed to the Dworkin-MacKinnon ordinance, as are many feminists, claiming that Dworkin/ MacKinnon's 'new category of 'pornography' would have codified a feminist anti-porn description into law', something anti-censorship feminists find dangerous; censorship,

201 Humm: *The Dictionary of Feminist Theory*, 57

202 Rubin, op.cit., in Assister & Carol, 34

says Wendy Moore,[203] is 'like freedom an entirely subjective term' (in ib. 26); for Claudia, Dworkin and MacKinnon rely too much on the assumed decency of the people in government to carry out their bill: '[t]he implicit message, of safety through vulnerability, is broadcast by all those from Ms Cartland to Dworkin and MacKinnon who believe in the readiness of the 'decent chaps' in the government and police departments to protect them from the misogynist bad guys';[204] and the interpretation of the Dworkin-MacKinnon Bill would vary from judge to judge, as Pratibha Parmar notes: '[a] second problem is that Dworkin's definition of what is pornographic can be interpreted in a variety of ways, depending on who is doing the interpreting';[205] for the Feminists Against Censorship, Dworkin gets too much coverage in the media – certainly Dworkin receives more attention than many feminists; Feminists Against Censorship write: '[i]rony is heaped on irony: Andrea Dworkin was given an hour to herself on television [a BBC *Omnibus* documentary in 1991] to explain her anti-porn position – no opposing voice was needed, it was said, because Ms Dworkin explained *our* view for us well enough. No equally one-sided hour has been offered to anti-censorship feminists, of course. Yet Dworkin and her friends and colleagues all complain that *their* view is being suppressed... Ms Dworkin claims her books are suppressed, and so on. In fact, most authors would dearly love to have been published as 'few' times as Andrea Dworkin';[206] Alison Assister and Avedon Carol suggest that Dworkin is mistaken about the relation between politics and sexuality: '[n]owadays, Andrea Dworkin and Sheila Jeffreys both seem to place intercourse and the phallus at the centre of oppression, as if reproduction and child-care had nothing to do with it', and they continue: 'both Dworkin and Jeffreys seem to believe that the purpose of heterosexism and sexism in general is a male conspiracy to get women to provide the maximum amount of sexual pleasure to males – but this hardly explains why society

203 Moore: "There Should Be a Law Against It... Shouldn't There?", in Chester, 140
204 Claudia, in Assister & Carol, 136
205 Parmar, in Chester, 128
206 in Assister & Carol, 147

deliberately limits female willingness to become involved in sex, nor why fellatio, male voyeurism, female exhibitionism, 'hand jobs' and the like are stigmatized. (If Jeffreys is correct, why aren't girls trained from birth to suck cock?) No, it's clear that our society has fetishized reproduction to the point that even where sex is clearly had when conception is not desired, we still fear to acknowledge outright that we're not in it for the babies';[207] Dworkin, it seems, sets herself up for attacks from other feminists, as well as all manner of commentators, journalists, comedians, critics and philosophers; we can analyze her arguments and pick holes in them; it is easy to do this, because Dworkin's arguments are simply too simple, too easily made; take, for instance, her various essays and speeches and lectures on pornography collected in *Letters From a War Zone*, for example the 1981 piece "Why Pornography Matters to Feminists", where Dworkin states that women are used as 'things': 'pornography says that women are things' (War, 203), well, so are men used as things, and children are used as things, and people in all manner of photographs are used as 'things': men and women modelling clothes in fashion magazine spreads are used as 'things', the 'thingness' of women in pornography is simply part of the 'objectification' of people in all manner of representation; the very nature of representation means that people are used as 'things'; Jesus in the Bible is used as a 'thing', characters in novels are used as 'things', heroes and martyrs in Renaissance paintings are used as 'things'; perhaps Dworkin means that women are degraded when they are used as 'things'; but, so is any human who is photographed or represented in the media, not just in pornography, for what applies to the æsthetics of pornography must apply, in one way or another, to the æsthetics of all image-making, all photography, cinema, television, radio, newspapers, magazines, books, billboards, all manner of representations 'objectify' and make 'thing-like' people; Dworkin writes, in "Against the Male Flood" that pornography is all about erection: '[w]hat is at stake in obscenity law is always erection' she writes (War, 260), isolating the main component of male desire in pornography, which may be true, for, certainly, desire is one of

207 in ib., 154-5

the main driving forces of pornography, as of all art, and all culture, but Dworkin as so often, gives her interpretation a biological slant, saying that pornography is for the promotion of erections, which may be true in a number of cases, but not in all, perhaps not even in most cases – 'erection' is but one component in a complicate web of desires, not all of which need to be expressed biologically by any means, for pornography is a series of signs and meanings, as well as anything else, which do not require manifestation physically to exist; a more interesting point is where Dworkin continues with her analysis and writes: '[w]hy they [men] want to regulate their own erections through law is a question of endless interest and importance to feminists' (War, 260), this is a crucial point: why does censorship of sexual relations exist? if Dworkin is right that it is mainly men who create pornography, why do they censor some of it, and not allow it to be sold openly in newsagents and video shops? if pornography is made by grown men, why can't other grown men have access to any or all pornography produced? if censorship by men exists to 'protect' certain sections of society, why do men wish to 'protect' other grown men? one can understand men not wanting certain people to see the pornography they produce or consume – they wouldn't want children to see pornography, for instance, or women, because, according to Dworkin, children and women would see the horrific acts depicted in pornography – but this analysis of why men censor pornography is not quite right, is it? firstly, it assumes that only men create and consume pornography, and, if we take the definition of pornography to be far wider than Dworkin's objectification and torture definition (that is, if we say that all manner of cultural productions contain pornography in them: fashion, 'style', TV soaps, pop music, etc), then pornography is censored for quite different reasons, for pornography is not censored only by men, but by mechanisms, such as the legal system, which are not identical to men, but are products of masculinist systems, which include both men and women; when she moves from purely biological and determinist interpretations of pornography, Dworkin is more effective, as when she says that pornography 'is a metaphysics of women's subjugation', a metaphysics it may be, for here Dworkin acknowledges the idea of pornography as a cultural event, but to say that pornography is a metaphysics of 'women's subjugation' is not true; one might say, rather, that pornography is a series of representations in which more women than men (in terms of numbers) are eroticized, used as the vehicles of fantasy and desire, but this fantasy mode does necessarily mean subjugation; Dworkin says that 'pornography says that women are sluts, cunts', but pornography does not say this and only this, or even this at all, pornography shows women as sexual beings, as the vehicles of sexual pleasure, as voracious, sexually, as the site of orgasmic pleasure, so that some feminists can see pornography as empowering women, a point of view Dworkin would find horrendous, because her reading of pornography is exactly the opposite; that, in pornography, women's power is taken away, because 'pornography turns women into objects and commodities', says Dworkin (War, 204), but does it? and what sort of objects? and are men in car adverts also objects? are characters in soap operas also objects, is the 'general public', when it appears on TV or in the letters page of a newspaper, also an object, does any form of art or representation turn people into objects? are people 'objectified' as soon as they commit part of themselves to an artwork? Dworkin says that 'pornography is violence against the women used in pornography' (ib, 204), but is it, is pornography violence? is, then, Renaissance painting violence? is a fish finger advert violence? is pornography violence because it is *sexual* representation, rather than representation of, say, economic status, or drawing skill? in "Pornography's Part in Sexual Violence" (1981), Dworkin insists that 'pornography *is* violence against women' (War, 207), but she goes on to make the connections between men's consumption of pornography and the battering of women, and rape and gang rape, and marital/domestic violence, so that, for Dworkin, pornography and physical violence are part of a continuum, one informing the other, and pornography, for Dworkin, plays a significant role in this culture of violence, but these connections are hotly disputed, and governments, critics, journalists, artists and thinkers and writers continually debate them, especially after a new case of domestic violence, the murder of a child and its connection with a

Hollywood film, for instance (as in the Jamie Bulger case and the movie *Child's Play 3*, in Britain, for instance, or the Bobbitt case in America), these debates go on and on, with the same simplistic arguments being put forward, and Dworkin is firmly on the side of the right-wing politicians who claim that the links between violent art and physical violence are real, palpable, actual, or as Dworkin puts it: '[t]his is the same system of power that condones the pornography that exalts rape and gang rape, bondage, whipping and forced sex of all kinds. In this same system of power, there are an estimated twenty-eight million battered wives' (War, 208), but is Dworkin right in asserting that only women are the 'victims' in pornography? what about male homosexual pornography? or pornography involving animals? is, anyway, all pornography hard core, and how much hard core pornography is consumed, and how much is produced? where are the statistics on the consumption of pornography? surely, if pornography is consumed 'in secret', how can you obtain fully researched statistics? if pornography is secret, few people will own up to consuming it; certainly when Dworkin asserts that '[w]hen your rape is entertainment, your worthlessness is absolute' (War, 279) her rage gets close to the true point of her polemic: that rape is utterly demeaning, and renders human life worthless, which is true, must be, it must be somewhere near the truth, for Dworkin is a humanist, and hates it when humanity fucks things up for itself, when people smash other people around, what's the point? Dworkin is simply another person who points out that there's a lot of pain that doesn't need to be there, so stop it, stop the pain, and rape is one part of that pain, though it's not the only sort of pain – there is political torture, there is child abuse, there is poverty and so on – but Dworkin's right to assert that when rape becomes mere entertainment, when it reaches the state of banal fun, it makes one's life worthless; but then, sidestepping the censorship issue, Dworkin with MacKinnon created the anti-pornography civil rights bill, where the actual existence of pornography was an act of 'terrorism': 'pornography is out in the world, where it is the officially established form of public terrorism against women' ("Silence Means Dissent", War, 249), is Dworkin going too far here, calling pornography terrorism? is, then, a Leonardo da Vinci painting also terrorism, a Leonardo painting that depicts women in an unflattering, or 'evil' fashion, i.e., the *Mona Lisa*: is the *Mona Lisa* pornography? well, yes, the *Mona Lisa* is perhaps the supreme, the most sublime piece of pornography Western 'high art' has produced – certainly many critics have noted the disturbing effect of Leonardo's painting, most famously was Walter Pater's likening of the *Mona Lisa* to a vampire, a sexually voracious demon, and this is exactly Dworkin's pornographic view of women; but what about other depictions of women in painting, what about, say, the women in Rembrandt, Velasquez, Caravaggio, Titian, Manet, Fra Angelico, Botticelli, Tintoretto, are they also pornographic? is *any* depiction of women terrorism? what makes a depiction pornographic and another not pornographic? who decides when terrorism is being committed in a representation of women? surely, in Dworkin's system, nearly all Western 'high art' is pornography? because so many of the great (male) artists have 'objectified' women, or emphasized their sexuality and passivity (Manet, Renoir, Picasso, Michelangelo, Titian, Courbet, Rembrandt, Raphael, Giacometti), these artists are purveyors of 'pornography' in Dworkin's definition of pornography, but we can extend the net beyond painting to all of representation, so that all (or most) of representation is pornographic, so that all (or most) of television, radio, advertizing, magazines, newspapers, etc, is pornographic, but is it? if so, then we live in a thoroughly pornographic culture, a pornographic society, a world in which pornography is the dominant mode of representation... but is this right? is this extensions of Dworkin's view to become all-inclusive of all forms of representation really accurate? is pornography the dominate mode of our (Western) society? Dworkin seems to think so, she thinks we live in a pornographic world, a world where pornography is a major factor in the oppression of women; Dworkin's views are extreme: for example, she says 'get pornography out of all prisons. It's like sending dynamite to terrorists' (War, 287) yet studies have shown that pornography calms people down; but Dworkin goes further, and claims that pornography is so pervasive that it is deadening much of life, so that she writes: 'pornography gives us no future;

pornography robs us of hope as well as dignity' (War, 205), but is this right? is pornography so powerful that it actually deadens so much of life, that it 'robs us of hope', as Dworkin claims? is our world really a suffocation of pornography? a world in which pornography infuses religion, ethics, politics, sociology, the media? perhaps; certainly Dworkin is convinced of the all-pervasive nature of pornography but finding pornography everywhere is one thing, blaming it for much of women's oppression is another: surely oppression creates expressive modes such as pornography, but pornography is not the *cause* of oppression, is it? surely pornography is an indication of oppression, a symptom, not a cause, an excrescence of an illness, in the Spenglerian/ Darwinian system, but not the source of it all, for the source of pornography, in Dworkin's system, is men, and male power, and masculine desire, this is the terrorism that Dworkin is really attacking, not pornography but male power, not pornography but a society that favours masculinism and men, not pornography but the injustices of patriarchal philosophy ('[w]e live in a system of power that is male-supremacist' says Dworkin in "Pornography and Male Supremacy", War, 226), but again and again, Dworkin maintains that sexuality is at the heart of masculinism, and that pornography is the weapon of sexual oppression, that men use pornography as a means of oppressing women, that pornography is the key to male power, so that sexual intercourse is for Dworkin the battleground of patriarchy, as she says in "Sexual Economics: The Terrible Truth" (1976): '[e]verywhere, then, the female is kept in captivity by the male, denied self-determination so that he can control her reproductive functions, fuck her at will, and have his house cleaned (or ornamented)' (War, 122); Anne Snitow agrees with Dworkin on the violences of pornography, but argues for a wider definition of pornography, one that would include, for instance, history, sociology, economics; Snitow writes: '[a] definition of pornography that takes the problem of analysis seriously has to include not only violence, hatred and fear of women, but also a long list of other elements, which may help explain why we women ourselves have such a mixture of reactions to the genre... Without history, without an analysis of complexity and difference, without a critical eye toward gender and its constant redefinitions, some recognition of the gap – in ideas and feelings – between the porn magazine and the man who reads it, we will only be purveying a false hope to those women whom we want to join us';[208] Dworkin says 'the acceptance of pornography means the decline of feminist ethics and an abandonment of feminist politics; the acceptance of pornography means feminists abandon women' ("Why Pornography Matters to Feminism", War, 204), and, again, here Dworkin surely puts too much emphasis on pornography, for, yes, pornography is powerful, but it is a part of art/ media/ representation, not life, and its existence does mean 'an abandonment of feminist politics' or that 'feminists abandon women', as Dworkin asserts; although, Dworkin may be right when she says that 'pornography further lessens our human value in the society at large' (War, 205), but that seems to assume that the very existence of pornography is enough to lessen the value of human life, but then, one might also say that if war still exists then human life is devalued, or if political censorship still exists then our lives are debased, and other issues may also devalue human life: racial harassment, economic inequality, ageism, classism, speciesism, etc; and, in another place, Dworkin says the same thing about pornography, but in a slightly different way: '[p]ornography can only develop in a variety that is viciously male-supremacist, one in which rape and prostitution are not only well-established but systematically practiced and ideologically endorsed' ("Pornography and Male Supremacy", 230), and Dworkin, in her pursuit of the death of pornography makes a mistake, claiming that '[p]ornography can only develop in a variety that is viciously male-supremacist', the subtext being that in a 'female suprematist' society, erotica, rather than pornography, would flourish, which is not the case, and, further, she claims that pornography can only occur in a '*viciously* male-suprematist' society (my emphasis), again, a claim that does not hold up, because a society does not need to be *viciously* anything for pornography to flourish, for, if pornography is, for many feminists, simply erotic representation, and is not necessarily (or

208 Snitow: "Retrenchment Versus Transformation: The Politics of the Anti-Pornography Movement", in *Women Against Censorship*, 117

even at all) exploitation, and is not necessarily as dangerous as Dworkin thinks; the famous feminists – Kate Millett, Dworkin, Catherine MacKinnon, Julia Kristeva, Hélène Cixous, Luce Irigaray, Susan Brownmiller, Maggie Humm, Nancy Friday, Shere Hite, Naomi Woolf, Betty Friedan, Gloria Steinem and Robin Morgan do not have a monopoly on powerful feminist statements; often the most incisive statements come from the 'general public', people who write to the letters pages of newspapers with simple but powerful things to say, such as this letter ('name and address supplied' it says in the newspaper), which says 'I like men, I hate patriarchy and I am sick of seeing women portrayed in so few and so limited aspects of our lives. In one recent issue of the *Guardian* I did not find a photograph of a woman until almost the back of the paper – a woman amongst a group of men, her head on the desk, asleep – vulnerability amongst stoic maleness? Next to this article there was another titled "Running standing still", in which Dea Birkett explores the possibilities of women "defeating" male athletes in future sports competitions. Why should we be even trying? Why not look at man's intense need or desire to win through by physical means alone? Why not turn it around and create our own "games" where men have to complete at different (i.e., not weaker) levels? I am fed up with the constant barrage of information that implies that I am weak, a victim, masochistic, hysterical, etc... When I reflect on all the thousands upon thousands of daily indignities, prejudices, and violent acts instigated by men against women (men who are terrified of their own vulnerabilities) it makes me really angry';[209] Dworkin is among other feminists who are optimistic about the future, despite the horror, as Françoise Parturier writes: 'I have the feeling that soon, in twenty years perhaps, there will be a revolt of feminine minds against a world made by men for men where so much horror, blood, weeping, and torture inflicted on what is alive proclaims that domination is a vice';[210] the problems that women face run from the superficial to the horrific, and feminists themselves are not free of problematic attitudes: if

209 *The Guardian*, 28 July 1992
210 Françoise Parturier: *Lettre ouverte aux hommes*, Albin Michel 1968, in Marks, 1981, 234

a woman is 'beautiful' or 'pretty', she is not taken seriously; it's a 'tendency to refuse to take seriously women who are conventionally beautiful; a tendency not absent from feminism, of course', as Margaret Marshment has it;[211] Dworkin knows that, even among feminists, issues of 'beauty' still get in the way of perceptive analysis, and some desperate critics, (often journalists) failing to criticize Dworkin in any other way, refer to her size; the middle class political left, says Michael Moorcock, sees Dworkin's work as a censorship issue, when it is really about civil rights, and the critics see her 'as attacking female sexuality, when in fact she is passionate in her vision of a world in which human sensuality is not only heightened but qualitatively improved by changes in the way we perceive and experience it';[212] it is her personal approach to feminism that makes her so powerful, though, the way she always involves herself and her own life in her disgust of pornography, for her commitment is total and unflinching, and nothing gets in the way of her telling it as she sees it, although she has been censored, many times, although she is loathed, by many people, she still holds firm to her fundamental hatred of pornography: 'life, which means everything to me, becomes meaningless, because these celebrations of cruelty destroy my very capacity to feel and to care and to hope. I hate the pornographers most of all for depriving me of hope' she writes in "Pornography and Grief" (War, 23); it is her ability to keep going, against all the odds, that is one of the things so impressive about Andrea Dworkin, for she never gives up on her crusade to tell the truth, to tell it like it is, how she sees it, even as she knows how much it costs her, for writing is a costly business, as her protagonist knows in *Ice and Fire*, and as Andrea Dworkin knows only too well: '[n]ow, at forty-one, the truth is that I am still a fool for writing. I love it. I believe in it. I do know now how hard it is to keep going' (War, 4).

---

211 Margaret Marshment: "Substantial Women", in Gamman, 37
212 Moorcock, 1989, 136

Bibliography

All books are published in London, England, unless otherwise stated

Dorothy Aaron: *About Face: Towards a Positive Image of Women in Advertizing,* Ontario Status of Women Council, Toronto 1975

Isobel Armstrong, ed: *New Feminist Discourses: Critical Essays on Theories and Texts,* Routledge 1992

Karen Armstrong: *The Gospel According to Woman; Christianity's Creation of the Sex War in the West,* Pan 1987

N. Armstrong & L. Tennenhouse, eds: *The Ideology of Conduct: Essays in Literature and the History of Sexuality,* Methuen, New York 1987

Geoffrey Ashe: *The Virgin: Mary's Cult and the Re-emergence of the Goddess,* Arkana 1987

Alison Assister & Avedon Carol, eds: *Bad Girls and Dirty Pictures: The Challenge to Reclaim Feminism,* Pluto Press 1993:

—ed: *Althusser and Feminism,* Pluto Press 1990

John Atkins: *Sex in Literature,* volume 2: *The Classical Experience of the Sexual Impulse,* Calder & Boyars 1973

Patrick Bade: *Femme Fatale: Images of Evil and Fascinating Women,* Ash & Grant 1979

Aliki Barnstone & Willis Barnstone, eds: *A Book of Women Poets: From Antiquity to Now,* Schocken Books, New York 1980

Kathleen Barry: *Female Sexual Slavery,* Prentice-Hall, New Jersey 1979

Georges Bataille: *Literature and Evil,* tr Alistair Hamilton, Calder 1973

Helen Baehr & Gillian Dyer, eds: *Boxed In: Women and Television*, Pandora Press 1987

Martin Barker, ed: *The Video Nasties: Freedom and Censorship in the Media*, Pluto 1984

Geoffrey Barlow & Alison Hill: *Video Violence and Children*, Hodder & Stoughton 1985

Ean Begg: *The Cult of the Black Virgin*, Routledge 1985

Catherine Belsey: *Critical Practice*, Routledge 1980

Leo Bersani: *A Future For Astynanax*, Boyars 1978

Frances Bonner, Lizbeth Goodman, Richard Allen, Linda Jones & Catherine King, eds: *Imagining Women Cultural Representations and Gender*, Polity Press, Cambridge 1992

R. Braidotti: *Patterns of Dissonance: A Study of Contemporary Philosophy*, Polity Press 1991

Jan Bremmer, ed: *From Sappho to de Sade: Moments in the History of Sexuality*, Routledge 1989

Robert Briffault: *The Mothers: A Study of the Origins of Sentiments and Institutions*, Allen & Unwin, 3 vols 1927

Susan Brownmiller: *Against Our Will: Men, Women and Rape*, Bantam, New York, 1976

J. Butler: *Gender Trouble: Feminism and the Subversion of Identity*, Routledge 1990

—& J.W. Scott, eds: *Feminists Theorise the Political*, Routledge 1992

Deborah Cameron, ed: *The Feminist Critique of Language: A Reader*, Routledge 1990

Joseph Campbell: *The Power of Myth*, with Bill Moyers, ed. Betty Sue Flowers, Doubleday, New York 1988

—*The Hero With a Thousand Faces*, Paladin 1988

Michael P. Carroll: *The Cult of the Virgin Mary*, Princeton University Press, New Jersey 1986

Whitney Chadwick: *Women, Art, and Society*, Thames & Hudson 1990

—*Women Artists and the Surrealist Movement*, Thames & Hudson 1991

Gail Chester & Julienne Dickey, ed: *Feminism and Censorship: The Current Debate*, Prism Press, Bridport, Dorset 1988

Laura Chester, ed: *Deep Down: New Sensual Writing By Women*, 1987

Hélène Cixous: *A Hélène Cixous Reader*, ed. Susan Sellers, Routledge, 1994

—& Catherine Clément: *The Newly Born Woman*, tr Betsy Wing, Manchester University Press 1986

Frances Colpitt: *Minimal Art: The Critical Perspective*, University of Washington Press, Seattle, 1990

Gail Cunningham: *The New Woman and the Victorian Novel*, Macmillan

1978
Mary Daly: *Pure Lust: Elemental Feminist Philosophy,* Women's Press 1984
—*Gyn/Ecology: The Metaethics of Radical Feminism,* Women's Press 1979
—*Beyond God the Father,* Women's Press 1985
G. Day & C. Bloch, eds: *Perspectives on Pornography: Sexuality in Film and Literature,* Macmillan 1988
—*Readings in Popular Culture: Trivial Pursuits?,* Macmillan 1990
M. de Certeau: *The Practice of Everyday Life,* University of California Press, Berkeley 1984
Chrisitine Delphy: "Andrea Dworkin", in Dworkin 1993, 1-6
Jonathan Dollimore & Alan Sinfield, eds: *Political Shakespeare,* Manchester University Press 1985
John Drakakis, ed; *Alternative Shakespeares,* Routledge 1988
Lene Dresen-Coendersed: *Saints and She-Devils: Images of Women in the 15th and 16th Centuries,* Rubicon Press 1987
Steven C. Dubin: *Arresting Images: Impolitic Art and Uncivil Actions,* Routledge 1992
Georges Duby & Michele Perrot: *Power and Beauty: Images of Women in Art,* Tauris Parke Books, 1989
Andrea Dworkin: *Mercy,* Arrow 1990
—*Ice and Fire,* Flamingo 1987
—*Intercourse,* Arrow 1988
—*Pornography: Men Possessing Women,* Women's Press 1984
—and Catherine MacKinnon: *Pornography and Civil Rights: A New Day for Women's Equality,* Organizing Against Pornography, Minneapolis 1988
—*Our Blood,* Harper & Row, New York 1976
—*Right-Wing Women: The Politics of Domesticated Females,* Women's Press 1983
—*Letters From a War Zone,* Secker & Warburg 1988
—"Andrea Dworkin parle d'Israël", *Nouvelles Questions Féministes,* vol. 14, no. 2, 1993
Richard Dyer: *Only Entertainment,* Routledge 1992
Mary Eagleton, ed: *Feminist Literary Criticism,* Longman 1991
—ed: *Feminist Literary Theory: A Reader,* Blackwell 1986
Hester Eisenstein: *Contemporary Feminist Thought,* Unwin Paperbacks 1984
Mircea Eliade: *Ordeal by Labyrinth,* University of Chicago Press 1984
—*Symbolism, the Sacred and the Arts,* Crossroad, New York 1985
M. Ellman, ed: *Thinking about Women,* Virago 1979
Julius Evola: *The Metaphysics of Sex,* East-West Publications 1985
R. Felski: *Beyond Feminist Aesthetics: Feminist Literature and Social*

Change, Hutchinson 1989
Feminist Review, eds: *Sexuality: A Reader*, Virago 1987
Peter Fingesten: *The Eclipse of Symbolism*, University Press of California 1970
John Fletcher & Andrew Benjamin, ed; *Abjection, Melancholia and Love: the Work of Julia Kristeva*, Routledge 1990
Michel Foucault: *The History of Sexuality*, vol. 1, Penguin 1981
—*The Use of Pleasure: The History of Sexuality*, vol. 2, Penguin 1987
Constance Franklin, ed: *Erotic Art by Living Artists*, Directors Guild Publishers, Renaissance, California 1988
S. Franklin *et al*, eds: *Off Centre: Feminism and Cultural Studies*, HarperCollins, New York 1992
Elinor Gadon: *The Once and Future Goddess*, Aquarian Press 1990
Lorraine Gamman & Margaret Marshment, eds: *The Female Gaze: Women as Viewers of Popular Culture*, Women's Press 1988
Pamela Church Gibson & Roma Gibson, ed: *Dirty Looks: Women, Pornography, Power*, British Film Institute 1993
Marija Gimbutas: *The Language of the Goddess*, Thames & Hudson 1989
Erving Goffmann: *Gender Advertisements*, Macmillan 1979
Robert Goldwater & Marco Treves, eds. *Artists on Art*, John Murray 1975
Eugene Goodheart: *Desire and Its Discontents*, Columbia University Press, New York 1991
G. Greene & C. Kahn, eds: *Making a Difference: Feminist Literary Criticism*, Methuen 1985
Clement Greenberg: *Art and Culture*, Beacon Press, Boston 1961
Germaine Greer: *The Obstacle Race: The Fortunes of Women Painters and Their Work*, Secker & Warburg 1979; Picador 1981
Gabriele Griffin *et al*, eds: *Stirring It: Challenges For Feminism*, Taylor & Francis 1994
Susan Griffin: *Pornography and Silence: Culture's Revenge Against Nature*, Women's Press 1981
Mary Beth Haralovitch: "Advertising Heterosexuality", *Screen*, 23, no. 2, 1982
M. Esther Harding: *Women's Mysteries*, Rider 1989
John Hartley: *Tele-ology: Studies in Television*, Routledge 1992
Marianne Hester: *Lewd Women and Wicked Witches: A Study of the Dynamics of Male Domination*, Routledge 1992
Janet Hobhouse: *The Bride Stripped Bare: The Artist and the Nude in the Twentieth Century*, Cape 1988
David Holbrook, ed: *The Case Against Pornography*, Tom Stacey, 1972
Anne Hollander: *Seeing Through Clothes*, Viking Press, New York 1980

Maggie Humm: *Feminisms: A Reader*, Harvester Wheatsheaf, 1992
—ed: *The Dictionary of Feminist Theory*, Harvester Wheatsheaf 1989
—*Feminist Criticism: Women as Contemporary Critics*, Harvester 1986
Luce Irigaray: *The Irigaray Reader*, ed Margaret Whitford, Blackwell, Oxford 1991
—*Je, tu, nous: Toward a Culture of Difference*, tr Alison Martin, Routledge 1993
—*Thinking the Difference: For a Peaceful Revolution*, Athlone Press, 1994
Mary Jacobus, ed: *Women Writing and Writing About Women*, Croom Helm 1979
C.G. Jung: *Memories, Dreams, Reflections*, Collins 1967
C. Kaplan: *Sea Changes: Essays on Culture and Feminism*, Verso 1986
S. Kappeler: *The Pornography of Representation*, Polity Press, Cambridge 1986
Bruce Kawin: *How Movies Work*, Macmillan, New York 1987
David Kinsley: *The Goddess's Mirror: Visions of the Divine From East and West*, State University of New York Press 1989
Cheris Kramarae & Paula A. Treichler, eds. *A Feminist Dictionary*, Pandora Press, 1987
Julia Kristeva: *The Kristeva Reader*, ed Toril Moi, Blackwell 1986
—*Desire in Language: A Semiotic Approach to Literature and Art*, ed Leon Roudiez, tr Thomas Gora, Alice Jardine & Leon Roudiez, Blackwell 1982
Annette Kuhn: *The Power of the Image: Essays on Representation and Sexuality*, Routledge 1985
—*Women's Pictures: Feminism and the cinema*, Routledge & Kegan Paul 1982
Weston La Barre: *The Ghost Dance*, Allen & Unwin 1972
—*Muelos*, Columbia University Press, New York 1985
Jacques Lacan and the *Ecole Freudienne*: *Feminine Sexuality*, ed. Juliet Mitchell and Jacqueline Rose, Macmillan 1982
Marghanita Laski: *Ecstasy*, Cresset Press 1961
D.H. Lawrence: *A Selection from Phoenix*, ed. A.A.H. Inglis, Penguin 1971
—*Selected Essays*, Penguin 1950
—*Lady Chatterley's Lover*, Penguin 1960
—*The Rainbow*, Penguin 1981
—*Phoenix*, Heinemann 1956
—*Phoenix II*, Heinemann 1968
Antoinette Le Normand-Romain, Anne Pingeot, Reinhold Hohl, Jean-Luc Daval, Barbara Rose: *Sculpture: The Adventure of Modern Sculpture in the Nineteenth and Twentieth Centuries*, Skira, Geneva, 1986
Carolyn Ruth Swift Lenz, Gayle Greene & Carol Thomas Neely, eds: *The*

Woman's Part: Feminist Criticism of Shakespeare, University of Illinois Press, Urbana 1980
Lucy Lippard: *From the Center: feminist essays on women's art*, Dutton, New York 1976
—*Six Years: The Dematerialization of the Art Object from 1966 to 1972*, Praeger, New York 1973
Edward Lucie-Smith: *Sexuality in Western Art*, Thames & Hudson 1991
Fiona MacCarthy: *Eric Gill*, Faber 1989
Catherine MacKinnon: *Towards a Feminist Theory of the State*, Harvard University Press, Cambridge, Massachusetts, 1989
—*Feminism Unmodified: Discourses on Life and Law*, Harvard University Press, Cambridge, Mass., 1987
Angela McRobbie, ed: *Zoot Suits and Second-Hand Dresses: An Anthology of Fashion and Music*, Macmillan 1989
—& M. Nava, eds: *Gender and Generation*, Macmillan 1984
Elaine Marks & Isabelle de Courtivron, eds: *New French Feminisms: an Anthology*, Harvester Wheatsheaf 1981
Gerardine Meaney: *(Un)Like Subjects: Women, Theory, Fiction*, Routledge 1993
Nancy Miller, ed: *The Poetics of Gender*, New York, 1986
Kate Millet: *Sexual Politics*, Doubleday, New York 1970
—*The Prostitution Papers*, Avon Books, New York 1973
Toril Moi: *Sexual/Textual Politics: Feminist Literary Theory*, Routledge 1988
—ed: *French Feminist Thought: A Reader*, Blackwell, Oxford 1987
Moira Monteith, ed: *Women's Writing: A Challenge to Theory*, Harvester Press, Brighton, Sussex 1986
Michael Moorcock: *Casablanca*, Gollancz, 1989
Robin Morgan: *The Word of a Woman: Selected Prose 1968-1992*, Virago 1993
Edward Mullins: *The Painted Witch: Female Body, Male Art*, Secker & Warburg 1985
Laura Mulvey: *Visual and Other Pleasures*, Macmillan 1989
Sally Munt, ed: *New Lesbian Criticism: Literary and Cultural Readings*, Harvester Wheatsheaf 1992
Lynda Nead: *Female Nude: Art, Obscenity and Sexuality*, Routledge 1992
Erich Neumann: *The Great Mother*, Princeton University Press, New Jersey 1972
Shirley Nicholson, ed. *The Goddess Re-awakening: The Goddess Principle Today* Theosophical Publishing House, New York 1989
Onlywomen, ed: *Love Your Enemy? The Debate Between Heterosexual*

Feminism and Political Lesbianism, Onlywomen Press 1981
Ursula Owen, ed: *Index on Censorship*, Writers & Scholars International, 1/2, May June, 1994
Rozsika Parker & Griselda Pollock: *Old Mistresses: Women, Art and Ideology*, Routledge & Kegan Paul 1981
Michael Payne: *Reading Theory: An Introduction to Lacan, Derrida, and Kristeva*, Blackwell 1993
Constance Penley, ed: *Feminism and Film Theory*, Routledge, New York 1988
Karen Petersen & J.J. Wilson: *Women Artists: Recognition and Reappraisal from the Early Middle Ages to the Twentieth Century* Women's Press, 1978
T. Piepe *et al*: *Mass Media and Cultural Relationships*, Saxon House 1978
Griselda Pollock: *Vision and Difference: femininity, feminism and histories of art*, Routledge 1988
Deidre Pribram, ed: *Female Spectators Looking at Film and Television*, Verso 1988
Terence H. Qualter: *Advertising and Democracy in the Mass Age*, Macmillan 1991
H.L. Radtke & H.J. Stam, eds: *Gender and Power*, Sage 1994
Janice Radway: *Reading the Romance: Feminism and the Representation of Women in Popular Culture*, University of North Carolina Press, Chapel Hill 1984
J.L. Reich: "Genderfuck: The Law of the Dildo", *Discourse: Journal of Theoretical Studies in Media and Culture*, vo. 15, no. 1, 1992, 112-127
Patrice Retro: "Mass Culture and the Feminine", *Cinema Journal*, 25, 1986, 5-21
Philip Rice & Patricia Waugh, eds: *Modern Literary Theory: A Reader*, Arnold 1992
Adrienne Rich: *Blood, Bread and Poetry*, Virago 1980
Arthur Rimbaud: *Complete Works, Selected Letters*, tr. Wallace Fowlie, University of Chicago Press, Chicago 1966
Bertrand Russell: *A History of Western Philosophy*, Allen & Unwin 1971
Gill Saunders: *The Nude: a new perspective*, Herbert Press 1989
Janet Sayers: *Biological Politics*, London 1982
C. Schwichtenberg, ed: *The Madonna Connection: Representational Politics, Subcultural Identities, and Cultural Theory*, Westview Press, Boulder,1993
Eve Sedgwick: *Between Men: English Literature and Male Homosexual Desire*, Columbia University Press, New York 1985
L. Segal & M. McIntosh, eds: *Sex Exposed: Sexuality and the Pornographic*

Debate, Virago 1992
Eric Shanes: *Constantin Brancusi*, Abbeville, New York 1989
Ruth Sherry: *Studying Women's Writings: An Introduction*, Edward Arnold 1988
Elaine Showalter, ed: *The New Feminist Criticism*, Virago 1986
—ed: *Speaking of Gender*, Routledge 1989
—*Sexual Anarchy: Gender and Culture at the* Fin de Siècle, Virago 1992
Penelope Shuttle & Peter Redgrove: *The Wise Wound*, Paladin/Grafton 1978/86
Monica Sjöo & Barbara Mor: *The Great Cosmic Mother*, Harper & Row, San Francisco 1987
Dale Spender: *Man-Made Language*, Routledge & Kegan Paul 1980
—*The Writing or the Sex? why you don't have to read women's writing to know it's no good*, Pergamon Press, New York 1989
Judith Still & Michael Worton, eds: *Textuality and Sexuality: Reading Theories and Practices*, Manchester University Press 1993
Susan Rubin Suleiman, ed: *The Female Body in Western Culture: Contemporary Perspectives*, Harvard University Press, Cambridge, Mass., 1986
J. Stoltenberg: *Refusing To Be a Man*, Fontana 1990
William Thompson: *The Time Falling Bodies Take to Light: Mythology, Sexuality and the Origins of Culture*, St Martins Press, New York 19811
Maurice Valency: *In Praise of Love: An Introduction to the Love-Poetry of the Renaissance*, Macmillan, New York 1961
Benjamin Walker: *Body Magic*, Paladin 1979
R. Warhol & D.P. Herndl: *Feminisms*, Rutgers University Press, New Brunswick
Marina Warner: *Alone Of All Her Sex: The Myth and Cult of the Virgin Mary*, Picador 1985
—*Monuments and Maidens*, Weidenfeld & Nicholson 1985
Valerie Wayne, ed: *The Matter of Difference: Materialist Feminist Criticism of Shakespeare*, Harvester Wheatsheaf 1991
Peter Webb: *The Erotic Arts*, Secker & Warburg 1983
Daniel Wheeler: *Art Since Mid-Century: 1945 to the Present*, Thames & Hudson 1991
Margaret Whitford: *Luce Irigaray: Philosophy of the Feminine*, Routledge 1991
S. Wilkinson & C. Kitzinger, eds: *Heterosexuality: A Feminism and Psychology Reader*, Sage 1993
Judith Williamson: *Consuming Passion: The Dynamics of Popular Culture*, Marion Boyars 1986

Colin Wilson: *The Sexual Misfits: A Study of Sexual Outsiders*, Collins 1989
Gerard Woods *et al*, eds: *Art Without Boundaries*, Thames & Hudson 1972

A new critical study of J.R.R. Tolkien, creator of Middle-earth and author of *The Lord of the Rings, The Hobbit* and *The Silmarillion*, among other books.
This new critical study explores Tolkien's major writings (*The Lord of the Rings, The Hobbit, Beowulf: The Monster and the Critics, The Letters, The Silmarillion* and *The History of Middle-earth* volumes); Tolkien and fairy tales; the mythological, political and religious aspects of Tolkien's Middle-earth; the critics' response to Tolkien's fiction over the decades; the Tolkien industry (merchandizing, toys, role-playing games, posters, Tolkien societies, conferences and the like); Tolkien in visual and fantasy art; the cultural aspects of The Lord of the Rings (from the 1950s to the present); Tolkien's fiction's relationship with other fantasy fiction, such as C.S. Lewis and *Harry Potter*; and the TV, radio and film versions of Tolkien's books, including the 2001-03 Hollywood interpretations of *The Lord of the Rings*.
This new book draws on contemporary cultural theory and analysis and offers a sympathetic and illuminating (and sceptical) account of the Tolkien phenomenon.
This book is designed to appeal to the general reader (and viewer) of Tolkien: it is written in a clear, jargon-free and easily-accessible style.

754pp ISBN 1-86171-057-7 £25.00 / $37.50

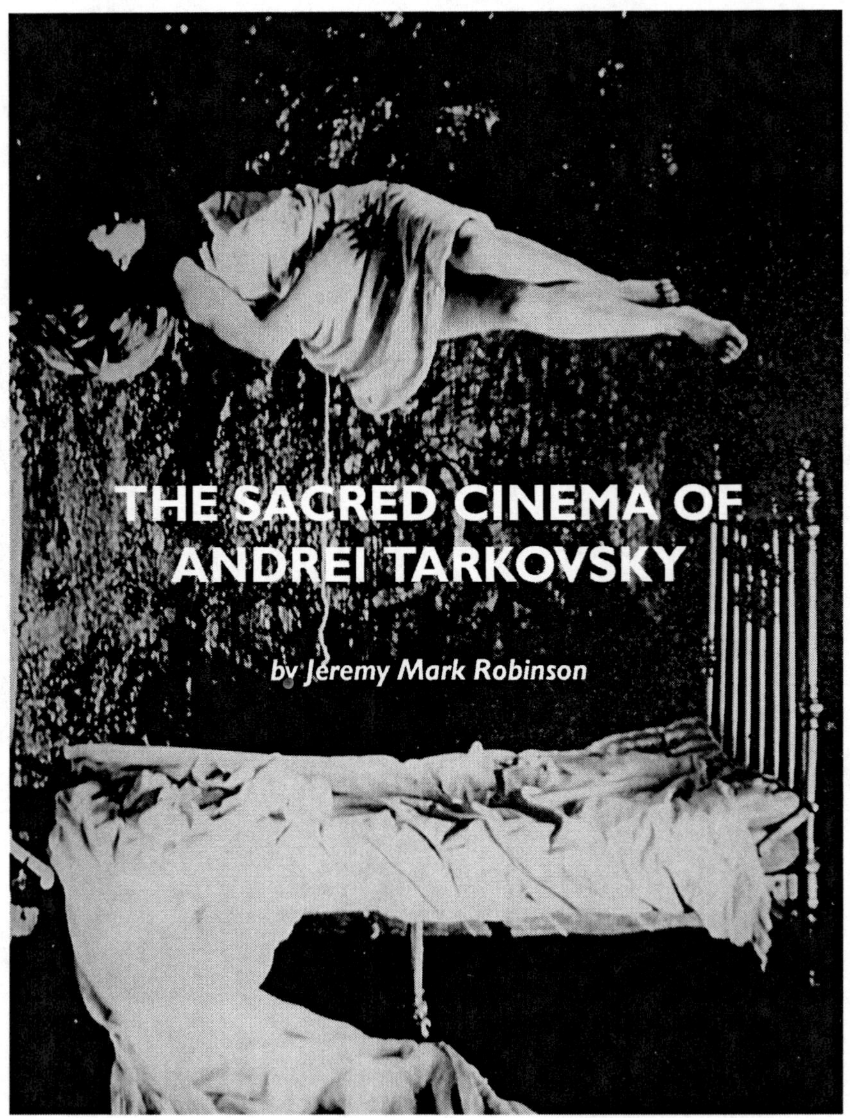

A new study of the Russian filmmaker Andrei Tarkovsky (1932-1986), director of seven feature films, including *Andrei Roublyov, Mirror, Solaris, Stalker* and *The Sacrifice*.
This is one of the most comprehensive and detailed studies of Tarkovsky's cinema available. Every film is explored in depth, with scene-by-scene analyses. All aspects of Tarkovsky's output are critiqued, including editing, camera, staging, script, budget, collaborations, production, sound, music, performance and spirituality. Tarkovsky is placed with a European New Wave tradition of filmmaking, alongside directors like Ingmar Bergman, Carl Theodor Dreyer, Pier Paolo Pasolini and Robert Bresson.
An essential addition to film studies.

Illustrations: 150 b/w, 4 colour. 682 pages. First edition. Hardback.

Publisher: Crescent Moon Publishing. Distributor: Gardners Books.

ISBN 1-86171-096-8 (9781861710963) £60.00 / $105.00

The Best of Peter Redgrove's Poetry
The Book of Wonders

by Peter Redgrove, edited and introduced by Jeremy Robinson

Poems of wet shirts and 'wonder-awakening dresses'; honey, wasps and bees; orchards and apples; rivers, seas and tides; storms, rain, weather and clouds; waterworks; labyrinths; amazing perfumes; the Cornish landscape (Penzance, Perranporth, Falmouth, Boscastle, the Lizard and Scilly Isles); the sixth sense and 'extra-sensuous perception'; witchcraft; alchemical vessels and laboratories; yoga; menstruation; mines, minerals and stones; sand dunes; mud-baths; mythology; dreaming; vulvas; and lots of sex magic. This book gathers together poetry (and prose) from every stage of Redgrove's career, and every book. It includes pieces that have only appeared in small presses and magazines, and in uncollected form.

'Peter Redgrove is really an extraordinary poet' (George Szirtes, *Quarto* magazine)
'Peter Redgrove is one of the few significant poets now writing... His 'means' are indeed brilliant and delightful. Technically he is a poet essentially of brilliant and unexpected images...he never disappoints' (Kathleen Raine, *Temenos* magazine).

240pp ISBN 1-86171-063-1 2nd edition £19.99 / $29.50

Sex–Magic–Poetry–Cornwall
A Flood of Poems

by Peter Redgrove. Edited with an essay by Jeremy Robinson

A marvellous collection of poems by one of Britain's best but underrated poets, Peter Redgrove. This book brings together some of Redgrove's wildest and most passionate works, creating a 'flood' of poetry. Philip Hobsbaum called Redgrove 'the great poet of our time', while Angela Carter said: 'Redgrove's language can light up a page.' Redgrove ranks alongside Ted Hughes and Sylvia Plath. He is in every way a 'major poet'. Robinson's essay analyzes all of Redgrove's poetic work, including his use of sex magic, natural science, menstruation, psychology, myth, alchemy and feminism.
A new edition, including a new introduction, new preface and new bibliography.

'Robinson's enthusiasm is winning, and his perceptive readings are supported by a very useful bibliography' (*Acumen* magazine)
'*Sex-Magic-Poetry-Cornwall* is a very rich essay... It is like a brightly-lighted box. (Peter Redgrove)
'This is an excellent selection of poetry and an extensive essay on the themes and theories of this unusual poet by Jeremy Robinson' (*Chapman* magazine)

220pp New, 3rd edition ISBN 1-86171-070-4 £14.99 / $23.50

THE ART OF ANDY GOLDSWORTHY

COMPLETE WORKS: SPECIAL EDITION (PAPERBACK and HARDBACK)

by William Malpas

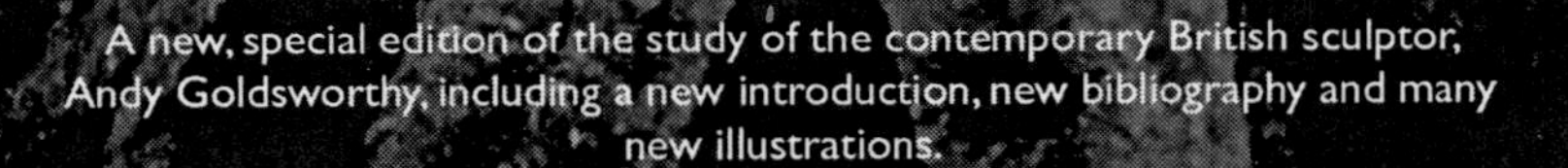

A new, special edition of the study of the contemporary British sculptor, Andy Goldsworthy, including a new introduction, new bibliography and many new illustrations.

This is the most comprehensive, up-to-date, well-researched and in-depth account of Goldsworthy's art available anywhere.

Andy Goldsworthy makes land art. His sculpture is a sensitive, intuitive response to nature, light, time, growth, the seasons and the earth. Goldsworthy's environmental art is becoming ever more popular: 1993's art book *Stone* was a bestseller; the press raved about Goldsworthy taking over a number of London West End art galleries in 1994; during 1995 Goldsworthy designed a set of Royal Mail stamps and had a show at the British Museum. Malpas surveys all of Goldsworthy's art, and analyzes his relation with other land artists such as Robert Smithson, Walter de Maria, Richard Long and David Nash, and his place in the contemporary British art scene.

The Art of Andy Goldsworthy discusses all of Goldsworthy's important and recent exhibitions and books, including the *Sheepfolds* project; the TV documentaries; *Wood* (1996); the New York Holocaust memorial (2003); and Goldsworthy's collaboration on a dance performance.

Illustrations: 70 b/w, 1 colour. 330 pages. New, special, 2nd edition.
Publisher: Crescent Moon Publishing. Distributor: Gardners Books.

ISBN 1-86171-059-3 (9781861710598) (Paperback) £25.00 / $44.00

ISBN 1-86171-080-1 (9781861710802) (Hardback) £60.00 / $105.00

CRESCENT MOON PUBLISHING

ARTS, PAINTING, SCULPTURE

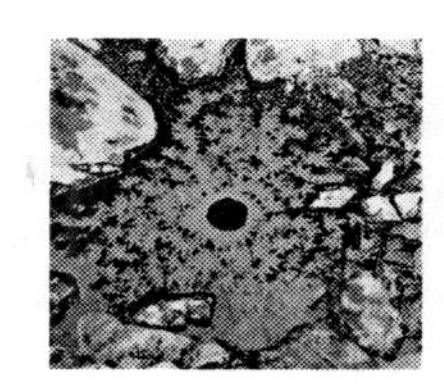

The Art of Andy Goldsworthy: Complete Works(Pbk)
The Art of Andy Goldsworthy: Complete Works (Hbk)
Andy Goldsworthy in Close-Up (Pbk)
Andy Goldsworthy in Close-Up (Hbk)
Land Art: A Complete Guide
Richard Long: The Art of Walking
The Art of Richard Long: Complete Works (Pbk)
The Art of Richard Long: Complete Works (Hbk)
Richard Long in Close-Up
Land Art In the UK
Land Art in Close-Up
Installation Art in Close-Up
Minimal Art and Artists In the 1960s and After

Colourfield Painting
Land Art DVD, TV documentary
Andy Goldsworthy DVD, TV documentary
The Erotic Object: Sexuality in Sculpture From Prehistory to the Present Day
Sex in Art: Pornography and Pleasure in Painting and Sculpture
Postwar Art
Sacred Gardens: The Garden in Myth, Religion and Art
Glorification: Religious Abstraction in Renaissance and 20th Century Art
Early Netherlandish Painting

Leonardo da Vinci
Piero della Francesca
Giovanni Bellini
Fra Angelico: Art and Religion in the Renaissance

Mark Rothko: The Art of Transcendence
Frank Stella: American Abstract Artist
Jasper Johns: Painting By Numbers
Brice Marden
Alison Wilding: The Embrace of Sculpture
Vincent van Gogh: Visionary Landscapes
Eric Gill: Nuptials of God
Constantin Brancusi: Sculpting the Essence of Things
Max Beckmann

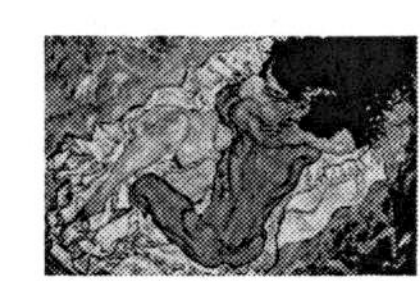

Egon Schiele: Sex and Death In Purple Stockings
Delizioso Fotografico Fervore: Works In Process 1
Sacro Cuore: Works In Process 2
The Light Eternal: J.M.W. Turner
The Madonna Glorified: Karen Arthurs

LITERATURE

J.R.R. Tolkien: The Books, The Films, The Whole Cultural Phenomenon
Harry Potter
Sexing Hardy: Thomas Hardy and Feminism
Thomas Hardy's *Tess of the d'Urbervilles*
Thomas Hardy's *Jude the Obscure*
Thomas Hardy: The Tragic Novels
Love and Tragedy: Thomas Hardy
The Poetry of Landscape in Hardy
Wessex Revisited: Thomas Hardy and John Cowper Powys

Wolfgang Iser: Essays
Petrarch, Dante and the Troubadours
Maurice Sendak and the Art of Children's Book Illustration
Andrea Dworkin
Cixous, Irigaray, Kristeva: The *Jouissance* of French Feminism
Julia Kristeva: Art, Love, Melancholy, Philosophy, Semiotics and Psychoanalysis
Hélene Cixous I Love You: The *Jouissance* of Writing
Luce Irigaray: Lips, Kissing, and the Politics of Sexual Difference
Peter Redgrove: Here Comes the Flood
Peter Redgrove: Sex-Magic-Poetry-Cornwall

Lawrence Durrell: Between Love and Death, East and West
Love, Culture & Poetry: Lawrence Durrell
Cavafy: Anatomy of a Soul
German Romantic Poetry: Goethe, Novalis, Heine, Hölderlin, Schlegel, Schiller
Feminism and Shakespeare
Shakespeare: Selected Sonnets
Shakespeare: Love, Poetry & Magic
The Passion of D.H. Lawrence
D.H. Lawrence: Symbolic Landscapes
D.H. Lawrence: Infinite Sensual Violence
Rimbaud: Arthur Rimbaud and the Magic of Poetry

The Ecstasies of John Cowper Powys
Sensualism and Mythology: The Wessex Novels of John Cowper Powys
Amorous Life: John Cowper Powys and the Manifestation of Affectivity (H.W. Fawkner)
Postmodern Powys: New Essays on John Cowper Powys (Joe Boulter)
Rethinking Powys: Critical Essays on John Cowper Powys
Paul Bowles & Bernardo Bertolucci
Rainer Maria Rilke
In the Dim Void: Samuel Beckett
Samuel Beckett Goes into the Silence
André Gide: Fiction and Fervour
Jackie Collins and the Blockbuster Novel
Blinded By Her Light: The Love-Poetry of Robert Graves
The Passion of Colours: Travels In Mediterranean Lands
Poetic Forms
The Dolphin-Boy

POETRY

The Best of Peter Redgrove's Poetry
Peter Redgrove: Here Comes The Flood
Peter Redgrove: Sex-Magic-Poetry-Cornwall
Ursula Le Guin: Walking In Cornwall
Dante: Selections From the Vita Nuova

Petrarch, Dante and the Troubadours
William Shakespeare: Selected Sonnets
Blinded By Her Light: The Love-Poetry of Robert Graves
Emily Dickinson: Selected Poems
Emily Brontë: Poems
Thomas Hardy: Selected Poems

Percy Bysshe Shelley: Poems
John Keats: Selected Poems
D.H. Lawrence: Selected Poems
Edmund Spenser: Poems
John Donne: Poems

Henry Vaughan: Poems
Sir Thomas Wyatt: Poems
Robert Herrick: Selected Poems
Rilke: Space, Essence and Angels in the Poetry of Rainer Maria Rilke
Rainer Maria Rilke: Selected Poems
Friedrich Hölderlin: Selected Poems
Arseny Tarkovsky: Selected Poems
Arthur Rimbaud: Selected Poems
Arthur Rimbaud: A Season in Hell

Arthur Rimbaud and the Magic of Poetry
D.J. Enright: By-Blows
Jeremy Reed: Brigitte's Blue Heart
Jeremy Reed: Claudia Schiffer's Red Shoes
Gorgeous Little Orpheus
Radiance: New Poems
Crescent Moon Book of Nature Poetry

Crescent Moon Book of Love Poetry
Crescent Moon Book of Mystical Poetry
Crescent Moon Book of Elizabethan Love Poetry
Crescent Moon Book of Metaphysical Poetry
Crescent Moon Book of Romantic Poetry
Pagan America: New American Poetry

MEDIA, CINEMA, FEMINISM and CULTURAL STUDIES

J.R.R. Tolkien: The Books, The Films, The Whole Cultural Phenomenon
Harry Potter
Cixous, Irigaray, Kristeva: The *Jouissance* of French Feminism
Julia Kristeva: Art, Love, Melancholy, Philosophy, Semiotics and Psychoanalysis
Luce Irigaray: Lips, Kissing, and the Politics of Sexual Difference
Hélene Cixous I Love You: The *Jouissance* of Writing
Andrea Dworkin
'Cosmo Woman': The World of Women's Magazines
Women in Pop Music
Discovering the Goddess (Geoffrey Ashe)
The Poetry of Cinema
The Sacred Cinema of Andrei Tarkovsky (Pbk and Hbk)
Paul Bowles & Bernardo Bertolucci
Media Hell: Radio, TV and the Press
An Open Letter to the BBC
Detonation Britain: Nuclear War in the UK
Feminism and Shakespeare
Wild Zones: Pornography, Art and Feminism
Sex in Art: Pornography and Pleasure in Painting and Sculpture
Sexing Hardy: Thomas Hardy and Feminism

In my view *The Light Eternal* is among the very best of all the material I read on Turner. (Douglas Graham, director of the Turner Museum, Denver, Colorado)

The Light Eternal is a model monograph, an exemplary job. The subject matter of the book is beautifully organised and dead on beam. (Lawrence Durrell)

It is amazing for me to see my work treated with such passion and respect. (Andrea Dworkin)

Sex-Magic-Poetry-Cornwall is a very rich essay... It is like a brightly-lighted box. (Peter Redgrove)

CRESCENT MOON PUBLISHING
P.O. Box 393, Maidstone, Kent, ME14 5XU, United Kingdom.
01622-729593 (UK) 01144-1622-729593 (US) 0044-1622-729593 (other territories)
cresmopub@yahoo.co.uk www.crescentmoon.org.uk

Printed in the United Kingdom
by Lightning Source UK Ltd.
132746UK00001B/244/P